ARYANS AND HINDU WOMEN

ENCYCLOPAEDIA OF WOMEN SOCIETY AND CULTURE SERIES-3

Aryans and Hindu Women

RAJ PRUTHI
&
BELA RANI SHARMA

ANMOL PUBLICATIONS PVT LTD
New Delhi-110 002

ANMOL PUBLICATIONS PVT LTD
4374/4B, Ansari Road, Daryaganj
New Delhi-110 002

Aryans and Hindu Women

First Edition 1995
Reprint : 1997
ISBN 81-7488-084-4

PRINTED IN INDIA

Published by J.L. Kumar for Anmol Publications Pvt. Ltd., New Delhi and Printed at Tarun Offset Printers, Maujpur, Delhi-53, Phone : 2260794

Acknowledgement

Some good work has been published on the otherwise neglected area of gender studies in the recent past. While compiling the present series we have collated relevant information to answer some of the present day queries pertaining to women studies. In doing so many distinguished contributors have earned our gratitude and we are deeply indebted to them.

Prof. Sheik Ali, Prof. G.C. Pande, Prof. M.N. Das, Prof. Romila Thapar, Prof. Aparna Basu, Prof. Vina Majumdar, Prof. Suvra Jaiswal, Prof. Leela Dubey, Prof. Devaki Jain, Prof. Sardamani have constantly inspired us. We are obliged to them.

Dr. (Mrs.) S. Pruthi, Dr. M. Lakshman and Dr. Neelam Khurana have facilitated the preparation of this series and we are sincerely grateful to them too.

Last but not the least, we are thankful to Shri J.L. Kumar without whose help and cooperation this series would not have seen the light of the day.

Editors

Preface

The role and status of women in society can best be understood within the cultural content by the operation of various historical, political, economic and educational factors moulding the society within the framework of time and space.

The present volume *Aryans and Hindu Women* is based on the informations collected and collated from various sources on different themes on Women Society and Cultures.

Devided into eight chapters this book has been written with an aim to highlight multi-dimensional aspects of women in Hindu society.

Suggestions and comments for the improvement of the book is always welcome.

Editors

Contents

Acknowledgement *v*

Preface *vi*

1. Women's Status and Gender Equality 1
2. The Construction of Feminity 43
3. Epics and Women 81
4. Place of Women in Ramayana 141
5. The Kama Sutra and Sex 164
6. Ligitimisation of Feminity 185
7. Feminists in India 211
8. Hindu Women and Society 221

1

Women's Status and Gender Equality

Right down to the early decades of the twentieth century, the progress of civilisation was often linked with the Aryan race, and the redemption of man with Aryan Supermen. In conformity with these notions, historians and anthropologists had given us vivid pictures of the primitive peoples of India to whom the benign Aryan conquerors brought the benefits of civilisation. Indo-Aryan literature mentions the peoples whom the Aryans conquered, as Mlecchas, Dasyus, Nishadas, Naktancharas, Rakshasas, Asuras, etc. the exact meanings of which are now lost to us, but all sufficiently notorious as indicative of evil. The absence of any living monuments or literature of pre-Aryan India, and the general acceptance, throughout the country, of the political, social and religious conceptions known as Indo-Aryan, strenthened the belief in the fiction of a wild pre-Aryan India.

In Europe, too, scholars generally held the view that the Persians, Greeks and Romans, all claiming Aryan blood, were the originators of civilisation, and before their conquest the Mediterranean and Persian Gulf regions were inhabited by inferior or barbarous races. In Europe, as in India, Aryan literature dominated scientific thought, and even Christian and Muslim theology, though drawing its dogma from the Jews, had its philosophic and emotional background in Greek literature. So deep-seated was the belief in the Aryan monopoly of civilisation that in northern Europe began to appear systems of philosophy based on conceptions of the inherent superiority of the Aryan blood which led to the dogma of Nazism with what result is now a matter of history.

In India, too, the salvation of humanity was linked with the spiritual leadership of the Aryans: the country they inhabited was known as Aryavartha, the best of all possible worlds; the way to liberation was called the Aryan Path even by the Buddha who was singularly free from ethnic illusions; the word 'Aryan', as a rule, stood for all that was best in humanity, and 'non-Aryan' or 'un-Aryan' for the worst.

These pious beliefs received a rude shock by the archaeological discoveries of the early decades of the twentieth century and the research work of scholars who delved into the history of the pre-Aryan world. Due, mainly, to their labours, it was discovered that the Aryans who conquered south-eastern Europe, the Middle-East and India were, in comparison with the great, settled civilisations of these regions nomads of a semi-barbarous type, more warlike but less civilised. The Aryan outburst on the civilised world, may, in fact, be likened to the barbarian invasion of Rome or the Mongol conquest of the great civilisations of Asia and Europe.

We are now told by historians that those Aryans who moved to the south-east of Europe and came to be known as Greeks, conquered the Minoan civilisation of Crete and other regions, while the Persians who conquered Mesopotamia came under the cultural influence of the Babylonians. That branch of the Aryans who made inroads into India and settled down in the Punjab, it would appear, came in contact with what is now known as the Indus Valley Civilisation; they seem to have assimilated what they could digest of this civilisation and called it Aryan without acknowledgements.

The Indus Valley Civilisation

Two great cities, Mohenjo-daro and Harappa, believed to be Metropolitan centres which controlled a pre-historic Indian empire, were unearthed in the Sind-Punjab region in the third decade of the twentieth century. These cities, we are told, flourished for centuries till their destruction in an invasion or cataclysm that took place about the middle of the second millennium before Christ; the empire controlled by the cities extended from Baluchistan to the

Doab, from the Punjab to the Arabian Sea. Since the excavation of Mohenjo-daro and Harappa, many sites have been discovered which show a wide diffusion of this culture, the latest being at Lothal in the Ahmedabad District; Lothal, it would appear, was a port of considerable importance which was destroyed towards the close of the second millennium before Christ, much later than the main centres of the Indus Valley Civilisation farther north.

It is now generally held by archaeologists that the Aryan invasion of India was responsible for the destruction of the Indus Valley Empire. The views of Sir Mortimer Wheeler, the well-known archaeologist, are of particular importance in this connection. He says :

> There is some material evidence that the Indus Civilisation was still in action within the first half of the second millennium B.C. and it is widely accepted that somewhat about the middle of that millennium occurred the Aryan invasion which is reflected in the earliest literature of India, the hymns of the *Rigveda.* It these hymns the invasion constantly assumes the form of an onslaught upon the walled cities of the aborigines, and the only fortifications of approximate date known to us are those of the citadels of Harappa and Mohenjo-daro and at certain of the smaller contemporary towns. It is tempting to relate the two circumstances to one another and to recognize in the destroyers of Mohenjo-daro, indifferent to the city they had sacked, some of these heroic but barbarian nomads, to whom city life was alien. It is not indeed impossible that the name of Harappa itself is concealed in the Hari-Yupiya which is mentioned in the *Rigveda* as the scene of a battle.

Our knowledge of the Indus Valley people is, at present, very meagre. The size, lay-out and architecture of their cities, their arts and crafts indicate a fairly advanced civilisation mainly supported by commerce, both inland and foreign, by overland and overseas trade routes. The construction of their streets and houses with public baths and elaborate systems of drainage and sanitation, their interest in histrionics, the careful attention paid to personal appearance as seen from the art treasures unearthed, their love of jewellery, the extensive use of seals to mark personal properly, all indicate a well-developed urban civilisation with a leisured class who possibly controlled the affairs of state.

The Indus Valley people knew the art of writing. The seals discovered bear writings in a script not yet deciphered. Apart from the seals no written documents have so far been discovered; even if the script of the seals are deciphered, we may not be able to gather from them much information concerning the social life of the people, as the seals seem to have been used to mark property for establishing ownership of goods.

Very little information can be gleaned from the evidence now available to us concerning the marriage laws and customs of the Indus Valley people, of the position of their women in society and other matters relevant to our subject. The many figures of goddesses discovered would suggest that the popular deities of the pantheon were female, and this would indicate matriarchal social conceptions. Phallic cults, the cults of the Lingam and Yoni, were also widely prevalent.

An interesting find from Mohenjo-daro is the bronze of a dancing girl. The features indicated in the find are like those of figurines discovered at Kulli in Baluchistan, and scholars even opine "that the merchants returning along the southerly caravan routes may have brought with them girls whose exotic dancing and unsophisticated charms might be thought to tickle the fancy of the tired businessmen of Harappa or Mohenjo-daro".

The elaborate attention paid to feminine adornments would show that connoisseurs had set high standards in fashions.

> All known semi-precious stones and metals were utilised for manufacturing various ornaments. Women wore a fan-shaped head-dress. Small cones of gold, silver, copper, faience, as also of shell, were worn on the sides of the head.

The forehead was decorated with a fillet or head-band. Earrings were made of coils of gold, silver, copper or faience. It is doubtful if any nose ornaments were used. There was a variety of necklaces having pendants in the middle, with a number of rows of beads of various shapes and materials artistically arranged using spacers and terminals. Finger-rings were plentiful, and bangles and bracelets were commonly used. Materials for bangles and bracelets were gold, silver, copper, bronze, faience, shell and potterv. Gold and silver bangles were penannular in shape with their hollows filled with a fibrous or lac core. Girdles, of which two fine specimens have been found, were worn round the waist. Various stones such as carnelian, steatite, agate, chalcedony, jasper, etc., were pressed into service in the manufacture of beads which evince fine workmanship and technical skill on the part of the lapidary.

We can also form some idea about the toilet and cosmetics of the people. The 'vanity case' found at Harappa with its combination of piercer, ear-scoop and tweezers, invites comparison with similar finds from Ur, Kish and Khafaje, both types showing the same peculiar construction of the looped head. Toilet jars were made of ivory, metal, pottery and stone. Small faience vessels having four compartments were used for keeping expensive perfumes or cosmetics. It appears that the ladies of Mohenjo-daro knew of the use of collyrium, face-paint and other cosmetics. Small cockle shell containing a red ochre rouge, lumps of green earth, white face-paint, and black beauty substance show that the belles of ancient Sind attended to beauty and toilet culture. It is interesting to note that Chanhu-daro finds indicate the use of lipsticks. Carbonate of lead, a face-paint, may also have been employed as a kind of ointment or hair-wash. Round metal rods in bronze and copper with both ends rounded and polished, were probably used for applying cosmetics. There were small toilet tables specially designed for women. Articles on the dressing table included mirrors, made of bronze, oval in shape, and combs of different shapes made of ivory.'

Compared with these sophisticated ladies of the Indian cities, Aryan women of the time were crude, hardy camp-dwellers who could neither understand nor appreciate these urbane luxuries.

The importance of mother-worship in religion, the abundance of female figurines with rich ornaments, the comparatively lesser importance given to males, would all indicate that society in ancient Indus Valley was more favourable to women than to men; it was possibly a matriarchate of the type of ancient Egypt.

Scholars are of opinion that the Indus Valley Civilisation was Dravidian. This Dravidian civilisation seems to have been widely distributed in India at the time of the Aryan conquest. In the initial vehemence of the Aryan impact in the north, South India possible became its main refuge. Isolated groups of Dravidian survivals even now exist in the north, the Brahuis of Baluchistan being a notable example; but South India is at present the most important stronghold of living Dravidian culture though Indo-Aryan civilisation has been super-imposed on it. But before dealing with this Dravidian culture, we shall see what Indo-Aryan literature has to say about the women of non-Aryans, prejudiced as it is against non-Aryans and their institutions.

Non-Aryan Women in Indo-Aryan Literature

The earliest literary compositions of the Hindus, the *Vedas*, are mostly religious in character and give us little insight into the social conditions of the people of India. But when we come to the epics, we get detailed accounts of Indo-Aryans and their non-Aryan friends and enemies, of their social life, customs, manners and moral and ethical conceptions. The *Mahabharata* and the *Ramayana*, the two epics of the Hindus, were compiled in their present form, as were some of the *Puranas*, during that formative period in Hinduism which intervened between the collapse of the Mauryan empire in the third century B.C. and the rise of the

Guptas in the fourth century of the Christian era. Most of the stories, legends and traditions narrated in the epics are as old as the race itself, while a good deal of the 'packing' to the main themes is drawn from events and ethical conceptions current at the period of their compilation; interpolations were made later by scholars and law-givers who wished to pass on their views under the high authority of the epics. A considerable part of the epics is, no doubt, the offspring of lively imagination inspired by a love of the miraculous, but they contain a good deal of history and geography dressed in fancy costume.

The epithets generally used in the epics to denote the non-Aryans, who were inimical to the Aryans and their gods, are Asuras and Rakshasas, both at times indiscriminately used along with their synonyms like Naktancharas to indicate the same people. In certain accounts the words are used for people of demonaic habits, while in others they indicate racial enemies who were, in prowess and the practice of virtues, as good as the aryans and even superior. Between the two, we have to make what sense we can, out of given contexts. Besides these terms, we come across several other nomenclatures like Yakshas, Gandharvas, Apsaras, Kinnaras and Kimpurushas who, at times appear as fairiess and celestials with occult powers, but, at other times, weaker than humans. Then there are the Mlecchas, Yavanas, Hunas and Nagas, with their ways of life different from those of people already noticed; the Yavanas were Ionians or Greeks, and the Hunas, Huns, and both had come to India later than the Aryans; the Nagas, on the other hand, were a race of snake-worshippers almost as ancient as the Dravidians and as widely diffused, while Mlecchas (the Indian equivalent of barbarians) were any people whom the Indo-Aryans did not like.

The mythical origins of some of the non-Aryans people of India are given in the *Mahabharata*. In the war between king Visvamitra and the sage Vasishta for the possession of the divine cow Kamadhenu or Nandini, from the tail of the cow began to pour forth armies and materials of destruction. After a shower of burning coal, the magic tail of the cow produced "an army of Pallavas; from her udders sprang forth armies of Dravidas and Sakas; from her womb, Yavanas; frrom her dung an army of Savaras; from her mouth came out hosts of Paundras, Kiratas, Simhalas, the tribes of Khasas and Shivukas, Pulindas and Chins with Hunas and Keralas, and numerous other Mlecchas". Other accounts tell us that the non-Aryans generally were the progeny of mixed marriages, condemned to live outside the pale of Aryan society.

Without being dogmatic, we may say that the general tendency of the epics would indicate that the Asuras and Rakshasas were the more powerful of the non-Aryans who opposed Aryan expansion in India, though some of them seem to have been won over by the Aryans through fear or conciliation. Their human personalities are clearly traceable behind the grotesque masks they are given in the epics. Besides, many Asuras, like Bali and Bana, live in the legends of certain communities who honour them as the emperors of a bygone age; the Asura Bali, in particular, was an honoured emperor of the south, and both in the Mahratha countries and Kerala festivals are even now celebrated in his honour. Similarly, the monkey tribes of South India who aided the Aryan hero Rama in his war on Ravana, as well as this worthy himself, appear to hide under their fantastic masks, some people and factual elements of historic importance.

One thing, however, stands out clear in all Indo-Aryan literature: That all the non-Aryans were blessed with a stronger sex nature than the Aryans, and these were better looking than their enemies. As a consequence, when a non-Aryan male found an Aryan lady under opportune circumstances, he made love to her, and when his suit was rejected, had recourse to rape. The plight of the Aryan males was almost as bad as that of their women; the moment Surpanakha, Ravana's sister, saw Rama and Lakshmana, she lusted after them, and the Aryan heroes had to save their virtue by cutting off her nose and ears; another Rakshasi, Ayomukhi, had to be mutilated in a similar manner while the passion of a third, Thadaka, could not be cooled by mutilation and she had to be killed.

The heroes of the *Mahabharata* were less virtuous and more chivalrous. When the Pandavas were wandering in the forests, the Rakshasa lady Hidimbi, we are told, met Bhima, and, taken by his size and looks, begged him to marry her. Bhima, not only married her but stayed in her house for a year, and returned to his brothers only after the birth of a son named Ghatotkacha. This would indicate that this particular Rakshasa tribe practised some sort of a matriarchal custom by which a man, on marriage, had to live with his wife in her own house. Arjuna had a similar adventure with a Naga lady by name Ulupi, and lived in her house for some time.

The *Mahabharata* refers to an age in which inter-racial marriages were common. Apart from the marriages of Bhima and Arjuna, already noticed, the sage Jaratkaru married a Naga princess, sister of the renowned Vasuki, and lived in her house; he left her only after she had broken her pledged word with him. Shantanu, the progenitor of Kuru-Pandavas, married Matsya Gandhi or Satyavati, a fishwoman, and the lunar line descended through her son Vichitravirya. Further, Krishna's grandson Aniruddha married the daughter of the Asura king Bana; in this case, there was some objection and a war, but the objection came not from the Aryans but from the Asuras who did not approve of this inter-racial marriage.

Another celebrated inter-racial union was between king Yayati and the Asura princess Sharmishta. In this instance there was, however, no regular marriage, but the sons born of the union became famous Aryan heroes. The intricate story needs some detailed notice, especially as it involves the only approved instance of a Pratiloma marriage, of which more presently.

Sukra, the Brahmin preceptor of the Asura king Vrishaparvan, so goes the story, had a daughter named Devayani on whom he doted. The girl, with Vrishaparvan's daughter, the beautiful Sharmishta, went on a picnic to a forest where, while playing, they started an argument as to who, between the two, was the superior. Sharmishta maintained that Sukra was merely a paid servant of her father and that Sukra's daughter was her slave. Devayani resented this, and started asserting her superiority, when the irate Sharmishta pushed her into a dry well, near by, and returned to the city as if nothing had happened.

As luck would have it, the Aryan king Yayati now came into the forest for hunting; hearing the moans of Devayani, he proceeded to the well and helped her out. Devayani thanked the king, went back to her father and told him all that had happened. She also wished to know of Sukra if she was really Sharmishta's slave. The mighty sage told his weeping daughter that he, Sukra, far from being the servant of the king, was his preceptor and master and that Devayani was in effect Sharmishta's mistress. On this Devayani asked her father to prove his statement by obtaining for her Sharmishta as a maid.

Sukra now went to the Asura king, told him all that had happened and threatened to desert him if he would not give his daughter as a servant to Devayani. Under this threat, and convinced of the guilt of Sharmishta in the affair, Vrishaparvan ordered his daughter to go and serve Devayani as a maid and companion.

While living merrily with her maid in her father's house Devayani, one day, felt like visiting the well from which she had been saved by Yayati; hence together with her friends and Sharmishta, the young lady went to the same forest for a picnic. And chance again brought Yayati to the spot; seeing her saviour, Devayani was naturally delighted, and started talking with him, and what with one thing leading to another the lady suggested marriage, and the king accepted the proposal. The king, who happened to see the lively Sharmishta, casually asked Devayani who she was, and the prospective bride curtly dismissed the query by remarking that she was her maid-servant.

The marriage ceremony was duly performed and Devayani went to live with her husband. Sharmishta naturally accompanied her mistress; not used to living in crowded apartments, she wished to have a separate residence for herself, which the obliging Yayati caused to be built for her. While Sharmishta was this living comfortably, one day, the king unaccountably wandered into her residence. Then time, however, was auspicious and opportune, for Sharmishta was in her Rtu or fertile period and she thought it a pity that her chance of getting an illustrious son should go waste. Hence she approached Yayati and confided to him her secret desire. Yayati showed reluctance; he was honour-bound to confine his sex relations to Devayani, he told Sharmishta, especially as Sukra had particularly warned him against having anything to do with his daughter's young maid. On this Sharmishta delivered a spirited discourse on morals, in which, among other things, she maintained that a woman's husband was also the husband of her friends and maids. As regards keeping the matter secret, Sharmishta quoted the authority of sages who permitted honest Aryans to tell lies to women in love affairs. The preaching of the passionate moralist convinced Yayati, and he yielded.

The intrigue continued and a son was born to Sharmishta. Devayani now asked Sharmishta for an explanation, and the fair liar told the simpleton that it was all on account of a very special boon granted to her by a sage. After three sons were born to Sharmishta the fraud was discovered, and Devayani fled to her father, that never-failing source of her consolation, and old Sukra cursed Yayati with premature decrepitude.

In most of these inter-racial marriages and philanderings, it will be noticed that the men were Aryans and the women, non-Aryans. Here, an ancient Indo-Aryan prejudice that has persisted through the ages to the present day has to be noted. The idea is perhaps linked with the patriarchal notions of property rights in women; anyway, the Aryans have always held the view that a woman marrying below her caste or status, demeans herself and her family, whereas no such stigma is attached to a man marrying a woman below his caste. It is this notion that has led to the condemnation of what is known as Pratiloma marriage (women marrying men of power castes) in practically all Hindu texts. Even at present this ancient prejudice is very strong among the Hindus who will readily approve of the marriage of a Hindu male with a Christian or Muslim lady, but find it extremely difficult to reconcile themselves to the marriage of a high caste Hindu lady with a Christian, Muslim or any man of a caste considered lower than hers.

In the whole Hindu literature it is difficult to find an approved case of a regular marriage between an Aryan woman and a non-Aryan man. In fact the only instance of a marriage of a Pratiloma nature is the wedding of Devayani and Yayati. In this connection, it must be remembered that Sukra was in the pay of an Asura, and Brahmins who lived in the court of the non-Aryans often adopted the ways of their patrons; the fact that it was Devayani who proposed to Yayati is a proof of this; for among most non-Aryans, the privilege of proposing was of the woman and the right of rejection or acceptance man's. As such the behaviour of Devayani and her marriage are more in keeping with Asura conventions that with aryan traditions.

Certain instances have, however, been related in the epics and the *Puranas* of Aryan ladies having given birth to monsters due to the activities of Asuras. But these were cases of forbidden relations, as the Asuras in question had either ravished the ladies or approached them at night in the guise of their husbands, and took their pleasure with the unsuspecting women who were disillusioned too late to prevent the conception and birth of their undesirable progeny. Aryan ladies are always mentioned in Brahminic literature as particularly loyal to their race, and not a single instance of an Aryan lady who married or bestowed her favours willingly on a non-Aryan out of wedlock will be found in it. So, the only course open to a non-Aryan who was taken by the looks of a charming Aryan lady was to cultivate the virtue of self-restraint or abduct the object of his desire, and many non-Aryans had recourse to the latter expedient when they could. The most notorious case of this nature was the abduction of Sita, wife of the Aryan hero Rama, by Ravana, the Rakshasa king of Lanka, which forms the main theme of the *Ramayana*.

The *Ramayana* deals with an age in which Brahminic ideals of religion and sexual morality were fully developed and non-Aryan practices were held in extreme contempt. At the time of the *Ramayana* there was a progressive racial degeneration southwards from Ayodhya, the kingdom of the solar Aryan heroes. The wild region immediately south of Ayodhya was inhabited by non-Aryan tribes known as Nishadas whose chief, Guha, was well disposed towards the Aryans in general and Rama in particular. The Nishadas, though much inferior to the Aryans, were human beings. Farther south were the monkey, bear and vulture tribes, described in the epic as the friends of Rama, but definitely sub-human. South of the Vindhyas the Rakshasas were numerous but their stronghold was the island of Lanka, the southernmost inhabited region known to the *Ramayana,* where ruled the mighty Ravana, king of the Rakshasas.

From the *Ramayana* we get an inkling of Rakshasa morality. War and women were the delight of the more powerful of the Rakshasas; while they appear as patriarchal communities their women were much more free than those of the Aryans. Among the Rakshasas, as, in effect, among all non-Aryan communities, marriage was not sacramental but a secular affair with freedom of divorce and re-marriage. It would appear that the women of a Rakshasa chief vanquished in battle generally passed on to the victor; if he was slain, due mourning had to be performed by the women after which they were free to accept the conqueror as a husband or protector.

Ravana is depicted in the epic as a ravisher of other people's wives and daughters, and a ferocious warrior. Even spoiling for a fight, he ranged the world in search of war, and challenged anyone he considered worthy of his steel; in most of these encounters he was successful though some reverses are also recorded. In these martial adventures if he happened to meet a pretty woman, he immediately approached her for marriage or pleasure, and if the suit was rejected, he seized her whether she was married or not. Thus he ravished the Apsara Rambha, the appointed wife of

Nalakuvera, his own cousin; Punchikasthala, the daughter of Varuna; Vedavati, grand-daughter of Brahaspati, the venerable Brahmin preceptor of the gods. In the fulness of his wickedness, he abducted Sita which led to his destruction.

Ravana would appear to be an interesting historical personality, from the mention of his activities in the *Arthasastra* and certain other pre-Ramayana texts, and it is unfortunate that we possess no impartial account of this indomitable emperor of Lanka, and his conquests. Any ways, we have to take the accounts of his life as we find them.

It would appear that among the Rakshasas there was a law by which strong rulers could seize the wives of their foes. Marriage by capture was a recognised institution among many ancient people including the Indo-Aryans; Indo-Aryan law as expounded in the epics would indicate that only the capture of unmarried women was permissible. Among the Rakshasas marriage ties were weak and it would appear that capture of another man's wife was permissible as indicative of the power of a warrior. Even among the Indo-Aryans such capture was recognised, if the captor had fought and defeated or slain the husband and relatives of the captured woman; in the case of the capture of Draupadi by Jayadratha and of Sita by Ravana, the main accusation against the ravishers was not capture as such, but capture without fighting and defeating the husbands of the ladies. What was blameable in the ancient world was cowardice, and might was a virtue that had an overriding effect on many a convention and law.

If Ravana was free to molest other men's wives, his sister Surpanakha, as we have seen, was equally free to force men. All Rakshasis were not, however, so wicked as Surpanakha. Mandodari, Ravana's chief queen, was a noble and virtuous lady, a devoted wife even by Aryan standards. She was the daughter of the celebrated Asura Maya, and almost the equal of Sita in virtue and beauty. She constantly warned her husband against seizing unwilling women for pleasure, but her good counsel was lost upon her husband. In spite of his inconstancy to her, she was ever devoted to him, and her lamentation on the death of her husband was as heartfelt as that of the most dutiful Aryan Sati. She wailed over the dead body of her husband:

> What had you found in this Sita that you risked your own life, the life of your subjects, and the welfare of your great kingdom? Verily, there are damsels in your palace more beautiful than Sita; but blinded by Cupid, you were indifferent to their charms. Impelled by fate, alas! this woman seized your fancy! She is not my equal, not in any way, my superior, in nobility of birth, in beauty and accomplishments; then what made you, O hero, court so great a danger for her? I am the daughter of the king of Danavas, my husband is the powerful lord of the Rakshasas, and my son Indrajit is the conqueror of Indra, king of gods...You, O hero, were invincible in battle,; even gods, Gandharvas and Yakshas had been conquered by you; then how is it that you were destroyed by Rama, a mere man? I can only put down all this to the working of fate from which there is no escape.

Mandodari is venerated by the Hindus as a saint, mainly because of her constant advice to Ravana to return Sita, just as Pilate's wife is considered a saint by the Christians. Another famous Asura lady noted for her virtue and devotion to husband was Vrinda, wife of Jalandhar; this Asura's claim for immortality was based on his wife's constancy, and the gods could despoil her of her virtue only through fraud. Thus, though, among the non-Aryans, marriage was not sacramental, there was no dearth of virtuous women who were devoted to their husbands.

In the *Ramayana* we have been given a description of the night life of Lanka, the greatest city of the time according to the accounts of the Indo-Aryans themselves. The Rakshasas, says the epic, were great lovers of pleasure. While for the Aryans sex life was guided by social duty and the desire for progeny, to the Rakshasas pleasure was the primary object of sex, and progeny secondary. So while the Aryans were more virtuous and pious, the Rakshasas were merrier people as is clearly seen in the *Ramayana*.

The monkey chief Hanuman in search of Sita reached Lanka during day-time, but in order to prevent detection, he started looking for Sita only after nightfall. The city of Lanka was the wonder of the age, and the Aryans had nothing to show in comparison; Lanka was built on a hill with lofty walls and moats surrounding it; it was a well-planned city with broad highways, and soaring mansions for the king and his nobles.

It must be mentioned here that the Rakshasas and Asuras appear as great builders in the epics. This is a fact borne out by archaeological and historical evidences too. The Indus Valley people, as we have seen, had well-planned cities and palaces built in brick while the early Aryan settlers were poor builders who had not got far beyond wood and thatch. They did not known the art of building in brick and stone. The first Aryan buildings in brick were the stupas, the tumuli constructed to enshrine the relics of the Buddha in the sixth century before Christ. The palace of the Pandavas at Indraprastha, we are told in the *Mahabharata*, was not built by an Aryan but by the renowned Asura architect Maya.

But to revert to the night life of Lanka. Hanuman found at the lofty arched gateways of the city infuriated elephants guarding the entrance. Walking through the broad, well-paved streets, Hanuman saw, on both sides, houses of citizens with golden doors opening into the street; there were spacious halls and courts in the mansions with mosaic floors and walls studded with bright stones, crystals and pearls. The tempo of the night life of the city was rising as Hanuman proceeded from street to street. From every house emanated the notes of stringed and wind instruments set to the melodious music of lovely singing girls. The streets resounded with the jingling of ornaments of light-footed dancers and the merry peals of laughter. Moving from house to house, Hanuman saw damsels, rivalling celestial Apsaras in beauty, dancing, drinking and merry-making with their lovers; he heard their laughter and clapping of hands, the foot-steps of lovers going up and down the stairs. As the pleasurable night advanced, the revellers, drunk with wine and sleep, sought their beds with their sweet-hearts. And Hanuman heard :

> ...the sweet music of stringed instruments lulling the lovers to sleep. As the Rakshasas are wondrous in their feats of valour, so are they in their sports and pleasures; and he saw the pick of the race, drunk with the choicest of wines, disputing, railing and gesticulating against one another, as the gay ladies laughed.... He also saw damsels daubing their faces with sweet-smelling unguents, fair-faced wenches smiling, others singing, while some bold Rakshasa, challenging another, striking his chest (in order to emphasise important in his), and inebriate ones sinking on the breasts of their reclining sweet-hearts; ladies, experts in dalliance, casting side-glances on their lovers, drinking choicest of wines, and showing love-signs to dashing gallants; blazing beauties, abandoned to love, entwining their arms round their lovers' necks; young lovers cooing like birds.... Some of these beautiful women, of the complexion of molten gold, lay listless with their garments disordered; others, on lonely beds with their flower-braids crushed, pining for their lovers. All these women were blooming with youth and vigour; adorned with ornaments and flowers, they were wonderful to look at; charmers, they had elegant eyes and long lashes; these flowery fays of Lanka lay in the delightful city, like lines of lighting in the autumn sky.

This description of Lanka would fit in well with the night life of some of our modern cities with their gay women, night clubs, wealth and splendour. But then, Lanka, under Ravana, was a prosperous city enriched by the spoils of war from the many kingdoms he had conquered, and the poetic fancy of the author of the *Ramayana* is based on some elements of fact.

Ravana's pleasure palace was mistaken by poor Hanuman for Paradise itself. Ravana had a very wide taste in the matter of selecting women for the seraglio. In Lanka, there were no Pratiloma taboos, and Ravana's women were mostly "daughters of Rajarshis, of Brahmins, of Daityas, of Gandharvas and Rakshasas who were either formally married to him or had agreed to serve him. There was none among them who was not of noble birth; none who was defective in grace and charm; none who was wicked or infirm; none who was not adorned with costly jewels; none who was not an object of desire to her lover". Ravana's harem was truly reminiscent of that of a medieval emperor the recruits to whose seraglio came from the four corners of his empire and from the palaces of vanquished monarchs. Seeing the great ladies of Ravana's palace, Hanuman almost unconsciously soliloquished that, but for the fact that she was abducted, Sita would have been a fit person to rule over those bevies of beauties, the greatest of the attractions of the marvellous city of Lanka.

So much for the Rakshasas and their women. The *Ramayana,* as we have seen, refers to the Vindhya mountains and the regions to the south as inhabited by monkey, bear and vulture tribes. It is difficult to make much sense out of the descriptions given in the epic, concerning the nature and culture of these inhabitants of the south. At times they are mentioned as mere animals and birds in appearance and habit, and at other times as regular human beings with social, political and religious institutions, and enjoying the gift of speech and the knowledge of the *Vedas.* Some of them are depicted as even superior to celestials in wisdom, prowess, courage and moral virtues. Their military organisation appears from the *Ramayana* itself as superior to that of the Aryans, and the term 'Sugriva Anjna' (the commands of Sugriva) is even now a byword in military discipline in India.

Leaving the epic for a moment, and coming down to history, we know for a fact, that South India, not only at the time of compiling the epic but even before, was a well-developed civilised region; if the findings of archaeologists are correct, it had enjoyed the benefits of the Dravidian civilisation of the Indus Valley even before the advent of the Aryans into India; so it is fairly certain that the Simian tribes mentioned in the *Ramayana* were human beings whom the lofty pretensions of the Indo-Aryans consigned to the four-footed kingdom. It is also probable that in the ancient skeleton plot of the *Ramayana* the tribes who aided Rama in his conquest of lanka were mentioned by their totems, and the lively imagination of the author of the present version furnished the tribes with the attributes of their totems. Further, it is noteworthy that in the post-Vedic development of Puranic Hinduism, Hanuman, one of the monkey heroes, found an honoured place in the Indo-Aryan pantheon. All told, we may presume with a fair amount of probability that the Simian tribe mentioned in the epic was some powerful people of southern India with their capital at Kishkindha.

Kishkindha was poor in structure and appearance compared with the magnificent metropolis of Lanka. Though not so good as the Rakshasas in building cities, the Simians were as good in martial virtues. Bali, the Simian chief whom Ravana provoked, easily defeated the lord of Lanka and imprisoned him; the prisoner was set free only after tendering an unconditional apology for his ill-advised, wanton aggression. Both Sugriva and Hanuman were more than a match for many of the generals of Ravana.

The *Ramayana* gives us an inkling into the sex life of the Simian heroes. Their moral codes, like those of the Rakshasas, were less strict than the rules of the Aryans. Matrimonial ties were loose, and both polygyny and polyandry seem to have been prevalent. Bali and Sugriva were born of the same mother but of Indra and Surya, both of whom had sexual relations with the lady. Society was generally patrilineal, and kings and chiefs had, like the Aryans and Asuras, well-stocked harems. It would appear that the harem of a defeated chief, wives, slave-girls, and all, passed on to the conqueror, and the ladies were expected to respect this convention, and attach themselves to their new lord with the same ardour they showed their erstwhile master. When Sugriva, mistaking his half-brother Bali for dead in an encounter with a Rakshasa, ascended the throne of Kishkindha, Bali's harem passed on to Sugriva. Bali was not dead but came back very much alive, after defeating the Rakshasa; he was enraged at the unseemly haste of Sugriva in seizing his throne and wives, gave him battle, defeated him, and sent him into exile, seizing Sugriva's wife Rumi, along with the other women of his harem. This trouble, however, did not end here. Prince Rama, in his search for Sita, met-Sugriva in exile entered into an alliance with him and killed Bali. On this Sugriva got back not only his own wife Rumi, but all the women of Bali including his chief wife Tara. And Tara, after performing formal mourning for Bali, started a life of pleasure with Sugriva almost immediately. after Bali's funeral.

In this constant change of wives, there was a subtle point of breach of morality which had been made much of by Sugriva. It would appear that it was lawful for the younger brother to marry the widow of the elder, as was the rule among many ancient peoples, but unlawful for the elder to marry the widow of the younger brother. This was the main complaint of Sugriva to Rama when he dwelt upon the wicked deeds of Bali. Bali's son Angada, on the other hand, thought it was the other way about. Once when he was led to brooding over the wickedness of Sugriva, he said: "Reverence, candour, mercy and patience are not in Sugriva; he who appropriates the wife of the elder brother, who is like a mother unto him and who has a living son, is hated of all beings". Between the two, the author of the epic does not pronounce any clear judgement.

Another interesting point to be noted is that Tara is not considered blameable in this affair between bali and Sugriva, which involved her change of allegiance several times. If anything, she is held in the greatest honour in the Indo-Aryan scriptures, and is even now venerated as one of the five paragons of feminine perfections. Though practising of morality different from that of the Aryans, Tara was a wise, forceful woman of the type of Draupadi, efficient in the management of men and affairs. She often controlled and guided her husbands, and on a particular occasion when the irate Lakshmana intruded into the privacy of Sugriva's palace, the monkey chief was frightened to face him and it was Tara who met him. The incident may be narrated in some detail as it shows the cool-headedness of Tara, and her ability to handle difficult situations; incidentally it also speaks well for the freedom women enjoyed in Kishkindha and their capacity to argue with unreasonable Aryans.

In the agreement between Rama and Sugriva, it was stipulated that Rama should kill Bali and reinstate Sugriva on the throne of Kishkindha; Sugriva, on his part, was to despatch his men to the different regions of the earth to search for Sita and regain her, when found. Rama fulfilled his part of the contract, but the season for the despatch of agents in search of Sita was not favourable and it was agreed that the search would start after a stipulated period. Sugriva, long starved for women in his exile, now gave himself up to the pleasures of the boudoir; after the stipulated period. Rama sent Lakshmana to remind Sugriva of his promise. Sugriva now gave instructions for calling, to his capital, competent people well acquainted with the geography of the regions to be explored, and, again, repaired to his harem for pleasure. When Sugriva was thus seeking satiation with his numerous wives, Rama who had lost the only one he had, was becoming impatient, and sent Lakshmana with a peremptory order to call Sugriva to a sense of his duty to his ally. Lakshmana was so worked up by Rama that he literally flew to Kishkindha and, ignoring the guards of Sugriva's palace, gate-crashed into his harem where the monkey chief, well plied with wine, was lolling in Rumi's lap. On this intrusion, Sugriva was so confused that he asked Tara to go and meet Lakshmana.

Tara appeared before Lakshmana and, in her sweet way, asked him why Kishkindha was honoured by the unexpected visit of the intimate friend of Sugriva. Lakshmana was not quite prepared for this encounter, but after the initial embarrassment found speech. "O lady!" said he, "don't you see, that Sugriva, abandoning virtue, has given himself up to pleasures; he has surrounded himself with parasites and pleasure-seekers, while we, Rama and myself, his friends, are immersed in grief. Having giving us his solemn word that he would institute enquiries concerning Sita four months after his coronation, Sugriva has forgotten his promise and is wasting his time on wine and women". Then followed a long-winded discourse on the twin evils of wine and women, and the consequences of dereliction of one's duty.

Tara now gave a spirited defence of pleasure. She said :

> I know the power of Kama, the irresistible god of pleasure, by whom Sugriva is now ruled. Even weak human beings, O hero, coming under the influence of that god, are inflamed with desire; then how much more should his power be on Sugriva, the strong man, made for action and for pleasure? Even austere sages whose delight is asceticism or penance, often come under the influence of Kama and foreit their spiritual merit; then what wonder is there if Sugriva, of royal power, seeks pleasure in his own palace with his own ladies?

In this censure there is a broad hint that the austere Lakshmana who had never fallen in love, was not competent to talk on pleasure, one of the four main objects of life. Tara closed her discourse with a mild rebuke:

> O prince, this ire hardly becomes you; Sugriva is your friend and it is unfair to rail against a friend without just cause. I know what you have done for him, and I know what is due to you from him. Nor has he allowed pleasure to interfere with his duty. He has already issued orders for all preparations to be made for the search for Sita. Monkeys and bears by the hundreds, nay by the thousands, have already arrived here, and many are on their way to Kishkindha.

This information was quite true, and Lakshmana felt extremely foolish, especially for his having rushed into Sugriva's harem without first ascertaining the real state of affairs. Seeing Lakshmana's embarrassment, the courteous lady politely invited him to see Sugriva in his harem with the soothing words: "It is not objectionable for a man to see the wives of his friend in the inner apartments of his house, in a spirit of friendliness and cordiality."

We have also been given in the *Ramayana* a picture of Sugriva in his harem.

> Seated on a superb couch laid on a costly carpet, the monkey chief resembled the sun-god himself in splendour. He was

> of a dignified presence, his person was adorned with brilliant jewellery, and he wore garlands and superb robes rivalling those of Indra. Surrounded by damsels wearing flower braids and elegant ornaments, his eyes reddened with the effect of wine, Sugriva looked like the Destroyer himself. Sitting beside him was his favourite wife Rumi.

The more powerful of the non-Aryan races and individuals, whether the friends or foes of the Aryan's are mentioned in the epics as of celestial origin, due mainly to the general Hindu conception that all great manifestation of power, for good or evil, essentially emanates from the Deity. As we have seen, Bali was born of god Indra, and Sugriva of Surya, in a monkey; Hanuman was the son of the wind-god Vayu and the monkey lady, Anjana.

Even Ravana had respectable parentage on the male line, though his mother Kaikasi was a Rakshasa lady. As the young Rakshasi came of age to be married, her father, Sumali, sent her to woo the mighty Brahmin sage Vaisrava, son of Pulastya. Kaikasi approached Vaisrava at an inopportune hour when the Brahmin, under the stress of a sacrifice he was performing, was blazing like fire; as a result, Kaikasi started giving birth to monsters. Ravana had ten necks and twenty arms; his brother Kumbhakarna was huge as a mountain, and sister Surpanakha, of hideous form; by the time Vibhishana was born, the effulgence of the saint, however, subsided, and this son of Kaikasi was, in consequence, of a milder mould both in aspect and nature; Vibhishana was, in the fact, so good that he deserted the Rakshasas, went over to Rama, disclosed many secrets regarding the defences of Lanka, and was rewarded by Rama, after the destruction of Ravana, with the crown of Lanka.

From the general trend of Indo-Aryan literature, it will be seen that the non-Aryans were less strict in moral matters than the Aryans. The Aryans themselves, had enjoyed a good deal of sexual freedom, but with the development of their religion, a tendency set in which idealised marriage and restricted the freedom of women. The non-Aryan, generally speaking, did not develop sacramental notions of marriage except when strongly influenced by the Indo-Aryans; as a rule, marriage for them was a mundane affair with certain legal, economic and biological privileges and responsibilities.

For a correct understanding of the position of women in the pre-Aryan cultures of India, more helpful than Indo-Aryan literature would be, perhaps, a study of existing non-Aryan cultures and survivals. Before dealing with this subject, however, we have to note certain trends in the development and expansion of what we call Indo-Aryan religion and culture.

South Indian Cultures and Aryans

Though the Aryans who conquered North India and settled down in the country were a race of semi-nomads who were culturally inferior to some of the peoples whom they conquered, they built up in the country, along with their political expansion, a distinctive religion and literature by developing their own ideals and borrowing freely from indigenous peoples and later invaders of India. Their composite culture came to be known as Indo-Aryan; in its full developed form. Indo-Aryan culture was perhaps more non-Aryan than Aryan, but the name has proved a convenient one.

Nor were the ancient Aryans, with the best efforts, able to maintain their racial purity in India. There were several reasons for this. This Aryan conquest of India was not a single outburst under a powerful conqueror like Alexander or Chengiz khan, but a series of tribal movements which extended over centuries. The Aryans, in their original homeland, had no conception of an administrative machinery, controlled centrally, which extended its ramifications to vast areas or masses of humanity. They were divided into numerous clans which were capable of uniting under a single leader in times of emergency, but were normally autonomous units that operated independently. As such, whatever confederacies they might have formed against a powerful adversary, the clans, once the common danger was past, reverted to their independent status. The idea of empire was essentially non-Aryan; the first Aryan empire was of the Persians who learnt the art and craft of empire-building from the Semites.

One peculiarity of the Aryan invasion of India was that, by the time the earlier tribes passed on to the Gangetic plain, the newcomers in the Punjab and Indus region were so far removed culturally from them that they had little in common except the name. Further, after the last of the Aryans had settled down in India, alien races found their way into the country from the west, east and north, while some of the indigenous people who got over the initial shock of the Aryan impact mustered strength and reconquered many Aryan clans and kings. These revolutions led to a good deal of mixed blood through intermarriage, rape and abductions, and the process went on in spite of the strictest taboos.

The Aryans, however, had retained their political supermacy in India sufficiently long to build up a powerful sacerdotal hierarchy which commanded the respect of not only the Aryans and the conquered peoples, but also of the people who conquered the Aryans. The Brahmins, as these hierarchy are known, emerged as a powerful class whom all feared and honoured: by the magical knowledge their jealously guarded scriptures were supposed to contain, by mysterious rites and elaborate sacrifices, they were believed to be capable of conferring merit and prosperity on whomsoever they cared to patronise, and hell and ruin on those whom they wished to destroy.

The cultural expansion of the Indo-Aryans was not a little due to this power and prestige of the Brahmins. While the Aryan kings vied with one another in securing the services of famous Brahmins, well versed in sacred lore, the non-Aryans considered it a greater honour and privilege to have Brahmin ritualists and sacrificers in their courts. Powerful Asura kings, as we have seen, had Brahmin preceptors and advisers. That this non-Aryan preference for Brahmin priests was not a myth is borne out by the fact that in historic times many courts of South East-Asia (Java, Cambodia, Siam and Burma, for example) had Brahmin hierarchy as their ritualists; even after Buddhism was well established in these regions and Buddhist patriarchs and prelates gave counsel to kings, Brahmins were retained to consult omens, fix auspicious days and timings for royal ceremonies, and to perform secret rites.

Another peculiarity of Brahminism that facilitated its expansion and, with it Indo-Aryan culture was its refusal to make religion cheap by showing an eagerness to spread it among the aliens. To the Brahmin, Vedic wisdom was essenitially esoteric, and it was a sin to reveal it to the aliens and low castes; as a result, they were particularly anxious to benefit by Vedic wisdom, and Brahminism spread throughout the country without much conscious effort by those who professed it.

The method of its diffusion was also unique. An alien who wished to come under the Indo-Aryan religious, influence did not have to discard his traditional beliefs, gods and way of life, as a heathen who accepted Christianity or an infidel who embraced Islam had to. The alien continued to worship his own gods, and followed his own traditional beliefs and practices, but merely accepted the competence of the Brahmins to perform priestly offices for him and recognised the revealed nature and infallibility of the *Vedas* which he was expected not to see or read. As a matter of fact, individual conversions were few, but entire communities came under Brahminism in this manner. The new community was accorded a caste status in keeping with its power, prestige and occupation, and learned Brahmins joined its service and generally superintended its rituals and worship. When the community was powerful enough to claim a particularly high position for its deities, obsequious Brahmins were ready to give these new deities honoured places in their pantheon, lay down rituals and invent feasts, festivals and fasts in their honour, and fabricate myths to identify them with some mighty gods of the Brahminic pantheon. Such free admission of alien deities soon changed the character of the ancient pantheon; old Vedic gods began to disappear or recede into the background while new gods came into prominence. Shiva is a remarkable example of a new god having replaced old ones. He was not a member of the old Vedic pantheon, and the worship of his Lingam was abhorrent to the more ancient tradition. But both Shiva and his Lingam came to occupy the most important position in Puranic Hinduism. It is significant that he was a favourite deity of the non-Aryans. His worship is said to be as ancient as the Indus Valley

Civilisation, if not more. Ravana was an ardent devotee of Shiva, and wherever he went he is said to have carried a golden Lingam with him.

All told, deities and nature of worship changed in Hinduism but the power of the Brahmins remained.

The Aryan civiliser of South India, according to both Indo-Aryan and Dravidian accounts, was the Brahmin sage Agastya. All the South Indians, however, do not seem to have accepted the undisputed supremacy of the Brahmins. We are told in the epics the story of the Asura Vatapi and his father, who were contemptuous of the Brahmins and obstructed their progress to the south. They were great wizards who considered Brahmin magic inferior to their own, and conceived an ingenious plan for the destruction of the Brahmins in general and those who came to South India in particular. They posed as the friends of the Brahmins and invited them by the hundreds to grand feasts; when the hungry Brahmins came, Vatapi converted himself into a sheep by his magic; he was then killed and the meat was served to the Brahmin guests. After the Brahmins were well gorged, Vatapi's father, repeating a spell called his son back to life, and each piece of Vatapi's meat tore the entrails of the Brahmin who had consumed it, joined together, and revived Vatapi. This thing happened so often that the Brahmins were killed in large numbers and the puissant sage Agastya, the genius of digestion, was requested to do something in the matter. Agastya, accordingly, went to the palace of Vatapi who politely received him with all the courtesy due to a Brahmin sage, and introduced him to his father who regaled the sage with a pleasant conversation; soon, dinner was announced. Agastya particularly relished the meat dish, and fell heartily to it. After dinner, while Agastya and his host were sitting together and talking, the latter, laughing at his guest called out to Vatapi to come out of the saint's stomach. Agastya, also laughing, let out a mighty wind, and told his guest that Vatapi for once, had been digested.

These stories would indicate that in certain quarters at least there was stiff opposition to Brahmin expansion. Some of the

South Indians, we know from historical data, stubbornly resisted Aryanisation; the Paraiyans who had considerable power in ancient South India may be pointed out as an example. They persistently resisted the Aryan expansion to the south, tenaciously clung to their ancient ways, and refused to submit to the supremacy of the Aryans. They are, at present, the only community of the Hindus in South India who eat beef. They had to suffer much on account of this, and even the untouchables considered them as the unapproachables. The Paraiyans were prepared to suffer all this rather than adopt the custom of the Aryans. Further, "the hatred that existed between the early Dravidians and Aryans is best preserved in the Kuricchan's (a hill tribe of Malabar corresponding to the Kuravas of the Tamil country) custom of plastering their huts with cow dung to remove the pollution caused by the entrance of a Brahmin".

Nor has the bitterness between the Aryans and the Dravidians in South India completely died down; the activities of the Dravida Munnetta Kazhagam, a socio-political organisation of the non-Aryans enjoying considerable influence in Tamil districts at present, often take the form of burning Hindu scriptures like the *Ramayana* in which the South Indians have not been depicted as highly civilised.

Such resistance, however, has not materially affected the spread of Aryan culture to the higher strata of the Dravidian society in South India. Generally speaking, the ruling classes, with negligible exceptions readily accepted the supremacy of the Brahmins, and these, on their part, interfered little with the internal working of the social organisations of the communities that came under the Indo-Aryan cultural hegemony. In some cases, the Brahmins even recognised the competence of the priests of these communities to perform certain traditional ceremonies and sacrifices, and allowed them a caste status in keeping with their priestly traditions.

Many of the high caste Hindus of the present are non-Aryans by race who were thus admitted into the Indo-Aryan fold. All this led to a considerable intermingling of blood, especially during the formative period of Puranic Hinduism.

Anyway, the term 'Indo-Aryan' lost its ethnic significance, and is now generally used in a cultural sense; by 'Indo-Aryan' we mean those people who have come under the Indo-Aryan cultural influence. Generally speaking, they are the three higher castes, the Brahmins, the Kshatriyas and the Vaisyas who have initiation ceremonies known as Upanayanam and wear the symbol of the twice-born, the sacred thread. They are much less in number than the Sudras and the vast body of outcasts (known as Chandals, Panchamas, etc.) and hill tribes, but much more powerful because of the leadership of Hinduism that has been vested in them down the centuries.

The Tamils

Of the non-Aryan peoples now extant, the Dravidian Tamils of the south are more important to our subject than the several communities of the north. South India had enjoyed, from time immemorial, considerable immunity from foreign aggression; few races ever invaded India by sea, the first in this category being the Europeans who came rather late in Indian history. The conquests of India were generally from the north-west, and by the time the conquerors settled down in the Gangetic plain, few were left with the energy and desire to extend their dominions to the south. From the time of the Aryan invasion, the first known to Indian history, till the Muslim conquest in the eleventh-twelfth century, many races have conquered and settled down in India, but all these conquests have conformed to this geographical factor in the history of India. Even the Muslim influence was felt late in the south, and never to the extent it did in the north.

The history of the Tamils is very ancient, co-eval, perhaps, with the Indus Valley Culture, already noticed. But the Tamil literature, now extant, is of post-Aryan origin and is influenced by Brahminic, Jain and Buddhist ideals, and none of the works now available to us pertain to a period earlier than the third century B.C. Some Tamil works, however, give us an inkling into South Indian society before the arrival of the Aryans.

From the *Tolkappiyam,* it will be seen that the approved form of marriage among the ancient Tamils was 'Kalavu' or secret. This was love marriage pure and simple. Marriage was a private affair between a young man and a girl, and no wedding ceremonies or nuptial rites were performed. No details are, however, available to us as to how 'Kalavu' worked without complications, though we have lengthy descriptions of vigorous 'Kalavu' courtship by lovers in works like *Silappadikaram.* If we are to believe Tamil texts, 'Kalavu' worked very smoothly in ancient India, as no man betrayed his mate and no father disowned his baby. But knowing human nature as we do, it is not likely that masculine integrity alone was the cause of the smooth working of 'Kalavu' marriages. The social pattern was possibly such that betrayal of women and disowning of babies by men did not lead to any grave consequences, which would indicate a matriarchal society. In matriarchates, as we shall see presently, the function of the male is mainly biological, without any economic or domestic responsibilities to his wife and children, and 'Kalavu' marriages could have been successful only in such a society.

The open form of marriage, 'Karpu' as it is called in the ancient Tamil literature, in which wedding ceremonies are performed in public before witnesses, was, we are told, introduced by the Ayars (Tamil corruption of Aryans or Aryans; in South India, the Brahmins are even now distinguished by the honorofic 'Ayar'). The Karpu, in ancient days, was considered an undesirable innovation, an exotic fashion from the north, not suitable for the warm climate of the south. "It is interesting to note that the approved form of marriage according to the Sanskrit Samhitas were the unapproved forms to the Tamils, and were, as such, known as Poruntak-kaman."

The ancient Tamils, it must be noted, were not the docile South Indians of today. They were a hardy, martial people, who thought it a disgrace to die a natural death, and always courted death in the battlefield. The triple object of their life was war, women and wine, and a story typical of the spirit of the ancient Tamil, is told in an old poem. A woman, when asked where her son was, answered: "I know not where my son is; but he will appear, without doubt, in some battle-field, for this (pointing to her abdomen) is the cave that gave birth to that tiger."

All told, available evidence would indicate that the South Indian women before Aryan influences curtailed their liberty were a free, hardy type not enslaved by sacramental notions of marriage, Sati, child-marriage, Purdah and other evil institutions of the Aryans of the north. Pre-Aryan society in South India, as already indicated, was possibly matriarchal; but except some tribes of negligible importance, no well-developed matriarchate has come down to us among the Tamils; for this we have to look to Kerala.

Matriarchy in Kerala

Kerala has been particularly fortunate in its enjoyment of age-long freedom from foreign aggression. Protected on the east by the Western Ghats and on the west by the Arabian Sea, this well-populated, fertile strip of land built up a culture of its own without much interference from the Indo-Aryans. The Aryan castes, confined mainly to the Brahmins, and the Kshatriyas in whom rulership was vested, far from influence the indigenous culture, had to recognise and accept it, and compromise on some of their most cherished ideals.

The traditions of Kerala would indicate that the Asura emperor Bali was the most powerful monarch of the people in the pre-Aryan days. Onam, a festival that has now assumed a national character in Kerala, has been celebrated in the land, down the centuries to the present day, in Bali's honour. The Indo-Aryan literature mentions Bali as a very powerful, just and generous monarch whom even the gods could not vanquish in a straight war; as regards his conduct, neither the Aryans nor their gods had any complaint. Unlike the Rakshasa chief Ravana, the personification of wickedness, Bali was as good as the best of the Aryan monarchs, and in many respects even better; he did not abduct any Aryan women; Bali's only sin was that he was a non-Aryan who could not be vanquished by the Aryan heroes or gods.

According to the Indo-Aryan literature itself, Vishnu brought about the ruin of Bali through a dubious stratagem which is extolled in the *Puranas* as one of the great achievements of Vishnu. This god, we are told, having heard of the generosity of Bali, appeared before the emperor as a Vamana or Brahmin dwarf, and begged of him three paces of land in which to sit down and meditate the Almighty, and the monarch immediately granted it; on this, the midget grew into a cosmic giant and measured the earth in two paces and exiled Bali from this region for not keeping his promise. Kerala legends say that the exile broke Bali's heart, as he had loved his subjects like his children; he requested his tormentor to allow him to visit his people once a year, which was granted. The popular belief is that Bali comes to Kerala during the ten days of the Onam festival, and the merry-making of the season is the reception given to the invisible visitor. The folk songs sung on the occasion include panegyrics of the utopian reign of Bali in which "there were no castes, no droughts, no floods and no famines, and all men were equal and good". It is interesting to note that the object of worship during Onam is Bali for the non-Aryan castes", and Vamana for the Aryans.

The most important and numerous sections of the Hindus in Kerala are the Sudras who are not subject to the Indo-Aryan *Dharma Sastras* but follow their traditional customs. The predominant social system has been matriarchal from the time anything is known about Kerala. So deep-rooted was the matriarchal tradition in the country that the kings of Kerala who were Kshatriyas, and as such Indo-Aryans, were compelled to follow it; in the royal houses of Cochin and Travancore, as is well known, the heir to the throne was not the Maharajah's son but his sister's son. Even the Namboodiri Brahmins to whom Parasurama is believed to have given Kerala as gift to be enjoyed in perpetuity, had to come to terms with the matriarchal social system sacrificing some of their cherished ideals and transgressing the laws of Manu and the other Indo-Aryan legislators.

The matriarchal system in India has now succumbed to the patriarchate but as recent as two decades back, it was a vigorous living institution in Kerala, and in her villages it still persists. During the British period there were special laws for Kerala, known as Marumakkathayam (inheritance through Marumakkal or nephews and nieces) applicable for Kerala communities, and these were only superseded by the Hindu Marriage Code of 1955 and Hindu Succession Act of 1956 which aim at legal uniformity for all people known as Hindus.

A detailed account of the matriarchal system in Kerala will be appropriate to our subject especially as it will show how the 'Kalavu' form of marriage of the ancient Tamils could work without impairing the good name of respectable ladies.

The Nayars, nominally Sudras, are the dominant matriarchs of Kerala. In the days when the word 'Aryan' stood for all that was noble in India, there were Nayar scholars who had put forth laboured evidence to show that they were Aryan Kshatriyas who were decasted by the spiteful Brahmin Parasurama, but with the recent discovery of Dravidian precedence over Aryan culture, the Nayars are beginning to feel that they are Dravidians. In all probability the Nayars were the ruling classes whom Parasurama conquered; some philologists trace the origin of the word 'Nayar' to 'Nagar' (South Indian plural of 'Naga'), and the wide prevalence of snake-worship among the Nayars would indicate that they have some claim to Naga culture. Whether the Naga culture was pre-Dravidian or post-Dravidian, whether it was a branch of the Dravidian or an independent culture that co-existed with the Dravidian, are all pet themes of discussion with the anthropologists; for our purpose it is enough to note that the Nayars belong to the non-Aryan group in our broad division of the Indians into Indo-Aryan and non-Aryan.

For a Nayar marriage was a simple affair. When a girl came of age, she was married according to a rite known as Sambandham (literally, auspicious connection). Sambandham was not sacramental; a few relatives were called on the occasion and the bridegroom presented to the bride a set of clothes called Pudava, and the guests were treated to light refreshments; there was none of that noisy music, the endless chanting of texts and the mysterious fire rites that drown the misery and seal the iniquity of an Indo-Aryan sacramental marriage.

The girl, after Sambandham, did not leave her house for that of the husband, but continued to live in her own house with her people; the husband, likewise, lived in his own house but visited his wife at night for conjugal rights and returned home in the morning. These marriages usually took place in the same village or town, the husband and wife living in houses not more than a couple of miles apart. Thus, the Sambandham did not involve any disruption of family life for the bride or bridegroom.

Children born of a Nayar lady belonged to the mother and lived with her in the same family; they were known by the mother's name and that of the eldest maternal uncle, and not by the father's name. A man had no responsibility to support his children but was duty bound to look after his sisters and their children who lived with him and his brothers. In fact, among respectable Nayars, the giving of any gift by a man to his wife or children was resented by the latter, as it constituted a reflection on the ability of the members of the family to support their women and children.

Divorces among the Nayars were easy and informal, and led to no social, economic or domestic complication. When a husband was no longer wanted, he was politely told that he was not welcome; when the man himself took the initiative, he stopped his nocturnal visits and his continued absence could mean only one thing. In spite of such freedom of divorce, there was considerable constancy, especially among the higher classes, and Sambandham was of a permanent nature among them. Some Nayar sub-castes and certain other Sudra castes in Kerala practised fraternal and regular polyandry; among them, a plurality of husbands often enhanced the reputation of a woman.

The impact of the Indo-Aryan moral notions on matriarchy led to some curious social patterns in Kerala. The Kshatriya communities, as we have already seen, accepted regular matriarchal standards.

The Namboodiri Brahmins came to some interesting compromises. Among the Namboodiris, it must be remembered, only the eldest son of the head of a family was competent to marry; this law of succession and marriage was probably established to order to prevent dissipation of ancestral wealth through division of property. The younger brothers of a Namboodiri heir were not, however, obliged to remain celibate; they could have Sambandham with Nayar or Kshatriya ladies but were not allowed to bring their wives to their families. The children born of the Sambandham naturally belonged to the caste of the mother, and the Namboodiri had no responsibility to support them.

Pratiloma taboos were observed by the Namboodiris, Kshatriyas and Nayars, and as a result, the Namboodiri ladies had all to be married to the eldest male members of the Namboodiri households, which meant unlimited polygyny. In fact, so great was the demand in the marriage market for the heir in each household, that every time he married he brought into the house, in addition to his bride, a large sum of money as dowry while, when he gave away his sisters or daughters in marriage, he parted with similar amounts.

The Kshatriya ladies, however, had no dearth of men. They were regular matriarchs and could have Sambandham with men of their own community and with Namboodiri men. In the royal families and in other wealthy Kshatriya households which had a large number of ladies, separate establishments for husbands were maintained where the men lived on a permanent or semi-permanent basis.

The interesting point to be noted about this arrangement, as far as the Brahmins and the Kshatriyas were concerned, is that the Indo-Aryan religious injunction that a man, to be saved from the hell called Put (of which more in succeeding chapters), should have sons of his own status, was conveniently set aside in Kerala.

Medieval travellers and casual observers with superficial knowledge of matriarchates have often described the Hindu communities of Kerala as promiscuous, adulterous and by other uncomplimentary adjectives. But it is not clear why polyandry should be considered disreputable and polygyny respectable, why taking paramours by women should be treated as criminal and keeping mistresses or resorting to courtesans by men, fashionable.

The sanctity attached to our sexual morals will be found, on analysis, to be based on the responsibility of a man to support his children and his insistence that the children he supports are born of his loins; when this responsibility is removed, sexual relations become natural and secular. The sanctity of matrimony, generally confined to patriarchates, is largely the sanctity of iniquity, of the slavery of woman to man. Just social institutions do not require sacraments to make them workable whereas unjust ones do.

Anyway, centuries of matriarchal practices have, in no way, adversely affected the Nayars and Kshatriyas of Kerala. Both have been martial classes from the very dawn of history, and all who have visited Kerala have testified to their military prowess, their loyalty and honour. I myself have lived among the Nayars for years and can say with confidence that in physique, intellect, honour, friendship, courtesy, in fact in all those virtues we would associate with culture, the Nayars are in no way inferior to any patriarchal community of India. The freedom the Nayar ladies have enjoyed from the tyranny of husbands, the patent vice of patriarchal societies, and from the baneful influences of Sati, child-marriage, Purdah and other perverted institutions, has endowed them with a self-reliance, independence and ability to manage men and affairs found nowhere else among women of their position in India.

The Todas of the Nilgiris

The Todas who inhabit the Nilgiri hills in South India offer an ethnic enigma to the anthropoligists. By isolating themselves in the forest regions difficult of access to the outsiders, the Todas have preserved their racial integrity for ages and show no ethnic affinity to any of the existing peoples of South India. They are of olive complexion and of fine physique; and some scholars have even identified them as the lost tribe of Israel, while the possibility of their being, like the Indus Valley Dravidians, of a Mediterranean stock çannot be entirely ruled out.

The horror of the Brahmin was a characteristic feature of the Toda sense of pollution. The Europeans were allowed entry into their houses and temples, but not the Brahmins. "At the funeral of a female", wrote an Englishman, "I provided a box of tandstickors for lighting the pyre. A fire-stick, which was in current use in the dairy, was polluted and rendered useless by the touch of my Brahmin assistant! It is recorded by Harkness that a Brahman was not only refused admission to a Toda dairy but actually driven away by some boys, who rushed out of it when they heard him approach."

The Todas were polyandrous and, to some extent, are so even now, in spite of the Hindu Marriage Act of 1955 prohibiting polyandry and polygyny, as the arm of the law is not long enough in India to reach all the hills and forests. Both fraternal and regular polyandry were practised; it was however, important to know the paternity of the children and for this a very arbitrary ceremony was performed for fixing fatherhood. When brothers lived together sharing a common wife and supporting her and her children, the ceremony was not obligatory, but when there were husbands belonging to different families it was necessary to fix responsibility for fatherhood and maintenance of the children.

The ceremony of fixing paternity was known as Purusatpimi (the bow and arrow). It was usually performed in the seventh month of pregnancy of a woman, after consultation among the several husbands of the woman who elected one man for the office. The woman, accompanied by her relatives, proceeded to a previously arranged site where she sat under a Kiaz tree (*Eugenia Arnottiana*); the appointed husband also went to the spot and sat near her. The husband then asked the father of the woman if he could bring the bow, and on receiving his permission went and brought a twig of a shrub (*Sophora Glauca*) which he bent like a bow; he then procured a blade of grass to represent the arrow, and presented both with certain minor ceremonies to the woman.

The rite thus completed made the man the father of the expected child and of any that followed, even years after his death, as long as another of her husbands had not performed the Purusatpimi. Such fictitious rites to fix paternity do, no doubt, appear ridiculous to us, but these survivals help us to understand the economic and legal origin's of marriage. For the Todas, it was not the biological function of the father that mattered, but his economic obligations; we shall see, in the next chapter, that the institution of marriage among the Indo-Aryans too started with the legal rights and economic obligations of the father, and the sanctity of sexual relations was later development.

Survivals and Variations in Northern India

The few communities mentioned above constitute but an infinitesimal part of the vast non-Aryan communities are even more numerous. The Himalayan region in the north and the Assam Hills in the north-east are the homes of many non-Aryan peoples of Tibeto-Mongoloid extraction, many of whom follow polyandrous traditions; by coming into contact with them, even some Indo-Aryan groups have, as we shall see presently, adopted the polyandrous social pattern. In addition, there are numerous tribes known as the Gonds, the Bhils, the Santals, etc. who follow their own social codes and have a wide distribution extending from Rajputana to the Bay of Bengal along the Vidhyan ranges. Besides these, are the non-Aryan castes who lived with the Indo-Aryans in subordination to them. Interesting as the institutions of these vast groups of Indians are, the subject falls into the domain of anthropology, and the scope of this book does not admit of any detailed description of them. I may, however, mention two communities here, the Khasas and the Khasis, as representatives of two interesting social variations.

The Khasis

The Khasis are mainly concentrated in the Jaintia and Khasi hills and in Shillong. They were regular matriarchs, but unlike the Nayars among whom husbands and wives lived in separate houses, the Khasi man on marriage went to the house of his wife and lived with her; here was a direct reversal of the patriarchal system.

A man had a right to his ancestral property, and any property brought by a married man into his wife's family was reverted, after his death, to his own family along with his ashes. What a man earned during his sojourn in his wife's house naturally went to his wife who maintained him.

Unlike the widely accepted standard throughout the world by which authority and inheritance go to the eldest, among the Khasis, it was the youngest daughter who inherited. "She is the custodian of the family property and performs the religious sacrifices. Thus property descends in the female line, and the youngest daughter inherits as a trustee for the family."

It is difficult to say exactly to what culture or ethnic group the Khasis belong. They are, at present, an isolated community of matriarchs with cultural affinities to some of the peoples of South East Asia who have matriarchal traditions. They are neither Indo-Aryan nor Dravidian ethnically or culturally. They repudiate alike "the authority of the Brahmins and the entire caste system". Having no great loyalty to Hinduism, a great many Khasis have become Christians.

The Khasas

Polyandry and matriarchy are not exclusively non-Aryan institutions, but were prevalent among certain Indo-Aryan tribes too, though with the development of their religion and social theories both were condemned as 'un-Aryan'. An interesting survival of what may be considered as Indo-Aryan polyandry is found in the marriage customs and conventions of the Khasas of Jaunsar-Bawar in the Dehra Dun District; till recently they practised fraternal polyandry and permitted a good deal of free love to married women while living away from their husbands. Whether the institution was an independent development in some Indo-Aryan tribe or was borrowed from some polyandrous Tibetan stock with whom the Khasas came in contact, we do not know.

The Khasas are an ancient people mentioned in the *Mahabharata*, but their exact caste status is not very clear from the epic. According to Dr. Majumdar they are 'Rajputs or Brahmins', observe caste, and are, as such, to be considered as Indo-Aryan. They are a well-to-do community.

A typical Khasa family "consists of a group of brothers as husbands with one, two or more wives, and children. Poor families cannot afford to have more than one wife whom the brothers share among themselves, but as the economic condition of the brothers improves, more wives may be added. Similarly, when a substantial family falls on evil days, and finds it hard to maintain a number of wives, the latter find it more convenient to leave the household and seek divorce on economic grounds."

The arrangement often led to a good deal of disparity in age between a wife and some of her husbands; the many husbands who shared a wife could be of different mothers, and a wife often found that while her eldest husband was well in his thirties, the youngest was an infant whom she had to nurse. Under these conditions, marital relations between a wife and some of her husbands became difficult.

As the younger brothers grow up, it becomes a headache for the eldest, as he has to find a wife for them, and the financial commitments of a marriage may prove too difficult to provide for. The latitude and license socially recognized in Jaunsar Bawar, both for men and women, make possible domestic life on a polyandrous pattern. So long as the elder brother, particularly the head of the family, does not secure a wife for the younger brothers, he does not object to intrigues within the village according to the local customs of exogamy.

For the purposes of intrigue, the Khasa made a nice distinction between a Dhyanti and a Ranti. It is not difference in the individual that determined this distinction but environments. A married woman who came to her father's house was a Dhyanti (daughter), while living with her husbands in their house she was a Ranti (wife). The Dhyanti, freed from the oppressive presence of her husbands, was in independent individual who was allowed, by social conventions, to lead a gay life in her village and could consort with whomsoever she pleased; but once she went to her husbands' house, she had to remain faithful to her marital bond and any interest she might develop in men other than her husbands was censured as a moral breach and dereliction of duty. As a rule, the husbands of a Khasa girl seldom took the trouble of enquiring about her activities when she lived in her father's house; such curiousity was considered an unwanted interference. These social niceties were always reciprocal, and a wife who was living in her father's house was not expected to show any curiosity about her husbands' nocturnal peregrinations in the village during her absence.

While polyandry and matriarchy have existed among many non-Aryan communities, the large majority of them follow, like the Indo-Aryans, patrilineal descent; a wide variety of marriage customs prevails among them ranging from savage practices to pecularities as among the Kumbis of Gujarat who can only marry their boys and girls during the auspicious season that come but once in twelve years.

There is, however, one thing common to all non-Aryan cultures. Except those who have come into close contact with the Indo-Aryans and have adopted their ways, the non-Aryans, as a rule, consider marriage secular and no sacramental; as such a good deal of freedom is allowed to women in non-Aryan cultures as compared with the rigidity of Indo-Aryan marital standards. Further, many non-Aryan communities are economically backward, which has its own advantage; for women, among them, have been wage-earners, working in the fields or factories like men and, more or less, economically independent. Thus freed from the twin oppression of religious suggestion and economic bondage, non-Aryan women have enjoyed better freedom than their upper class Indo-Aryan sisters, and are not generally subject to the ideals of Pativrityam, Sati, child-marriage, life-long widowhood, Purdah and other social evils that ate into the vitals of the Indo-Aryan society.

Many laws have been enacted to bring about equality of sexes among all the sections of the Indians, now known as Hindus, irrespective of caste and race; polyandry, polygyny and caste privileges and disabilities have all been abolished by law. But we must remember that legal reforms are always easier than social reforms. The vast millions of rural and aboriginal India, oblivious to what happens in the Parliament at New Delhi, even now live and die just as their ancestors have done through the centuries.

2

The Construction of Feminity

The Aryan conquest of India, was not a single event under one leader, but a series of tribe movements extended over centuries, the earlier settlers moving east and south as fresh invaders came in. What caused these tribe movements is not known; perhaps, pressure from more warlike nomads from the north and east drove these dwellers of the Caspian region to the west and south or, impelled by those mysterious nomad dynamics which, during several periods in history, had swept off civilisations, the Aryans overran Mesopotamia, India, Asia Minor, and the Aegean region.

At what precise date the Aryan invasion of India started is not known, but it is believed that either direct from their homeland or from their settlements north of Mesopotamia, the Aryan tribes started making inroads into India by the middle of the second millennium before Christ. They were, in all probability, the people who destroyed the Indus Valley Civilisation, as we have already seen.

The earliest known literary compositions of the Indo-Aryans are the hymns of the *Rig Veda*. Though the nucleus from which the *Rig Veda* developed had its origin in the homeland of the Aryans, the work in its present form is definitely a product of the Indian soil. The composition is essentially religious in character and only incidentally treats secular subjects. As such it is difficult to obtain from the hymns of the *Rig Veda* an authentic account of the social life of the Indo-Aryans, though stray references to women and marriage are made in the text.

Based mainly on the *Rig Veda* and on the other three *Vedas* (or which more presently) a vast body of literature, known by the generic name 'Vedic literature', developed in India, but this too is mainly concerned with rituals, sacrifices and meta-physics. In the post-Vedic *Grihya Sutras* we have, however, some detailed accounts of the domestic life of the Indo-Aryans, as they deal with various ceremonies a householder was expected to perform in his life; in these texts we get some information, about marriage rituals, the status of women and other matters relevant to our subject. But more comprehensive accounts of the lore of the Indo-Aryans, the origins of their institutions, etc. are found in the *Mahabharata,* that repository of Indo-Aryan tradition. For information concerning the development of marriage and allied institutions among the Indo-Aryans, this epic is much more helpful than Vedic literature.

Aryan Marriage in its Earliest Form

If we are to believe the theory of evolution, there was a time in the development of primitive society, when men and women lived like animals without the institution of marriage. Jealousy and muscular strength were the main deciding factors in courtships, mating and living together; marriage was a later social development closely linked with the formation of political organisations that ensured individual rights through some sort of an administrative machinery.

It would appear from Indian literature that the notion of marriage among the Indo-Aryans rose out of a recognition of property rights in women and not out of sexual jealously. A woman was more or less the property of some man, and as long as she lived with and worked for him, and as long as her children were his property, he had no right to restrict her sexual freedom. Sexual relationship was purely an individual affair, but property right in women and children public responsibility involving legal definitions. To understand this conception of marriage it is necessary for us to divest our minds of the accretions of centuries of religious inhibitions which have mystified and sanctified sex and invested it with a complex that makes its very mention a taboo. But to the primitive man sex was a natural function like eating, drinking or playing, and there are many primitive and fairly well-advanced peoples, even now, who are inclined to treat marriage as a juridical institution involving property rights only.

Anyway, there are clear statements in the *Mahabharata* to indicate that there was a time when marriage, among the Indo-Aryans, had nothing to do with the sexual freedom of women. Many references in Vedic literature also confirm this view. One passage in the *Mahabharata* is of particular importance in this connection. In a highly intriguing moral situation, king Pandu, prohibited by a curse to consort with his wives, desired to have sons and requested his wife Kunti to have relations with another man for the sake of progeny. Elucidating the ancient matrimonial customs of the Aryans, Pandu lectured his wife thus :

> I shall now tell thee the practice of old, indicated by illustrious sages fully acquainted with every rule of morality. Women, in the olden days, were not immured within their houses, nor were they dependent on their husbands and male relatives. They went about freely enjoying themselves. They did not then confine themselves to their husbands, and yet they were not considered sinful; for that was the sanctioned custom of the age. This practice, sanctioned by precedent, is applauded by great Rishis. The custom is even now regarded with respect among the Northern Kurus. Indeed, that custom, so lenient to women, has the sanction of antiquity. The present practice (of a woman being confined to one husband for life) has been established but lately.

Two sages are named in the *Mahabharata* as having altered the ancient usage. One was Uddalaka Swetaketu and the other Dirghatamas. By Swetaketu's time, it would appear, marriage and family life had been well established, and husbands were beginning to think it improper that their wives should consort with whomsoever they pleased, and the practice was becoming surreptitious. Swetaketu, it is said, found his mother being led to her bed-chamber by a guest, and protested against this behaviour; on this, Swetaketu's father called the young man aside and told him that the practice was lawful for his clan, ancient and honoured, and no blame rested with his mother or the guest. Swetaketu, however, thought that the time had come to put a stop to it, and legislated as follows: "One woman can make love to one man only....If a woman is unfaithful to her husband, from today onwards, it will be a sin, equivalent to the killing of a foetus, bringing unhappiness to her."

Dirghatamas' objection to promiscuity was founded on personal vendetta against the fair sex. The sage was born blind and married a vivacious young lady named Pradweshi; promiscuity, permitted to married women, was commercialised by the couple, and Pradweshi followed the ancient custom more for profit than for pleasure, especially as Dirghatamas, disabled for active work by his blindness, could not support his wife and children. But the activities of the family became a scandal in the village in which they lived, and Pradweshi decided to give up the practice, and told her husband that it was preposterous that a woman should support her husband and children. This so angered the sage that he told her if her activities were not to bring him profit, she should confine her sexual relations to himself. These indecisive arguments led to blows and Pradweshi, with the help of her sons, seized the blind old man and threw him into the Ganges. But the sage saved himself by clinging to a floating log, and lived long enough to legislate against women's extra-marital freedom.

But old traditions and usages die hard, and the practice of 'attending on honoured guests' and entertaining lovers by women lingered among the Indo-Aryans for a long time, at least among some clans, and we have echoes of the practice in the *Brahmanas* and *Upanishads*, ritualistic and philosophic treatises attached to the main *Vedas*. In the Varunapraghasa sacrifice, for instance, jointly performed by the husband and wife, the latter had to confess to her husband the number of her paramours by dropping an equal number of blades of grass; after this confession, she was considered pure for performing the sacrifice. The ritual for the destruction of paramours is also mentioned, indicating the changing attitude towards ancient practices. The wife was advised by her husband to destroy her lovers by placing fire in a moist earthen pot, by spreading Kusa grass besmeared with clarified butter and by performing the sacrifice sitting in a direction opposite to the one she would otherwise adopt.

Then we have the interesting story of Satyakama Jabala narrated in the *Khandogya Upanished.* The young Satyakama went to a Brahmin teacher for instruction. Before accepting the student, the teacher very naturally asked him for his parentage and clan name. Satyakama was not well instructed in these matters, and so he went back to his mother Jabala to find out his father's name. But unfortunately Jabala was no wiser than her son. "During the time I got thee", said she, "I was attending on many guests and had no opportunity of finding out your paternity; hence I know not of what Gotra (clan) you are; Jabala is my name and Satyakama thine. Say, therefore, of thyself Satyakama, son of Jabala."

As the text is not quite clear on the subject, there is a difference of opinion among scholars as to whether Jabala was a widow or unmarried lady. That she had no living husband, when she conceived Satyakama, is fairly certain; for in that case Satyakama would legally belong to the Gotra of her husband, whoever might have been his actual father, as, according to early Indo-Aryan notions, the son of a married woman belonged to her husband just as the crop in a field would belong to the owner of the field and not to any one who might have ploughed it and sown the seed. Such legal fictions continued to the time of the law-giver Manu who says that "men who sow their seed in the soil of others benefit the owner of the woman" just as "if one man's bull were to beget a hundred calves on another man's cows the calves would belong to the owner of the cows; in vain would the bull have spent his strength."

Anyway, it is clear from the text that neither Satyakama nor his mother was looked down upon for his uncertain paternity. For we are told that the teacher declared Satyakama to be a Brahmin and accepted him as a pupil on the broad principle that only high-born Brahmins were capable of telling the truth on such delicate points.

Incidentally, it may be pointed out that in the ancient Indian literature we come across many celebrities and clans who took their names from their mothers and not from fathers. Jaratkara, son of Jaratkaru, Paruchchapa, son of Devadasi, Sariputra, son of the lady Sari, Vainateya, son of Vinata, Daityas, sons of Diti, and Kadraveyas, sons of Kadru, are some notable examples of those who took their names from their mothers.

Anyway, the motive behind the legislation of Swetaketu which restrained women from indulging in extra-marital sex activities is clear. Men were feeling that children whom they were expected to support should be born of themselves and not of anyone else. Since conception was supposed to take place only during a woman's Rtu, she was to observe the restriction only during her Rtu, and outside it she was free to follow the ancient custom. Pandu clearly stated this, soon after mentioning Swetaketu's legislation. "A woman should be faithful to her husband during her Rtu only. This is the Dharma laid down by those who know the law. At other times, a woman is free; this is the ancient rule."

Thus, morality among the ancient Aryans originated from the notions of economic responsibilities and property rights in women and children, and had little to do with sex relations as such.

The Rig Vedic Age

The story of the Indo-Aryan women is a tragic tale of gradual subjection beginning from the legendary age of free love and ending up in the middle ages when they had lost all individuality and were even made to mount the funeral pyres of their husbands. The story of this subjection is closely linked with the development of Brahminism and its eschatological notions which placed the needs of the hereafter before those of life on earth.

Rig Vedic Aryans, as we may conveniently designate the earliest Aryan settlers in India, were semi-nomads who had no great religious systems; the occupations connected with a strenuous life of expansion among alien peoples prevented them from falling into many superstitions which are essentially the offspring of indolence. For them the needs of life on earth were all important; they ate and drank well, tilled the soil, bred cattle and fought their enemies with a vigour that made them the masters of a good part of India Rig Vedic gods were full-blooded martial deities who helped them in their campaigns, confounded their enemies, protected.their fields and cattle and were generally worshipped for enhancing their welfare. They had no notions of sacrificing the pleasures of this life for those of the next world; nor had they any clear ideas of life after death. They found life on earth good, and all that they asked of their gods was an earthly life of hundred years and ten sturdy sons to a man. For the rest, they seem to have thought that the wicked ended up in the grave while the Aryan heroes, on death, were translated into vague regions of bliss where they drank their favourite Soma liquor with the gods.

For such people, women were no ornaments but co-partners in life, in its pleasures and hazards, in its joys and sorrows; they had no use for weaklings and the sickly, and exuberance of vitality and vigour guided them in forming their institutions of marriage and family life.

Child-marriage was unknown in early Vedic period, inas much as the notion that pre-marital menstruation would consign people to hell had not developed. Widows were not expected to remain single in memory of their dead husbands. The early Aryans could ill afford to let the fertility of their women go waste; as the needs of building up the numerical strength of the family and clan were paramount, the widow, being a member of the family of her husband, was married to her husband's brother. It is a common feature of all ancient patriarchal societies that once a woman was brought into the family of her husband after marriage, she became 'the field' of this family for raising crops, and the death of her husband was not considered a sufficient reason for depriving the family of her potentiality for bearing members for it; hence if she was widowed at child-bearing age, the brother or a near relative of her deceased husband married her. Even when she was not actually married to the brother, the latter was expected to raise issues to her in levirate, a usage we will have to notice later.

As an indication of the prevalence of marriage of the widow to the brother of her deceased husband, the following hymn of the *Rig Veda* is of particular importance. It is addressed to the widow by the brother of the husband who led the weeping woman from the grave of the deceased to his home :

> Rise, come into the world of the living, O woman;
> Come, he is lifeless by whose side thou liest.
> Wifehood with thy husband was thy portion,
> Who took thy hand and wooed thee as a lover.

The wedding ceremony described in the *Rig Veda* gives us an inkling into the marriage customs of the early Indo-Aryans, and the status and age of the bride. Rig Vedic Aryans were patriarchal, and a man had almost absolute power over his wife and children; in spite of this, the position of women in Rig Vedic society was much higher than in later times.

A girl, after marriage, went and lived in her husband's house. Marriage was generally arranged by parents; the bride was a full-grown girl, and consummation took place on the fourth night after marriage. In some of the hymns of the *Rig Veda* the marriage ceremony has been described in detail. It was not so lengthy as it became later, but the religious and sacramental conception of marriage was present. Before the ceremony, the god Visvavasu (who, in later literature, is mentioned as a Gandharva who protects maidens) was requested to leave her and make her over to the bridegroom.

The bride was adorned with ornaments and the bridal garments consisted of three pieces of cloth, of which one, a wrapper, had to be given away as a gift to the officiating priest. The bride was to have two bridemaids, one called the companion, and the other the attendant. In the ceremony proper, the bridegroom took hold of the bride's right hand and recited the following verse: "I take thy hand for good fortune, that thou mayst attain old age with me, thy husband. The gods Bhaga, Aryaman, Savitr and Paurandhi have given thee to me, that I may be the master of a household."

Further, "there is nothing to indicate that the ceremony was performed before the fire; nor can we suppose that the bride had been led round the fire." Thus, the most important rite, the taking of the seven steps (Saptapadi) before the fire, which alone later came to be considered to seal the union, was absent in the Rig Vedic marriage ceremony. It must be remembered that Rig Vedic Aryans buried their dead, and the importance of fire in the ceremonials of the Indo-Aryans was a later development.

The marriage ceremony usually ended with a joint prayer by the bride and bridegroom for long life and progeny. After the ceremony the following verse was repeated, formally transferring the bride from the house of her parents to that of her husband. "I set thee free from hence, but not from thence. I place thee there, firmly bound."

After this, and the invitable feasting, the bride with the bridegroom and the party left for her new home. Before her departure, the bride was thus addressed: "May Puṣhan lead thee hence, taking thee by the hand; may the Asvins convey thee in their car; go to the dwelling of thy husband, as thou art the mistress of his house; submissive to thy husband, give orders to his household." On the departure of the bridal car, a prayer was recited for their safe journey.

> On reaching her new home, the bride was thus welcomed:
> Bliss-bringer, furthering thy husband's welfare,
> dear, gladdening thy husband and his father,
> enter this home, mild to thy husband's mother.
> Be pleasant to thy husband's sire, sweet to thy
> husband, thy lord;

To all this clan be gentle, and favour these men's prosperity.

The consummation of marriage took place on the fourth night which would show that child-marriage was not prevalent in Rig Vedic times.

Nor were all the marriages arranged by parents and guardians in Rig Vedic times. As girls were of mature age, we can be sure that love played an important role in some marriages at least; there is a mention, in the *Rig Veda,* of festivals like the Samana to which young women went 'well-adorned with ornaments and bright garments' and possibly met eligible young men; many a marriage negotiation might have started off from here.

The marriage of Urvasi and Pururavas mentioned in the *Rig Veda* would indicate that contract marriage was not unknown to Rig Vedic Aryans. King Pururavas, we are told, married the dancer Urvasi who was living in free love with the Gandharvas, on a condition that he would not appear naked before her as it disturbed her aesthetic sense. Hence, all their sexual activities were conducted in the dark, but the Gandharvas, who wished to reclaim Urvasi, contrived to wake him up at night in a hurry without putting on his clothes, and Urvasi saw him in a flash of lightning. On this, Urvasi, we are told, left him and lived with the Gandharvas.

The *Rig Veda* does not give us a detailed account of the forms of marriage prevalent at the time, but there are indications, in the hymns, of Swayamvara and marriage by capture. The twin Asvins, we are told, married the lady Surya in a chariot race they won, which is possibly the nucleus of the celebrated Swayamvara (own choice) form of marriage of the Indian epics. Further, we read in the *Rig Veda* the story of Kamadyu, daughter of king Purumitra, whom Vimada captured and married; Vimada, it would appear, was not strong enough to fight Purumitra and capture his daughter, and hence he prayed to the Asvins who brought his sweetheart to him.

Monogamy seems to have been the general rule in Rig Vedic times, but chiefs and sages practised exceptional morality. Expressions such as 'like a king among his spouses' and 'as a common husband doeth his spouses' would indicate the prevalence of polygyny; incantations are also mentioned for removing rival wives. Though rare, polyandry too seems to have existed in Rig Vedic times. The twin Asvins as we have seen, had a common wife in Surya; Rodasi is mentioned as a lady attended by numerous husbands in the form of the Maruts (storm gods).

There are many pleasing passages in the *Rig Veda* describing the beauty and charm of women, of men vying with one another for the favours of the fair ones, of courtesans displaying their histrionic talents in public, and of eloquent women taking part in the deliberations of the assemblies of clans. "The wife is the home." says one hymn. In another hymn, Usha, the goddess of dawn, is described as a blooming beauty, dressed in superb finery, revealing her splendour on a public stage. In the hymn to the Maruts, these are mentioned as lovers courting Vak (the goddess of speech), who is likened to a courtly, eloquent woman.' According to Max Muller, the hymn "throws a curious light on the social character of Vedic times, as it presupposes two classes of wives--not necessarily simultaneous, however—a housewife who stays at home and is not much seen, and a wife who appears in public and takes part in society and conversation of the Sabha, the assembly room, and the Vedathas, the meetings".

Women also took part in the intellectual and spiritual life of the community. Sacrifices were performed and oblations offered to the deities, jointly by the husband and wife. One prayer runs as follows: "Gods! May the husband and wife who, with one mind, offer oblations and purify them, propitiate you with the Soma ever mixed with milk; constantly associated, may they acquire appropriate sacrificial viands; may they be able to offer sacrifices."

Some of the hymns of the *Rig Veda* were composed by women. Visvavara, Apala, Lopamudra, Shashiyasi, Ghosha, Indrani and Sachi are mentioned, among others, as composers of hymns. But unfortunately, we know few other details about these ladies; for that matter we know, however, little about the male composers of hymns too. Anyway, the fact that women were considered competent to compose religious hymns is proof enough that they had few religious disabilities at the time.

Women who lived in free love and professional dancers are mentioned in the *Rig Veda*. They were not looked down upon by society but were sought after by heroes and gallants. Urvasi, as we have seen, was a dancer whom king Pururavas married.

In the Rig Vedic age, marriage does not appear to have been compulsory for women; women could grow old in their parents' houses without public censure, and in case a man had an only daughter she was considered as good as a son and was not given away in marriage to another household. In such cases it is not clear whether the girl's husband married into the family of the heiress or she had children by Niyoga or appointment, a custom we will have to notice in detail later.

Illegitimacy, that bane of patriarchal societies, is as old as the *Rig Veda* as some hymns would indicate. Considerable stigma was attached to illegitimate children and we come across references in the *Rig Veda* to exposure of infants; the god Indra is said to have rescued some of these innocents.

All told, the position of women seems to have deteriorated considerably by the Rig Vedic times when compared with the earlier age when marriage was not sacramental and women had practically unlimited freedom in sexual matters.

Later Vedic Period

From the Rig Vedic times to the later Vedic period it was yet another descent down the rungs of the ladder. The main reason for this is the development of certain eschatological notions which led to a belief that sons alone were competent to redeem their parents from hell and daughters were incapable of performing this spiritual function. As these ideas began to take root, women were valued only as the vehicles for bearing sons, and when they were unfit for or unwilling to perform this function, they were considered useless.

The idea is emphasised in the *Atharva Vedas* the *Brahmanas* and the *Upanishads*.

Though the *Vedas* are at present reckoned as four, in the older tradition they are mentioned as three; of these the *Rig Veda* is the most ancient and original. The other two Vedas, *Sama* and *Yajur*, were compiled by arranging some of the hymns of the *Rig Veda*, mainly for the purposes of sacrifice and ritual, in certain order and sequence.

The fourth Veda, known as the *Atharva*, is a later addition; though it contains many of the hymns of the *Rig Veda*, it has an individuality and originality of its own. It would appear that the *Atharva Veda* was the scripture of some Aryan tribes who settled down in India later but were powerful enough to enforce on the older settlers their religious ideas and social theories. There is, in the *Atharva Veda*, a good deal of magic and witchcraft, spells and incantations, not found in the *Rig Veda*.

Just because the *Atharva Veda* came to be recognised as regular scripture later, it should not be imagined that it is essentially a later compilation. There were ancient commentators who maintained that the *Atharva Veda* was superior and anterior to the *Rig Veda* and some of the primitive teachings of the former would support this view. Anyway, when the *Atharva Veda* was accepted as a scripture of the Indo-Aryans, the text was modified to suit the requirements of the Rig Vedic tradition, and many of the hymns of the *Rig Veda* were added to it.

Two other important branches of later Vedic literature were the *Brahmanas* or ritualistic precepts, and the *Upanishads* or metaphysical writings attached to the four *Vedas*. Though chronology of Indian literature is difficult, the *Brahmanas* may be said to have been dominant in the sixth century B.C. when Buddhism and Jainism rose in revolt against sacrificial Brahminism, and the *Upanishads* shortly after.

Position of Women

The religious ideas embodied in the *Atharva Veda* had a direct bearing on the change of attitude of society towards women. In the *Atharva Veda* we find a firm belief in the survival of personality after death, and clear notions of hells and heavens. The souls of the dead, we are told, went to the regions of the manes; since these souls were new born, albeit in another world, they needed, like all infants, feeding by others as they were unable to feed themselves, and for their nourishment it was considered necessary for the living to oblations of food and drink. Another revolutionary change brought about by the followers of the *Atharva Veda* was the introduction of the practice of burning the dead in place of the old custom of burial mentioned in the *Rig Veda.* Considering how tenaciously people cling to their time-honoured funeral customs, the power of the Atharva Vedic tribes on the older settlers can very well be imagined from this change alone. But the *Atharva Veda* had no antagonism towards those who buried their dead. In one of the hymns we read: "They that are buried, they that are scattered away, they that are burned and they that are set up—all these fathers, O Agni, bring them to eat oblation." The only ancestors debarred from partaking of oblations were the non-Aryans. In the world of manes, it would appear, there was, as in ours, a scramble for food, and the non-Aryan manes who looked like Aryans, often took advantage of the resemblance, and going about as Aryans feasted on the oblations offered by the Aryans. Hence Agni was asked to save Aryan manes from these non-Aryan frauds, in the following hymn :"What barbarians, having entered among the fathers, having faces of acquaintances go about eating what is not sacrificed (for them), those who wear subtle bodies, let Agni blast forth from the sacrifice."

In the absence of these oblations, the spirits of the dead were feared to go to hell, which is described in the *Atharva Veda* as the "abode of female goblins and sorceresses, the place of blind and black darkness." Thus, while the Rig Vedic Aryans offered libations for their gods, the emphasis in the *Atharva Veda* is on oblations for the manes and not for the gods.

The dogma of metempsychosis is a somewhat later development. We find the idea fully developed in the *Brahmanas* and the *Upanishads;* when these new notions were assimilated, the ancient belief in heaven and hell was not entirely discarded. What happened was a compromise. A person, on death, was invested with a subtle body which needed nourishment by oblations; it was then made to suffer in hell for the evil the person had done or to enjoy the reward of his good deed, after which it was reborn on earth or some other plane on its eventful journey towards liberation.

What is important to our context is the development of the idea of nourishment for manes by means of oblations offered by the living. When the idea was mooted, the question was raised as to who was competent to offer these oblations, and it was decided that a son and a son alone could validly offer them. In a patriarchal community, the importance of a son is recognised all round, as the daughter is given away to another family in marriage and had to sever her connection with her parents' sooner or later. Besides, notions of ceremonial purity were fast advancing among the Indo-Aryans as the caste system developed, and the Brahmins, freed from the need for working for a living, was building up fantastic theories as to what was clean and unclean. Women were beginning to be considered generally impure, and particularly so during their menstrual periods, pregnancy and child-birth. Besides, 'below her navel a woman is always unclean.' Such impure creatures, it need not be emphasised, were not competent to perform the highly clean and spiritual function of offering oblations to the pure souls of the dead.

Now in addition to the old incentive for sons as the fighters for the family and the clan, there arose a new, all-important, use for male children. The son was an investment for the future without whom no man or woman could hope to go to heaven. As such the plight of the man without a son can very well be imagined. He had no heir to inherit his property and look after him in his old age, and no hope of a valid funeral ceremony being performed; in the absence of the last, his soul was feared to turn into a Preta or deformed ghost and eventually descend to hell whence it had but a chance deliverance in time.

These highly intricate eschatological notions, while raising the importance of the male, lowered the position of the women, never very high as things stood. A woman was considered important only as long as she was able to bear sons. As for daughters, the gods were requested to give them elsewhere. Henceforward, the prayer of the Aryan was for sons and more sons. "O Prajapati, Anumati, Sinivali," prays one hymn of the *Atharva Veda,* "give a daughter elsewhere, but here a male." The universal desire thus having been for sons, the birth of a daughter was considered a misfortune. Apart from her uselessness as far as redemption from hell was concerned, social censure was becoming very strict on erring women and, child-marriage not having come into vogue, the guarding of girls from improper conduct was becoming a very grave burden on parents. And we find a curious notion developing in later Vedic literature, that embryos were essentially male, and the birth of daughters was due to the perverse activities of malignant spirits who, during the course of the development of the foetus turned it into female. "O Pinga," pleads the *Atharva Veda,* "defend thou the child in the process of birth; let not the evil ones turn the male into females."

Ceremonies

Further, elaborate ceremonies began to develop during the Brahmana period for ensuring the birth of sons.

> In the New and Full Moon sacrifices of the Taitereya *Brahmana,* a ritual is specially instituted for avoiding the birth of a daughter. The main ceremony constituted of throwing a piece of Kusa grass upwards, by repeating a Mantra, signifying that all upward movements are connected with males and the reverse with females ... The whole of the fourth Brahmana of the sixth chapter of the *Brihada ranyaka Upanishad* is devoted to the ceremonial for a son ... Woman is conjectured as the Vedi of the sacrifice, and the son the fruit of the offering obtained for benefit in the next world.

Here then is the origin of the Pumsavana (male-producing) ceremony even now performed by the Hindus in the third month of gestation.

The need for having sons having thus become paramount, indiscriminate asceticism and celibacy were condemned in no uncertain terms, and every Aryan who loved his soul was compelled to marry. The importance of sons was emphasised at every step. In the *Aitareya Brahmana* we read the story of king Harischandra who had one hundred wives and no son; the learned Brahmins of his court thus revealed to him the greatness of a son. "The father pays a debt to his son and gains immortality when he beholds the face of his son who is born to him.... The son is a boat of salvation, a light in the highest heaven. A wife is a comrade but a daughter, misery."

Though the *Atharva Veda* deprecates the birth of daughters, we do not find in it mention of infanticide. The *Brahmanas* are generally more unfavourable towards women what with their ideas of ceremonial purity and the omnipotence of rituals and sacrifices, and in these texts we come across people who have started disposing of their unwanted daughters in infancy.

In the *Satapatha Brahmana* we are told that a wife should take her meals after her husband had finished his, and a wife who does not answer back to her husband even under grave provocation is praiseworthy; elsewhere, disobedient wife is enjoined to be taught obedience by physical force. "The *Maitrayani Samhita* places woman on a par with dice and drink, and describes her as one of the major evils in society. She is declared to be untruth itself in human society, and is connected with Nirriti, the genius of darkness. The *Taitareya Samhita* and *Satapatha Brahmana* rank her as inferior to a bad man."

Sterility in women was considered an evil and the continued bearing of daughters a worse evil. In either case, it became obligatory for a man to marry again and raise sons to himself. While sterility in women thus offered no insurmountable obstacle to the obtaining of sons for a man, impotence in men offered a more serious problem. In such cases, ingenious expedients were invented to invest the important with sons, and some fourteen kinds of sons are mentioned in some texts from whom the manes were likely to accept oblations. Of such sons the more important were those obtained in Niyoga or appointment. The brother or near relative of the unfortunate man was 'appointed' for raising sons to him; in the absence of these, the services of the learned Brahmins were obtained for this office.... Adoption was another expedient. But none of these sons was as good as a son of one's own loins, and to a Hindu impotence was a curse in this world and the next.

Position of Women

With all this, it must be emphasised that the position of women during the later Vedic period was much better than during medieval times. For one thing, the injunctions of the texts were not binding on all Indo-Aryans, and local usages and customs have always had, in Hinduism, over-riding effect on written ordinances. Nor were all authorities agreed concerning the position of women, their social and spiritual functions, and we find many conflicting views on these subjects. The *Upanishads*, especially, with their metaphysical leaning towards pantheism, were somewhat indifferent to the injunctions of the *Brahmanas*, and accorded to women a better status than that given in some of the *Brahmanas*.

Certain *Brahmanas*, however, mention women as competent to perform sacrifices and read the *Vedas*. Some sort of initiation for women, as the Upanayanam for men, is also mentioned in the *Brahmanas*, which later fell into disuse the marriage ceremony being considered the equivalent of Upanayanam, for women.

Though sons were generally preferred, the desirability of having a learned daughter was not entirely lost sight of, as we find mention of ceremonies performed with this end in view. Though later commentators defined the word 'learned' in the context to mean proficiency in the culinary art, the reference is likely to be to the Brahmavadins or lady philosophers mentioned in the *Upnishads*.

In the *Brihad Aranya Upanishad* is a narrated the story of the celebrated lady philosopher Gargi Vachaknavi who challenged Yajnavalkya, the al-knowing president of a philosophic conference, held under the auspices of king Janaka. At the end of the polemical discussion Yajnavalkya initiated Gargi into the highest spiritual truth, the jealously guarded esoteric doctrine of the *Upanishads* that was revealed only to the favoured few.

It would appear that during the age of the *Unanishads* women were not debarred from the study of the *Vedas;* learned Rishis, as a rule, initiated their wives into the sacred sciences, as in many rituals the husband and wife had to perform certain rites together, and even Sudra wives enjoyed this privilege. Janasruti, a wealthy Sudra, we are told in one of the *Upanishads,* wished to study the Vedas and presented the sage Raikva with a thousand cows, a necklace and a pair of bulls yoked to a chariot, but the sage refused to teach the *Vedas* to the Sudra. On this Janasruti offered his beautiful daughter in marriage to Raikva and the sage took the tempting bait. The learned man was then obliged to initiate his wife into the study of the *Vedas,* and the lady instructed her father in Vedic lore.

The evidence of the *Upanishads* regarding the initiation of women is also supported by later commentators who wrote after the practice was prohibited. Some of them mention that the wearing of the sacred thread, the utterance of sacred texts and the study of the *Vedas* were permissible for women in ancient days but were given up due to the degeneration of women.

Certain texts would indicate that in exceptional cases daughters were competent to perfrom funeral rites in the absence of sons. The institution of the 'appointed daughter' of the Rig Vedic times seems to have continued, as there are references in later Vedic literature to 'Putrika' (only daughter), and to Putrika Putra (son of Putrika), who was almost as good as one's own son.

Early Indo-Aryan Women

In the *Atharva Veda* there is a curious passage which would indicate polyandry in the next world if not in this one. The situation is similar to the one the Sadducees, who did not believe in resurrection, wanted Jesus to clarify; polyandry being prohibited to the Jews, the Sadducees wanted Jesus to tell them with which of her several husbands a woman, much married in this life, would live in resurrection. Jesus told his tormentors that there would be no marriage in the kingdom of heaven. But in Hindu heaven, there is marrying and giving in marriage, and the *Atharva Veda* states clearly that both the husbands of a twice-married woman would share her in heaven provided the second husband with his wife had sacrificed a goat and offered the meat with five dishes of rice to the manes of the first.

The Graihya Sutras

Coming to the post-Vedic period in Hindu literature, we get a clear picture of Indo-Aryan domestic and social life from the *Grihya Sutràs* (Grihya means 'pertaining to household,' and Sutra means 'aphorism') which deal in detail with the rules of conduct to be observed and ceremonies to be performed by an Indo-Aryan householder. The *Grihya Sutras* pertain to that period in Brahminism when the Vedic religion was well established in the south as well as the north of the Vindhyas; the Sutra writers, several in number, had written to meet the needs of the Indo-Aryan communities following different customs and usages, but efforts were made to create some basic unity in fundamentals.

Historically speaking, the main Sutra period may be said to have started by about the sixth century B.C. and continued till the rise and spread of Buddhism under Asoka in the third century B.C. The earlier Sutras were contemporaneous with the *Brahmanas* and *Upanishads;* in the main, the *Grihya Sutras* owe much to the *Brahmanas* as both emphasise the importance of ritual as distinct from the intellectualism of the *Upanishads*.

The *Grihya Sutras* would indicate that religion for the Indo-Aryan householder had become a daily ritual and a round or ceremonies to be performed at every stage in life's progress from conception till death; after death, ceremonies for the departed were continued by the living.

Of the writers of the *Grihya Sutras,* the more important were Asvalayana, Apastambha, Sankhayana and Bharadwaja. They were not contemporaries, but lived in different periods and wrote for different rigions taking into consideration local traditions but there is no great disagreement in existing texts attributed to them, concerning fundamentals.

Forms of Marriage

For the first time in Indo-Aryan literature we get, in the *Grihya Sutras,* a definite classification of the different forms of marriage prevalent among the Indo-Aryans. Asvalayana classified them into eight and this classification has been followed, in the main, by other Sutra writers as well as the authors of the epics, and the law codes. These eight forms of marriage were : (1) Brahma, (2) Daiva, (3) Prajapatya, (4) Arsha, (5) Gandharva, (6) Asura, (7) Paisacha, and (8) Rakshasa.

Brahma

The Brahma form is described as the giving away of a daughter by her father to a bridegroom of his selection after decking the bride with ornaments and 'pouring out libations of water' as in the case of valuable gifts. This was the most common form of marriage prevalent among the Brahmins, and even now it is a variation of this form that widely prevails among all sections of the Indo-Aryans.

Daiva

In the Daiva form, a girl was given in marriage to a learned priest officiating at an important sacrifice in recognition of his vast learning and efficient performance of the sacrifice. In this case, the girl was not necessarily the daughter of the householder, though usually she was; anyway, it was in his capacity as the host in the sacrifice that the man gave away the girl and not as her father. Well-known Brahmins got many wives in this way when sacrificial Brahminism was the prevailing religion, but as sacrifices fell into disrepute with the rise of Buddhism, the custom also fell into disuse.

Prajpatya

The difference between the Brahma and Prajapatya forms is not quite clear from existing texts. It would appear the bride, in Prajapatya rite, was not given away by her father but by a guardian, and this possibly necessitated its being treated as a separate form of marriage.

Arsha

In the Arsha form the girl was married according to the prescribed rites after her father received a pair of cattle, a cow and a bull. This has led to a good deal of controversy among the later commentators some of whom held the view that the giving of the cattle was tantamount to bride-purchase and the Arsha was a blameable form of marriage, while others maintained that the giving of the cattle was a token gift of goodwill with no commercial motives behind it. Anyway, this form of marriage has not come down to us; it was prevalent in Mauryan India. and Megasthenese, the Greek envoy to the court of Chandragupta Maurya, mentioned it in his accounts of India.

Gandharva

The Gandharva is love marriage, pure and simple. As a rule, Hindu moralists have been reluctant to admit that young people are competent to exercise a wise choice in the matter of selecting their life-partners and have ordained that young men and women should abide by the decision made by the elders; but there have always been, in society, independent young people who thought that they knew better than their parents, and often married as they wanted, and presented their parents or guardians with a *fait accompli,* and such marriages were reluctantly recognised as valid. Though the general preferences in Indo-Aryan society, all down the ages, have been for arranged matches, from the Rig Vedic times to the present day there have been cases of Gandharva marriages persistently appearing in Indo-Aryan literature, and some of these will be noticed later.

Asura

Asura is bride-purchase, pure and simple. Here it is not a token present of a cow and a bull, but a regular bride-price, negotiated and settled, and paid before marriage. Among certain clans of the Indo-Aryans, Asura was the general form of marriage, and some of the celebrated ladies of the *Mahabharata,* as we shall see later, were bought by payment of a bride-price, and married. This was widely prevalent in India, especially before polygyny was prohibited, and many elderly men of wealth who wished to have young wives took advantage of the Asura system, and bought and married desirable young virgins from their impecunious parents.

Paisacha

Paisacha is drugging and rape of bride; the *Grihya Sutras* do not explain how rape could be legalised, but in Vatsyayana's *Kama Sutra* valid excuses for Paisacha are given.

Rakshasa

Rakshasa is married by capture. This kind of marriage, as we have seen, was widely prevalent in the ancient world, and in the heroic age of the Hindus it was almost a point of honour for the martial classes to capture there brides after fighting and vanquishing their guardians and relatives.

Of these eight forms. Asvalayana considered the first four alone as becoming of the righteous. The Brahma form, he maintained, ennobled ancestors for twelve generations, Daiva for ten Prajapatya, eight and Arsha, seven. The other four kinds of marriage were reckoned blameable and unworthy of the pious.

Arrange Marriages

We also get from the *Grihya Sutras* many details as to how marriages were arranged among the Indo-Aryans. In arranged matches, the boy seldom met the girl before marriage, and negotiations took place through intermediaties. As young men led an outdoor life, they were much better known to people than girls who were brought up, more or less, in seclusion. As such, defects in boys could easily be found out, but a good deal of enquiries had to be made and judgement exercised in finding out the eligibility of a girl. In most cases, the boy's party met the girl only once or twice after which the marriage proposal had to be accepted or rejected. According to Sankhayana, the eligible girl should possess certain good characteristics; "her limbs should be proportionate, hair smooth; she should have at her neck, two curls turned to the right." Such a girl, we are told, would give birth to six sons. "The girl who looks like the animal Sarabha, one who has wicked or cunning eyes, a hunchback, an ugly girl, a bald-headed girl, and a girl whose skin is like the frog's, is to be avoided." Other undesirable girls were "one who has deserted her people, one who has too many friends, a girl given over to sensuous pleasures, a girl who has a pretty younger, sister, or whose age is the same as that of the bridegroom." A girl whose name ended in the syllable `r' or `l' was also to be avoided.

It must be mentioned that the marriageable girl of the Grihya Sutra period was not a child but a young lady, and usually she obtained from her friends or gossips some information about the boy who was to be her husband and lord; and if the report was bad, she tried in her own way to derange the match. For instance, when the boy's party came for negotiating the marriage and formally interviewing her, she created a scene in the house, cried or yelled, or walked out of the house when called to appear before the wooing party. Hence we are told in the *Grihya Sutras* that a girl who cried pretended slumber, or left her house while the wooing party called her or was noticed guarded by her relatives, should not be accepted.

How to choose a girl

In modern times we find that horoscopes play an important role in arranged matches, among many Hindu communities. Boys and girls with compatible horoscopes are generally accepted as eligible, but in the Grihya Sutra period astrology had not developed well enough to be considered a reliable guide to marriage. But some enquiries had to be made and some reliable evidence adduced concerning the desirability of a bride. For this purpose, Asvalayana had a curious test prescribed. After satisfying themselves that a girl was physically fit and desirable, the wooing party was asked to place before the girl eight lumps of clay. These were taken from: (1) a field yielding two crops (signifying fertility), (2) a cowshed (indicating possession of cattle), (3) a sacrificial ground (denoting spiritual lustre), (4) a pool (for plenty), (5) a gambling den (indicative of inconstancy and vice), (6) the junction of four roads (indicative of a love of wandering), (7) a barren plot (denoting sterility), and (8) a cremation ground (indicative of widowhood). Only if the girl happened to choose one of the first four was she to be accepted.

Bharadwaja was an authority on auspicious and inauspicious marks in girls, but in the matter of Gandharva marriages, "whomsoever his soul would take delight, in whomsoever his eyes would take delight, her he would consider as blessed with good marks. What shall he do with marks?" Similarly, Apasthambha, after giving elaborate instructions as to how to choose a girl, very sensible concluded that "a wife who is pleasing to his mind and eye will bring happiness to a man; let him pay no attention to other things; such is the opinion of some".

Marriage Ceremony

By the Grihya Sutra period, the marriage ceremony had developed into an elaborate affair; Agni or the fire-god had become the presiding deity of the ceremony which was performed in his presence throughout. The ceremony, established in the Grihya Sutra period has come down to us, and at present the ceremony performed among the orthodox Hindus of the higher classes more or less conforms, in its broad outlines, to the ritual of the *Grihya Sutra.* As such a short description of the salient features in the ceremony will not be out of place here.

The ceremony, then as now, took place in the house of the bride, before the sacrificial fire. To the west of the fire was placed a milestone and to the north-east a water-pot.

The first important item of the ceremony was the Kanya Dan (giving away of the bride) by the father or, in his absence, by the guardian with the recitation of appropriate texts; the gift was ratified by pouring out libations of water. The groom accepted the gift, and recited the Kama Sukta hymn in propitiation of Kama or the love-god. After this the father of the bride exhorted a promise from the groom that in the pursuit of the triple object of life, Dharma (religion), Artha (wealth) and Kama (pleasures), he would not transgress her.

Next was the Vivaha-Homa rite in which the bridegroom offered oblations to fire while the bride held the hand that offered the oblations.

Then followed the important Pani-Grahana (hand-holding) ceremony. The bridegroom took the hand of the bride and repeated the Vedic text: "I take thy hand in mine; yearning for happiness, I ask thee to live with me as thy husband till both of us grow old. Know this that the gods Bhaga, Aryamat. Savita and Purandhi have bestowed thy person upon me, that I may fulfil my Dharma of a householder with thee." The Pani-Grahana is so important that marriage in many texts is referred to as Pani-Grahana. The way the bridegroom held the hand of the bride was also thought to decide the sex of the forthcoming progeny; if the man gripped the whole hand of the girl, including the thumb, he was to be rich in offspring of both sexes; if he desired only males he merely held the Thumb of the girl; if he wanted daughters, he left the thumb free and held the fingers.

After Pani-Grahana, Laja-Homa was performed. This was intended to release the bride from her bondage to certain gods, and it was effected by the brother of the bride, or in his absence, by someone specially appointed for the purpose, by his placing grain in her hand which she threw into fire.

The twin rites of Agni-Parinayana (walking round the fire) and Asmarohana (mounting the millstone) were now performed. The bride and bridegroom walked round the fire, repeating texts, the groom leading; in the process he led her to the millstone, kept for the purpose, and made her mount it for constancy, repeating a verse asking her to be firm as granite.

The next important ceremony was the celebrated Saptapadi (seven steps) which irrevocably sealed the union. The bride-groom led the bride in a north-easterly direction, and took seven steps repeating the following text:

> Let us pray together,
> For life-sap, as we tread one step,
> For power as we take two steps,
> For wealth as we take three steps,
> For happiness as we take four steps,
> For offspring as we take five steps,
> For a prolonged life together, as we take six steps,
> And be thou now my mate as we take the seventh step.

This completed the major items of the ceremony. Additional minor ceremonies were performed for the general happiness and prosperity of the couple, thanksgiving ceremonies for the guests, and blessing ceremonies by the guests who wished prosperity to the newly weds. After these ceremonies, there was the inevitable feasting, not essential to the ceremony proper, but, considering the expenses involved, the most important feature of a marriage.

Ceremonies were again performed at the time of the departure of the bride for her new home, and on her reaching here, greatings were offered in further ceremonies. All told, the *Grihya Sutras* indicate a period in which marriage had become a highly spiritual, idealised sacrament in which carnality had no place. Progeny was the only aim of marriage, but unfortunately progeny, even at the time of the *Grihya Sutras,* does not appear to have been possible without a good deal of carnality, and hence the Chaturthi Karma (ceremony of the fourth day) was performed on the fourth day of marriage for its consummation. Three nights the newly weds had to practise continence; according to Asvalayana, it was good to prolong it for twelve days, but if the couple wanted a Rishi or mighty sage to come out of the union they had to practise continence for one full year. Ordinary Aryans, however, had limited ambitions and the Chaturthi Karma was generally performed on the fourth night when consummation took place.

Marriage after Mensuration

This would indicate that child-marriage had not come into vogue by the Grihya Sutra period. Further, some Sutras make provision for the girl being in her menstrual period at the time or marriage. The minimum age for marriage is nowhere clearly laid down in the *Grihya Sutras*. In some texts, it is stated that a girl should be a Nanika. But the meaning attributed to this word by commentators is so wide as to include a 'naked girl of six or seven playing in the dust' and a young adolescent of sweet sixteen, and as such 'nagnika' leaves us no wiser.

But indications are clear that consummation generally took place in the fourth night; further, the behaviour of girls to be noted by wooing parties, as already stated, would show that they were capable of acting independently. So, though there are some vague references in later Vedic literature to married virgins who lived in their husbands' houses, the indications are not clear enough to suggest child-marriages; all available evidence, on the other hand, would show that girls, as a rule were married after menstruation, during the Grihya Sutra period.

No Property Right

Sacramental notions of marriage were fast effacing the individuality of woman and reducing her to an appendage on man. Asvalayana prohibited the performance of rituals by married women. Her right to independent ownership of property was also questioned. Some authorities maintained that she could own, in her own right, the Stridhan or dowry she brought with her at the time of marriage, and as such was competent to have sacrifices performed, by paying for them from her own wealth, but others objected that stridhan was but petty wealth not good enough for paying sacrificers. Anyway, it is clear from the *Grihya Sutras* that a married woman could not inherit wealth nor have any right to the property of her husband; all that she could own was some moveable property in the ornaments and other things brought from her parent's house by way of dowry.

All told, the position of women, in the Grihya Sutra period, deteriorated still further from the later Vedic period.

The Artha Sastra and the Evidence of Greeks

Ancient Indian literature, voluminous as it is, is mainly religious, and we have but few works extant which are of a purely secular nature. Of these few works, the most important and, perhaps the most ancient, is the *Artha Sastra* of Kautilya.

Though differences of opinion exist, it is now generally admitted that the *Artha Sastra* was written by Chanakya (another name of Kauṭilya), the minister of Chandragupta Maurya (fourth-third Century B.C.) the first Indo-Aryan emperor so far known to history. Before Chandragupta's period, the Indo-Aryans were generally content to follow their clan conceptions of the kingship and, though some efforts were made by ambitious monarchs like Ajatasatru to unite or subdue the neighbouring clans and found great kingdoms, no one succeeded in founding an empire of any considerable size; the imperial claim to world dominion advanced, in Indo-Aryan texts in favour of certain legendary heroes, is founded more on the love of the fabulous than on facts.

Tradition says that Chanakya who had some knowledge of the Persian and Macedonian empires was the man behind Chandragupta's political expansion, and the *Artha Sastra* is a work worthy of his genius. Chanakya was a philosopher-statesman who held the view that the progress of humanity was linked with a powerful state ruled by a king who enjoyed dictatorial powers; he maintained that in ruling an empire, the ruler was to be guided not by the wisdom of the ancients but by a powerful army and an efficient spy system that kept the king well informed of what was happening in his kingdom. He was an upholder of caste for political reasons, though he raised his protege Chandragupta Maurya to kingship from a low origin. Chanakya's respect for religion was generally confined to its utility for enhancing the power of the sovereign. In the Artha *Sastra,* it is clearly stated, that all sciences, sacred or profane are subordinate to statecraft, as without an efficient state there could be no law and order and in anarchy nothing could flourish.

Such a work has certain unique attractions not found in the ancient religious literature of India. Unlike writers on religious themes who were mainly concerned with the Indo-Aryans and their spiritual welfare, Chanakya wrote for a secular emperor whose sway extended from the Hindu Kush to Bengal, from the Himalayas to Mysore, and who ruled vast populations drawn from diverse ethnic and cultural elements. Hence the *Artha Sastra* is singularly free from the narrow-mindedness of most of the religious writers of the time whose pious views often warped their judgement. Chanakya was however sufficiently religious to employ priests as spies who were ordered to teach the people doctrines advantageous to the state whether such doctrines were in conformity with the teachings of the *Vedas* or not.

In Chanakya's time, it would appear, the greatest danger to the state (to Chanakya, the state and the king were identical) was the king's harem and not foreign armies or internal rebellion. Hence the first book of the *Artha Sastra,* deals with the efficient management of the harem. We are told:

> Hidden in the queen's chamber, his own brother slew king Bhadrasena; hiding himself under the bed of his mother his son killed Karusha; mixing fried grain with poison, as though with honey, his own son poisoned Kasiraja; with an anklet pained with poison, his own queen killed Vairantya; with a gem of her zone bedaubed with poison his own queen killed Sauvira; with a looking glass painted with poison his own queen killed Jalutha; and with a weapon hidden under the tuft of her hair, his own queen killed Viduratha.

After giving this impressive list, Kautilya laid down detailed instructions as to how to run the harem without danger to its master. The harem was to be guarded by trusted women; spies were appointed to test the loyalty of every responsible office holder of the harem, and spies spied on spies. Every person in the harem was to strictly keep to the place assigned to him or her and was never permitted to wander out of bounds. No important inmate of the harem was allowed to interview an outsider, man or woman.

The personal attendants of the king were all women. "On getting up," the *Artha Sastra* lays down, "the king shall be greeted by troops of women armed with bows and arrows."

Independent evidence also supports the *Artha Sastra.* The Greek envoy Megasthenese who lived in the court of Chandragupta Maurya wrote that amazons guarded the emperor's harem and formed the main body-guard of the king when he moved out, and the people went in fear of them. Any food to be eaten by the king, any garments, flowers or ornaments to be worn by him, any scents or unguents to be used by him, had to be tested by his trusted women before it was given to the king.

These women constituted the security force for the personal safety of the king. Then there was another class of women kept for the splendour of the court, pageants and for the pleasure of the king. These are mentioned in the *Artha Sastra* by the not very respectable epithet of prostitutes. In India the institution of prostitutes had enjoyed considerable power and prestige from the Rig Vedic times down to the British period. They were employed in large numbers by kings to sing and dance on ceremonial occasions in the court, to hold the royal umbrella and to fan riding royalty in pageants and processions. The *Artha Sastra* allots a full chapter for describing prostitutes employed in the palace or free-lancing in the great cities.

One of the important state officials mentioned in the *Artha Sastra* was the Superintendent of Prostitutes. His jurisdiction seems to have extended both to the palace and city prostitutes. From the detailed description of the duties of the dignitary we get some interesting accounts of the institution in and out of the palace as existed in Mauryan India.

The Superintendent was enjoined, in the *Artha Sastra,* to select, for the court, a Ganika or super-courtesan, noted for her looks accomplishments, and charming manners, and appoint her as the chief of prostitutes of the court, on a salary of 1,000 panas. A rival courtesan was appointed on half her salary. The numer of girls employed under them was quite considerable; even children were taken and trained in the profession, and we are told that a girl from the age of eight was to learn the art of dancing.

The court prostitutes were classed into three, the high, the low and the middling. Their main duties were "to hold the royal umbrella, golden pitcher and fan, and attend the king seated in his royal litter, throne or chariot". Their salary was fixed according to this classification. It would appear that these women and their progeny were the slaves of the king. The king could order any of them to surrender herself to anyone to whom the king wished to grant such a favour, and refusal without just cause entailed a fine; infectious disease, it would appear, constituted a valid cause for refusal. Prostitutes who had lost their attraction through age were appointed as nurses attendants and storekeepers in the place establishment.

The Superintendent had to keep a strict watch over the activities of the prostitutes who operated in the cities. They had to submit to him a correct account of their income and expenditure, and about 15 per cent of the profits of the trade was paid to the government as income-tax. Further, every prostitute had to send to him confidential reports about her clients, their political activities, if any, and their estimated income. Foreigners and political suspects were specially watched, and prostitutes were often employed as species to find out their intentions and partisan affiliations.

Special laws were in force to regulate the relations between prostitutes and their clients; as a rule punishments for most of the offences were fines, as Kautilya had always an eye on the stability of the royal exchequer. "When," however, "a prostitute murders her paramour, she shall be burnt alive or thrown into water".

Though the court and the city were teeming with courtesans, and the network of wandering prostitutes who worked as species was far flung, temples were free from Devadasis. This institution had become an integral part of temple worship in medieval India, but the *Artha Sastra* does not mention it, which would indicate that it was a later growth.

Marriage in Mauryan India

In Kautilya's time, marriage and property rights in women seem to have caused a good deal of litigation, for the *Artha Sastra* opens the chapter on marital rights with the curious remark that "marriage is the basis of all disputes."

The *Artha Sastra*. like the *Grihya Sutras* mentions eight kinds or recognised marriages, and approves of the first four as traditional to the Indo-Aryans, but adds that any kind of marriage "is approvable, provided it pleaseth all who are concerned in it." This naturally indicates the tolerance and recognition of customary law in marriages which has been a peculiar feature of the legal position of marriage in India.

It would appear that at the time of marriage a certain amount, varying according to the status of the party, was settled on the bride by her people, and this, known as the Sulka, she could use for maintaining herself and her children, if her own husband had made no provision in the matter.

A widow had the right of remarriage, but in this case she had no right to any property left by her first husband, and she had to surrender to her relatives or children any that was in her possession. In Chanakya's scheme, a woman could own property in her own right though some of the *Grihya Sutras,* as we have seen, were of a different view.

Polygyny was permitted by Chanakya but every time a man

married he had to settle a certain amount on the superseded wife and pay an amount to the state; this must have worked as a sound deterrent to over-marrying. Kautilya was so comprehensive that he even made provision for a man who found that all his wives, on a particular night, were having their monthly affliction. Nor was the chance of adding to the king's revenue by people failing in their marital duties lost sight of; for "if a man neglects to lie with his wife in her Rtu, he shall pay a fine of 96 panas".

Divorce was not permitted in the first four kinds of marriage but a woman could abandon her husband "if traitor to his king, or is likely to endanger the life of his wife or has fallen from his caste or has lost his virility." The right of physical correction of their wives was conceded to men. Refractory women could be brought to a sense of their marital duties "by administering three beats with a bamboo bark, rope or the palm of the hand, on her hip" anything more than this fell under the law of assault and was punishable.

Divorce by mutual consent was permitted where customary law allowed it. Widow marriage was permitted to all castes; nor was it necessary that a husband should be dead before a woman could remarry; when he was missing or gone abroad without any chance of returning, she could remarry. "Wives who belong to the Sudra, Vaisya, Kshatriya or Brahmana caste and who have not given birth to children, should wait as long as one year, two, three and four respectively, for their husbands who had gone abroad for a short time; but if they are such as have given birth to children. They, irrespective of caste, must, want for their absent husbands for more than a year." If however, the man who had gone abroad was in the service of the king, his wife was not to remarry, as, according to Kautilya, the exigencies of the state had priority over individual needs, and the man might have been sent on some secret mission for an indefinite period without the knowledge of his wife. She was, however, allowed to have children in his absence by a relative "with a view to avoid the extinctions of the race and she shall not be liable to contempt thereof."

In the case of husbands who renounced the world, wives, had the right of remarriage or getting children in levirate, Remarriage in such cases was strictly confined to a brother or near relative of the husband. "If the woman violates the above rule and marries a man who is not a kinsman of her husband, then, the woman, her new husband and all who have participated in the marriage are liable to fines." This would show that the ancient Vedic custom of a widow remarrying her husband's brother was recognised and prevalent in Kautilya's time.

The age of consent, according to Kautilya, was twelve for a girl and sixteen for a boy. Early marriage was prevalent, though not child-marriage. Marriage proposals were generally made and fixed when the girl was about the age of twelve, and the ceremony took place immediately after menstruation. It was obligatory for a man to get his daughter married before the passing of her seventh menses; for, according to Kautilya, intercourse between an unmarried girl who had passed here seventh menses and a man was not punishable; nor was the fornicator to pay any compensation to the father of the girl, "for her father has lost his authority over her in consequence of having deprived her so long of the result of her menses". Here, again, we come across the persistent Indo-Aryan idea that wasting the fertility of women was sinful and culpable. Further, Kautilya, like Manu in later times, ordained that a girl who remained unmarried for three years after her first menses, could marry a man even outside her caste at her own choice, as her father had completely failed in his duty towards her.

Punishments for adultery and allied offences were generally fines. The laws regarding these may be quoted in some detail as it will give us a rough idea of the offences of this nature generally committed in Mauryan India.

> If a woman engages herself in amorous sports or drinking, in the face of an order to the contrary, she shall be fined three panas. She shall pay a fine of six panas for going out at daytime for sports to see a woman or spectacular shows. For the same offence committed at night, the fines shall be

double. If a woman goes out while her husband is asleep or under intoxication, or if the shuts she door of her house against her husband, she shall be fined 12 panas. If a woman keeps him out of his house at night, she shall pay double the above amount. If a man and a woman make signs to each other, with a view to sensuous enjoyment, or carry on secret conversation with the same purpose, the woman shall pay a fine of twenty-four panas and the man double the amount; a woman holding out her hair, the tie of her dress round her loins, her teeth or her nails, shall pay the first amercement, and a man doing the same, twice the first amercement. For holding conversation in suspicious places, whips may be substituted for fines. In the centre of the village a Chandala (outcaste) may whip the adulteress five times on each side of her body. She may get rid of being whipped by paying a pana for each lash.

The Writings of the Greeks

Alexander the Great, as is well known, invaded Sind, North-Western Indian and a good part of the Punjab in 326 B.C. and some of his historian wrote accounts of the people they met in India. Later, the Greek king Seleucus to whom the eastern portion of Alexander's empire fell, made a political alliance with Chandragupta Maurya, and sent to his court an envoy named Megasthenese who wrote an account of India and the Indians. But unfortunately Megasthenese's work was lost and only fragments and quotations preserved in the works of later writers are now available to us.

The accounts of the Greeks, though generally political and geographical, have some references to social conditions in India. Megasthenese, as we have seen, mentioned Arsha marriages wherein girls were married after their parents received a pair of cattle. Another interesting observation by Megasthenese was the exclusion of women from the study of sacred texts. "The Brahmins," he wrote, "do not admit their wives to their philosophy; if wives are wanton, they might divulge mysteries to the profane; if they are good, they might leave their husbands, since no one who has learnt to look with contempt upon pleasure and pain upon life and death, will care to be under another's control." It would thus appear that the denial of Vedic wisdom to women was partly inspired by fear of sacrilege and partly by the selfishness of men. Megasthenese also noticed that "the son succeeds the father". The wealthy were polygynous in Mauryan India.

Megasthenese mentions child-marriage as existing in South India where girls of six or seven were married. In Mauryan empire, however, the minimum age for marriage would appear to have been twelve as fixed by Kautilya.

According to Nearchus, "girls were secured as prizes of victory in physical feats". The references is perhaps to the Swayamvara, prevalent among certain royal clans, in which a princess was usually married after suitor had proved his skill in arms, an institution we will have to notice later.

Sati (Suttee) was mentioned by the Greeks :

> Onesicritus saw it among the Kathai or the Kathas. Diodorus also states that among the Kathaians prevailed the custom that widows should be burnt with their husbands. Aristobulus relates that in 316 B.C. an Indian military leader who had gone to Iran to fight under Eumenes, accompanied by his two wives was unfortunately killed in battle, whereupon the two wives vied with each other to become Suttee. The elder being with child, the other one proceeded to the pyre and 'lay down beside her husband. As the fire seized her, no sound of weeping escaped her lips'.

It is interesting to note that neither the *Grihya Sutras* nor the anterior Vedic writings give any instructions regarding the performance of the Sati ritual; references in the *Rig Veda* would indicate the prevalence of Sati among the primitive Aryan communities but by the time the Aryans had settled down in India and custom had already been given up. It was probably prevalent in some northern tribe that arrived later but the practice had no sanction of the Indo-Aryan authorities of the Vedic period. We will have occasion to notice this institution in detail in later chapters; for the present, it is enough to say that it was not generally prevalent among the Indo-Aryans in the Vedic period.

3

Epics and Women

Jainism and Buddhism successfully challenged the authority of the Brahmins and the sanctions of the old Vedic religion. The popularity of the new religions made the Brahmins think; they could see plainly that it was practically impossible for them to continue the practice of the old Vedic religion with its exclusive rituals, ceremonies and esoteric doctrines which denied the common man not only participation in, but even the knowledge of, religion.

Hence the Brahmins too made a vigorous attempt to combat the spread of the new religions by enlisting popular support. They did not, however, cater to popular desire for participation in religion by abolishing caste and making the esoteric Vedic text exoteric. The abolition of caste would have led to their own ruin, as the Brahmins had derived their authority from the religious sanctions of caste; moreover they had found from the practical working of Buddhism and Jainism, that caste had taken root in India, that their own supremacy as the custodians of the ancients wisdom of the race had been well established, and that there was no need to abolish caste to gain popular support. So what they did was to write a series of popular books the contents of which were made familiar to the common man by incorporating in them, together with Vedic ideas, a good deal of popular lore drawn from the religious beliefs of the people; feasts and festivals were instituted in honour of the gods and goddesses of the people, and grand temples were built for them and ritualistic worship performed by the Brahmins. These innovations highly flattered the non-

Aryans, both of indigenous and foreign extraction. The process went so fast that the old pantheon, crumbled, and on its ruins rose new gods the most important of whom were Shiva, Vishnu and goddess Devi.

This new Hinduism was known as Puranic, mainly because the popular texts were called *Puranas.* These texts, eighteen in number, are ascribed to a single author, Dwaipayana Vyasa, but in ascribing authorship to their scriptures, the Hindus are guided more by a desire for high authority than considerations of veracity, and eighteen *Puranas,* in reality, pertain to different periods in Hinduism.

In addition to the *Puranas*, the two epics, *Mahabharata* and *Ramayana,* also form text-books of Puranic religion. Of all these twenty works, the *Mahabharata* is the most voluminous, running into some 100,000 verses, the longest single poem in the world. It is, as we have seen, a repository of traditions, sacred and profane, Aryan and non-Aryan, and deals with all conceivable problems of life, social, domestic political, religious and philosophical; a summary of the *Ramayana* is also found in it, obviously a later interpolation. So great is its authority in the Puranic religion that the *Mahabharata* is revered as the fifth Veda, and is read in Hindu homes today together with the *Ramayana* as the Bible is read in Protestant households. But, as in many religious texts, mortals and immortals in the epic move almost on the same plane, and it is difficult to ascertain how far the practices described, ordinances prescribed and events narrated in the *Mahabharata* had actual bearing on Indian society at any particular period in its history.

The war of succession which forms the main theme of the epic is said to have taken place towards the close of the *Dwapara Yuga,* the third of the mythical time divisions of the Hindus. The fourth age, *Kali Yuga,* is now, according to orthodox computations, in its sixth millennium, and as such the *Mahabharata* war was fought some six thousand years ago; making due allowance for the discrepancies inherent in mythical chronology, available evidence would indicate that the main events narrated in the epic relate to a period near about 1,000 B.C. when practically all northern India had been conquered by the Aryans, and powerful Indo-Aryan kings held sway from Afghanistan to Bengal, from Kashmir to the Vindhyas.

The nucleus of the story from which the epic has been developed, in all probability, contains a historical element. The main theme is a war between Kauravas and Pandavas, cousins, belonging to the ancient lunar dynasty of kings whose traditional seat of government was at Hastinapura (near modern Delhi). Most of the kings of northern India took part in the war and fought on one side of the other. Originally. it would appear, the Kauravas were depicted as the persecuted heroes and the Pandavas as the villains, but the story was rewritten and, as it stands at present, the Pandavas are shown as heroes and the Kauravas as villains.

The original story, as indicated, is about 3,000 years old; in the Buddhist Canon, Jain texts and in Vedic literature some of the characters of the epic are mentioned under the same or slightly different names. The *Artha Sastra* has a reference to Duryodhana and the abduction of Sita, though the *Mahabharata* and *Ramayana* as such are not mentioned.

The ancient tale started growing as each generation passed, poets and bards hooking on to it the exploits of their pet heroes and heroes and sages who were supposed to have lived at the time of the great war. Many popular stories and folk tales were added to it, and the method of weaving tales into tales, a convention beloved of the eastern story teller, made it possible to incorporate in the text anything whether it had any bearing on the main theme or not.

The *Mahabharata*, as it stands at present, is the work of that period in Indian history which intervened between the collapse of the Mauryan empire in the second century B.C. and the rise of the Guptas in the fifth century A.D. This was a period of confusion for political India, but of glory for literary India. It was an age of war and romance, of invasions and revolutions, of shifting frontiers and racial fusions, the formative period of Puranic Hinduism, famed for its brilliant literary output. It was during this period that the two epics and most of the *Puranas* were written. The work of later Indian writers was generally confined to imitation, interpretation and interpolation. The hand of the interpolator is clearly discernible in the didactic portions of the *Mahabharata,* which make the epic, in many ways, a standing monument of contradiction in teachings.

War too takes on a new meaning in the *Mahabharata.* Till now, to Hindu kings, as will be seen from the *Artha Sastra* of Kautilys, war was but a means for expanding the frontiers of kingdoms, for enhancing the glory of the king and generally advancing the prosperity of the state. What was important was the result, and if this could be gained without loss of life and property, the king, in the *Artha Sastra,* was advised the eschew war and resort to other methods including treachery. But in the *Mahabharata* war appears as end in itself, the fulfilment of life for the Kshatriya. In the *Bhagavad Gita* (the poem appears in the *Mahabharata*) it is expressly laid down that the soldier is not to concern himself with the result of the battle, but only with his conduct in action. In fact, a war undertaken with the object of furthering one's kingdom is even deprecated; for the Kshatriya, fighting was a duty or Dharma, and its result is to be left open for the gods to decide.

The *Mahabharata* essentially represents the Kshatriya spirit, the spirit of action; the heroes and heroines of the epic are full blooded individualls revelling in the joys and pleasures of life, little interested in the ascetic views which dominated certain section of Hinduism. The morals of most of the characters in action are, as such, in keeping with the needs of this life rather than those of the life to come.

As a rule, the *Mahabharata* represents a flexible tradition in marriage and morals, and as such there is no attempt at standardisation or uniformity. The writers were well acquainted with the social theories and moral codes of different cultures and races following diverse conceptions of sexual morals, and to them all seemed to cherish their own practices and to get on well in spite of their widely differing standards. "Morality is subtle, incomprehensible even to sages," is the burden of the teaching of the *Mahabharata,* and it is in no great hurry to condemn any practice, however, outlandish it might appear to individuals.

The Vedic moral codes, no doubt, were held as orthodox in the *Mahabharata* but variation seem to have been more popular in the age represented by the epic. The reason for this is not far to seek. The Vedic conceptions were mainly meant for a certain section of the people, in fact, the conquerors who wished to preserve their individuality and supermacy over indigenous races who formed the vast majority of the general population of India. But by the time the *Mahabharata* came to be written, Aryan individuality was beginning to become a conception rather than a reality; the Indo-Aryan kingdome especially in the north and west were being fast conquered by Parthians, Greeks, Scythians and other tribes who were getting assimilated into Hinduism, Jainism, and Buddhism, and their customs, manners, religion and social theories were penetrating even the Gangetic communities. Indigenous non-Aryan races were also coming into prominence in the south and east and their ideas were colouring Aryan concepts. The spread of Buddhism and Jainism too convinced the Brahmins of the need for borrowing the more popular of their theories and practices in order to regain their lost supremacy over the people.

In this melting pot, it was difficult to preserve the Vedic ideals of marriage and morals intact. Hence we find in the *Mahabharata,* a ready recognition of the strangest practice of the time as ancient and valid, though condemned by sages before and after. Inter-racial, and inter-caste marriages, polyandry and polygyny, all have the sanction of the *Mahabharata,* and a community that practised any of them was not shut out of the benefits of Puranic religion on that account. Some of the greatest figures of the epic were born of Sudra or worse women. Nor was illegitimancy a handicap to eminence as we shall see presently.

The Melting Pot of Morals

It may not be quite correct to say that all the important characters in the *Mahabharata* were born illegitimate or of extra-marital relations, but most of them were born outside conventional morality. In fact so large is their number and so great the eminence of most of them that it is possible that the author of the epic considered conventional morality inadequate to produce geniuses. This view becomes all the more plausible when we consider the peculiar circumstances under which Dwaipayana Vyasa, the reputed author of the epic, was born. He was the son of the mighty Brahmin sage Parasara, and Matsyagandhi (fish-smelling), an untutored fishermaid. The story of union of these two incompatibles is narrated in the *Mahabharata* itself. Parasara, we are told, was, one day, crossing a mountain ferry, when he found the fishermaid sporting half-naked in the stream. Though she smelt of fish, Matsyagandhi was good to look at, Parasara, by his occult powers, came to know that the rustic beauty was in her Rtu, and an auspicious conjunction of the heavenly bodies indicated the birth of a prodigy; Parasara, hence, prophesied to the girl and expressed his desire for immediate union with her. The girl was hafe-willing, but raised certain objections; as she smelt of fish, she said, she felt somewhat embarrassed at the prospect of the approach of the holy man. On this Parasara, by his powerful magic, changed her fish-odour into a fragrance. The girl, now convinced of the greatness of the man and the truth of his prophecy about her forthcoming son, was prepared to submit of the embrace of the saint, but pointed out to him the undesirability of copulation in the open. Parasara now created a screen of smoke around them, and under its cover lay with Matsyagandhi. After the business was over, the sage went his way.

Matsyagandhi's father was delighted to find that his daughter's fish-odour had been changed into an aroma, but was not equally happy when he discovered that she was pregnant. Anyway, to avoid a scandal, he had her confined in an island; Vyasa was born and brought up here and was, hence, called Dwaipayana (of an island).

The legend is significant of the spirit of the times. Both in the vedic period and in later Hinduism such an affair would have been considered highly reprehensible. A Brahmin, according to certain law-givers, could take a fourth wife from the Sudra caste, after he had married three from the higher castes, but any relation between him and a woman of a caste lower than Sudra was taboo. And fisherfolk, for all practical purposes, were outcastes. Further, it is specifically stated by many lawgivers that the progeny of mixed marriages sink below the caste status of the lower of the parents. Here then, we have a case in which a most holy Brahmin, without even waiting for the formalities of a marriage ceremony, had casual relation with a fishermaid; and the result? Not an outcaste, but the most illustrious literary genius and Rishi Hinduism ever produced!

The story would show how desperately the Brahmins courted the lower castes; the literature of the period, in fact, has many instances of condescension by the high, and legends are not wanting that tell us of the great gods of the pantheon who assumed the form of the hunter, the fisherman or some other outcaste.

It is also noteworthy that Satyavati (this is another name of Mastsyagandhi) suffered little by her adventure with Parasara. While this affair may possibly be attributed to a passing fancy, moral lapse, or the anxiety of the sage to take advantage of the stellar conjunction and act quickly lest the chance slip away for ever, Satyavati's subsequent marriage with Shantanu, the leading light of the lunar race, had none of these extenuating circumstances. Shantanu, while out hunting in the forest, saw the girl, feel in love with her and approached her father for her hand. Satyavati's father was prepared to give her in marriage to Shantanu but demanded that her son and not Bhishma, Shantanu's existing son by his first wife Ganga, should by the heir to the throne. Shantanu did not agree to this, but Brishma, like a good son, voluntarily gave up his title to the throne, and arranged his father's marriage. In conformity with this contract, Vichitravirya, Satyavati's son, succeeded Shantanu and not Bhishma.

Another illustrious illegitimate was Karna. He was born of princess Kunti (mother of the Pandavas) before her marriage to Pandu. In the epic we are told that Pritha or Kunti was in charge of the arrangement for the stay of the irascible sage Durvasa at her father's house. The sage was so pleased with her hospitality that he granted her a boon by which she could call any five gods of the pantheon by repeating a spell and make them do her bidding. As soon as the sage was gone, Pritha, out of curiosity, repeated the incantation and called forth Surya, the gun-god. The luminary immediately appeared before her and wished to know what she wanted of him. The girl had no particular mission for the god just then, and told him so. The sun-god, however, thought it a pity to go back with a wasted day, and tried to make love to the pretty maid. The revolted girl pointed out to the celestial that she was a maiden and not a free agent. "It is only one's father, mother and other superiors who are competent to bestow a maiden on a man," she said. Surya met her objection with an impassioned address:

> O thou of sweet smiles, neither thy father, mother nor any other superior is empowered to give thee away. Listen carefully to my words! It is because a virgin desires the company of every man that she is called Kanya, from the root 'Kam' meaning desire. Therefore, O young lady, a virgin is free in this world. Thou shall not be guilty of any sin by complying with my request. And how can I, a well wisher of all creatures, desire an unrighteous act? That all men and women should be free in their sexual desire is the law of nature; the opposite is the perversion of the natural law.

This statement, while basically correct, does not appear to have been true of society in which Pritha lived. Anyway, all the objections raised by Pritha were satisfactorily settled for her by Surya, and she yielded.

Pritha became pregnant and in due course gave birth to Karna whom she had to abandon. The child was picked up by a Suta (caste of charioteers) and brought up as his child. Karna, when he grew into manhood, played an important role in the Mahabharata war. He fought his half-brothers, the Pandavas, chance driving him into the rival camp where he became the ally and trusted friend of Duryodhana, the leader of the Kauravas.

An institution mentioned in the *Mahabharata* and widely prevalent among the ancient Indo-Aryans was Niyoga or 'appointment' of agents for raising sons to dead or impotent men. The idea was closely linked with property rights in women, the notion that crops raised in the field of a man belonged to the owner of the field and not to the sower of the seed. We have seen that in Rig Vedic times, the widow, as a rule married the brother of her husband; in later Vedic times too, widows had rights of re-marriage, and a woman could ask for divorce on the ground of impotence in her husband. But during the Mahabharata time, widow marriage and divorce were becoming unpopular among the Indo-Aryans, but the need for sons remained paramount. Hence Niyoga began to be widely practised as a legitimate method of procuring sons for dead men and for those who were rendered incapable of begetting sons.

The lady Satyavati, as already noticed, married Shantanu. Two sons were born of this marriage when Shantanu died; of the two, Chitrangada was killed before marriage, and the other, Vichitravirya, married two sisters, Ambika and Ambalika but he died before any of them could conceive. When the lunar line thus stood in danger of extinction, Bhishma was requested to raise issues to his half-brother's wives in Niyoga, but he had forsworn himself to life-long celibacy and would have nothing to do with Ambika and Ambalika in spite of the ancient law which permitted sex indulgence to celibates when a woman's Rtu stood in danger of going waste. In this predicament, Satyavati confided to Bhishma the relation between Vyasa and herself, and it was decided between the two that the sage's services should be requisitioned for raising progeny to Vichitravirya.

Dwaipayana Vyasa was, accordingly, addressed in the matter. The sage was at the time practising penances without eating, shaving or washing, and while he agreed to the proposal of his mother, he asked for some time to qualify himself for the office and make himself presentable to the young queens. But Satyavati, who was in a hurry to have grand-children, would brook no delay, and requested the sage to go into her daughter-in-law immediately.

This feminine impatience, with which Vyasa complied, produced dire results. For the appearance of the amorous anchoret was so forbidding that Ambika, when the sage embraced her, closed her eyes, and her son was born blind. The bolder Ambalika did not close her eyes but only turned pale and her son Pandu was in consequence born pale. Satyavati wished for one more grandson, but by now the queens had had enough of Vyasa, and they sent their Sudra maid-servant to him; of her was born the wise Vidura.

Now Dhritarashtra, the blind son of Ambika, was the father of the Kauravas. Pandu, again, could not have sons. He married two ladies, but was prevented by a curse from having sexual relations with either. While he was hunting, it would appear, he shot by mistake, a sage who was mating with his wife in the forest, and the dying saint cursed that Pandu would die the moment he embraced a woman. Pandu now asked his senior wife Kunti to have recourse to Niyoga; but Kunti, as we have seen, could make gods serve the purpose, and she called forth three gods, Yama, Vayu and Indra, and had three sons by them, Yudhishtira, Bhima and Arjuna respectively. As the sage Durvasa had given her the power of calling forth five gods (one already availed of), she could still obtain one more son but this power she generously transferred to her co-wife Madri, who called up the twin Asvins and had the twins Nakula and Sahadeva. Thus the origin of the five Pandavas who, biologically speaking, were not the sons of Pandu.

In Niyoga, usually a brother or nearest of kin of the dead or impotent man was appointed. In the absence of these, saintly Brahmins could perform this pleasant office. In fact, in the *Mahabharata* it is related that the whole male population of the Kshatriyas was destroyed by the Brahmin warrior Parasurama to avenge the murder of his father by a Kshatriya, and the so-called Kshatriyas who fought the epic war were, in effect, the children of the Brahmins produced in the live fields of the Kshatriyas in Niyoga.

Several stray cases of Niyoga by which Brahmin sages produced sons for the Kshatriyas are also mentioned in the *Mahabharata*.

Vasistha is said to have produced a son, Asmaka, in the field of Kalmashapada, king of Ayodhya, and Dirghatamas sixteen, in that of Vali.

We have already noticed how Dirghatamas was thrown in the Ganges and how he floated down the river on a log; the sage eventually reached the kingdom of Vali. This king was greatly delighted by the arrival of the holy man in his kingdom as, at that time, he was in particular need of one. He had no sons and there was no possibility of his ever having one. So the sage was appointed to supply sons for Vali, but the young queen was so repulsed by the sight of the wrinkled, blind, old saint that she sent her Sudra maid-servant to him. Being blind, Dirghatamas was not in a position to distinguish the royal from the vulgar, and started producing sons for his patron. The maid-servant gave birth to eleven sons, one after another, while the queen remained sterile as ever, which roused the suspicions of the king who made detailed enquiries and discovered what was happening. The king now asked the sage if, by any chance, the maid-servant's sons could be legally considered his, inasmuch as the woman was his property and not the sage's; Dirghatamas, however, declared that the eleven sons were his and not Vali's. So the king gave peremptory orders to his wife to behave herself; on this, the queen reluctantly approached the saint who, by merely touching her, produced in her five mighty sons each of whom founded a kingdom. The origin of Anga, Vanga, Kalinga, Pundra and Kumbha was ascribed to these five princes.

Originally there was no limit to the number of sons that could be got in Niyoga, but by the time the epic was compiled three were considered the ideal. But there were practical difficulties in the way of limiting production to an exact three sons; apart from factors such as the possibilities of begetting twins, in spite of the male-making ceremonies performed by the best of the Brahmins there were chances of daughters intervening, and there are few cases mentioned in the *Mahabharata* in which the number three was strictly adhered to. Anyway, as centuries passed, Niyoga began to be viewed with increasing disfavour; soon after the epic period, only one son was permitted to be born in Niyoga, and ultimately none, as the strict later moralists held the view that it was better for a man to go to hell than let his wife be carnally known by another, whether relative or saint, for the sake of sons to perform his last rites.

Draupadi

The most interesting character in the *Mahabharata* to our subject, is its heroine Draupadi, also called Panchali as she was the daughter of the king of the Panchalas. She was a forceful personality, able, brave and grateful but revengeful against enemies, showing none of the meekness and Pativrityam that became the later ideal of womanhood in Hinduism. And what is most important, she had five husbands, not one, and ruled all the five with an iron hand.

This polyandry of the heroine is the most intriguing moral situation in the whole epic. She seems to have been a historic character, the central figure, in fact, in the ancient story from which the *Mahabharata* developed. Ancient Buddhist and Jain literature too, as we have seen, mention her. As such, it was clearly impossible to have written the *Mahabharata* without her; if there was any such possibility, the author, who lived in an age which viewed polyandry with horror, would have certainly compiled the epic without her. But as things stood, he could only invent excuses, explanations and precedents for the exceptional morality of Draupadi.

Justification of Draupadi's Polyandry

The main justification given in the *Mahabharata* for draupadi's polyandry is that it was adopted by the Pandava brothers out of consideration for the word of their mother. To understand this explanation it is necessary for the reader to have some idea of the peculiar circumstances that attended the marriage of Draupadi.

Draupadi, we are told, was born in accordance with a special vow of her father who wanted to bestow her in marriage to the Pandava prince Arjuna, the greatest archer of his age. But by the time Draupadi came of age to be married, the trouble between the Pandavas and Kauravas took a serious turn and the Kauravas set fire to a house in which the Pandavas were living with their mother, and the five princes and Kunti were reported to have perished in the conflagration. Draupada, king of the Panchalas, on hearing that Arjuna was no more, decided to give his daughter in marriage to an archer as skilled as Arjuna; hence for the marriage of the princess he had a moving target constructed at a great height which the suitor had to shoot through five times in quick succession; only an archer of the skill of Arjuna was believed capable of performing the feat. Drupada then invited all eligible princes of India for the Swayamvara of his daughter.

The Pandavas, however, had not actually perished. The plot to burn down the house was discovered, and the five princes, along with their mother, escaped before the house was set on fire, not wishing to show themselves up immediately, lest the wicked Duryodhana should do them further harm, the Pandavas travelled incognito as mendicant Brahmins and lived, with their mother, as the guests of a poor Brahmin in the village of Ekachakra. Their intention was to continue their disguise till they had made some alliances strong enough to resist Duryodhana and his gang.

While they were thus living in Ekachakra they heard about the marriage of Draupadi. As the Brahmins were welcome to all feasts, the five brothers went along with other Brahmins to the capital of the Panchalas, leaving their mother at Ekachakra.

On the date fixed for the marriage of Draupadi, numerous royal suitors arrived at the palace of the Panchala king. One after another the princes tried to shoot the target, but none was successful. Karna was, perhaps, the only bowman who could have shot the mark; he too was present at the Swayamvara as he had been elevated to the kingship of Anga by his friend and patron Duryodhana, but when he strung the bow to shoot the target, Draupadi objected. Even if he were to win, she said, she would not wed the son of a Suta, no better than a Sudra, so he could just as well spare himself the trouble. Karna threw down the bow in disgust and went back to his seat.

Arjuna now entered the arena from the Brahmin gallery. He took the bow, strung it with ease and shot five arrows in quick succession through the target.

Draupadi accepted him, but this time the objection came from her Kshatriya suitors. "Swayamvara," they declared, "is meant only for Kshatriyas and not for Brahmins. If this damsel does not desire to wed a Kshatriya, let us cast her into fire and return to our kingdoms." The Panchala king did not appreciate this line of argument. If the Kshatriyas proved themselves imbeciles, he said, a Brahmin youth, skilled in the use of arms, was competent to marry his daughter. The Kshatriyas tried to drive home the point by an appeal to arms, but they were put to rout by the Panchalas and the Pandavas. After this fight, Arjuna collected this bride and, along with his brothers, proceeded to Ekachakra to meet Kunti.

Arjuna, wishing to break the news to his mother personally and prepare her for the reception of her daughter-in-law, went in advance of the main party. On meeting his mother, the jubilant prince said: "Mother, I have won today, something very precious". "Well, my son", said Kunti, "share it, as usual with your brothers". It was after this command that the lady knew what exactly the precious possession was. When the matter was reported to the marriage party, there was consternation all round, but the consensus of opinion was that in deference to Kunti's words, Panchali had to be shared by all the five brothers.

A council of elders was then convened. The Panchala king opposed his daughter's marriage to five. Yudhishtira, however, was of opinion that polyandry was not entirely unknown to the Aryans. Jatila, he said, of the race of Gotama, had married seven sages. "So also, an ascetic's daughter, born of a tree had, in former times, united herself in marriage with ten brothers all bearing the same name of Prachetas, who were of souls exalted by asceticism". The sage Vyasa, now called Drupada aside and passed on to him a piece of important information; Draupadi, he confided to him, was in a former life the common wife of five celestials, and these were now reborn as the Pandavas. This celestial origin of the Pandavas swung Panchala's decision in favour of his daughter marrying all of them.

Another explanation given of Draupadi's polyandry is that the princess, before her marriage, had propitiated Shiva for a suitable husband, and when the deity made his appearance she, in order to prevent misunderstanding, repeated, five times, her request for a husband, which the god mistook for a prayer for five husbands and granted as a special favour.

Anyway, Draupadi was formally married to all the five brothers. They also chalked out a plan as to how she was to be shared. Only one of her husbands was to have her company at a time, and while she was with him no other brother was to intrude even by accident. The penalty for breaking this domestic rule of conduct was one year's exile; we are told in the *Mahabharata* that Arjuna, who happened to be in urgent need of arms, once entered the armoury where Yudhishtira was enjoying the company of Draupadi, and had, consequently, to go into voluntary exile for a year.

Draupadi's Character

Draupadi is the one feminine character in the *Mahabharata* typical of the age. Confident of her own strength of mind and will, she was the most forceful and consistent personality of the epic. While her husbands on many occasions lost hope of winning their case by war, were cowed down by suffering and wished for a peaceful life even submitting to humiliating terms. Draupadi was ever unflinching in her determination of refusal to compromise with evil-doers and of bringing about the defeat and destruction of foes. No amount of suffering, no even exile, starvation, public denudation, and kicking in an open court by an infatuated sadist could break her indomitable will, and it was often she who whipped up the fagging spirit of her husbands when misfortune broke them. To bring out her character to the best advantage, it is necessary for us to narrate some of the principal events of her life in the correct sequence.

After her marriage, Draupadi lived for some time with her husbands as an exile, but there followed a period of truce between the Kauravas and the Pandavas during which the latter were allowed to live in a palace at Indraprastha, near the capital Hastinapura, and rule half the kingdom. Neither Duryodhana, the eldest of the Kauravas, nor his friend Karna could quite forget her loss to Arjuna in the Swayamvara. Karna, as we have seen, was particularly humiliated by her on the occasion; though generally chivalrous, he took this insult to heart and never forgave her.

Duryodhana now suffered an additional insult. He was, one day, invited to see the Pandavas' palace at Indraprastha. As Megasthenese said of Chandragupta's palace, there were many wonders in Indraprastha. It was built by the renowned Asura architect, Maya, and water in certain pleasure-baths looked like crystal and crystal floors created the illusion of sheets of water. While being taken round the palace, the dignified Duryodhana mistaking water for crystal fell into a tank, and Draupadi, who was near by, burst out into laughter. This hilarity was neither deliberate nor pre-meditated, but Duryodhana, already smarting under her loss to Arjuna, took it grievously to heart. In fact, the desire of Karna and Duryodhana to humiliate Draupadi played no small part in widening the gulf between the Pandavas and Kauravas which eventually ended up in the dreadful holocaust of the Mahabharata war.

Soon after the laughing matter at Indraprastha, Duryodhana challenged Yudhishtira to a gambling contest. In those days, among the Indo-Aryans deciding the fate of kingdoms by an appeal to dice was a recognised method of contest; Yudhishtira accepted the challenge and started playing at dice. Duryodhana's uncle and partisan, Sakuni, was notorious for sharp practice in the game, and he started winning for Duryodhana the personal property of Yudhishtira one after another. After private property, part of the kingdom was staked and lost; in the end Yudhishtira lost all his possessions when Duryodhana asked him tauntingly if he would like to offer as a stake the freedom of his brothers and himself. The mad gambler accepted the challenge, lost the game and, together with his brothers became slave of Duryodhana. "I give you one more chance", said Duryodhana, "will you care to offer your wife for a stake against all that you have lost"? Yudhishtira agreed, and the dice were thrown; the Pandava, again lost.

So, at last, Duryodhana got the chance he had been waiting for. He would now insult Draupadi as no man had ever insulted woman before or after; in fact, he decided to denude Draupadi in the assembled court, in presence of all the dignitaries of the kingdom!

Accordingly, a messenger was sent to Indraprastha to summon Draupadi to Duryodhana's presence. The messenger was told by Draupadi that Yudhishtira had no power to gamble her away, and as such she was a free woman and not Duryodhana's slave. On this, Duryodhana sent his ribald brother Dussasana to bring the woman to Hastinapura by physical force if necessary. Dussasana performed the task with alacrity. He caught Draupadi by her hair, dragged her all the way from Indraprastha to Hastinapura and presented her before his imperial brother. And Dussasana, by Duryodhana's order, started disrobing the screaming wretched woman, when the learned assembly of elders entered into a lengthy, illuminating discussion about property rights in women.

This is one of the most incomprehensible and disgusting sections in the *Mahabharata*. Draupadi, wriggling, shrieking and resisting the attempt of Dussasana to disrobe her, argued that Yudhishtira had no right to gamble her away, as at the time of the last throw of dice, he had already lost his freedom and was not a free agent. Duryodhana maintained that in gambling away his brothers and himself, Yudhishtira had also gambled away his wife, since a wife had no independent status apart from her husband or husbands; the final throw of dice was merely in the nature of confirmation of an existing title. Karna, usually chivalrous but now smarting under the insult suffered in the Swayamvara, stoutly defended Duryodhana's right to do what he liked with Draupadi, especially as a woman with five husbands had lost her claim to decency and was to be treated as a prostitute; he even told her that, as a slave, she was relieved of her matrimonial bonds and could bestow her favours on any one she pleased including himself. On this, Duryodhana bared his left thigh, reserved for women of pleasure. Bhishma, whose discourses on morals run into several sections of the epic, and the no less loquacious Vidura, sat blinking like a pair of owls blinded by sunlight. On the lad Vikarna, a younger brother of Duryodhana, protested against the outrageous behaviour of his elder brothers, but he was told to shut up.

What all the moralists in the assembly, great and small, as well as the author of the *Mahabharata* seem to have forgotten is that the question involved in the denudation of Draupadi is not the right of Duryodhana to treat Draupadi as a slave-girl but the common law of obscenity. To put the matter in a different way, if Duryodhana, in order to punish a slave-girl of his harem, took it into his head to exhibit her naked in his court, would not all respectable people including Karna have walked out? If Duryodhana had disrobed Draupadi in his harem in a drunken bout with his gang of voluptuaries, the question of property rights in women would have had some meaning in the context; but here the sentiments of the assembly in which sat the grave and elderly celibate Bhishma and other dignitaries of the realm, had to be respected but no one seems to have thought of this, but all were busy babbling about the rights of gamblers.

Anyway, Draupadi was saved the disgrace of complete denudation by a miracle. She also won her freedom and that of her husbands by an appeal to Dhritarashtra, Duryodhana's father, who, alarmed by portents, complied with her request. Duryodhana, finding that the free Pandavas could be a perpetual menace to his safety, offered Yudhishtira a tempting bait. "A last throw of dice", said he, "and the chances are even for both of us. If I lose, I abandon my kingdom and with my relatives will repair to the forest and live there twelve years and pass the thirteenth in disguise; if, during the thirteenth year, I am recognised or identified, I will accept another twelve years' exile as forfeit. If you lose, you will do the same". The foolish Yudhishtira took the bait; the dice were thrown, and the Pandava prince lost the last chance.

The Pandavas with Draupadi went into exile. But the fate of the Kauravas and of all Indo-Aryan kingdoms was sealed. War and war alone could now settle the issue. Panchali swore that she would not anoint her dishevelled hair except with the blood of Dussasana who had dragged her by the hair. From now on she lived for revenge.

In her exile Draupadi had to suffer many things of many men. One day, for instance, Jayadratha, husband of Duryodhana's sister Dussala, while he was on a hunting expedition, happened to come to the cottage where Draupadi was living. Her husbands were away, and seeing Draupadi alone in the house he tried to make love to her; on rejection, he abducted her but before could get out of the forest, the Pandavas came on the scene and saved her. As they were unable to capture Jayadratha himself, they discussed among themselves as to what course of action was to be taken in respect of him. Bhima and Arjuna were for pursuing and killing him, but Yudhishtira, a man of peace, advised them to desist, out of consideration for their old aunt Gandhari and for Dussala, their cousin. Draupadi's reply was characteristic: "If you care to do what is agreeable to me, you must slay that mean, despicable wretch, that stupid, sinful, infamous chief of the Saindhava clan. The foe who forcibly carries away a married woman or who wrests a kingdom should never be spared, though he would supplicate for mercy."

Though in theory, the slave and property of her husbands, in actual practice, Draupadi often dominated her husbands and their councils. She is even mentioned in the epic as Pandita (learned). Her forceful, domineering personality often clashed with the ideals of the peace-living Yudhishtira. One day, for instance, while he was giving her a sermon on the greatness of God, Draupadi replied:

> I see the noble and the good in distress, and the wicked enjoying the good things of life. You, my lord, are righteousness personified, and yet are always in misery. Your wicked foes, the Kauravas, on the other hand, are ever fortunate and enjoy regal splendour....God does not

> show for all mankind the love of a parent or the concern of the wise and the intelligent guardian. God is partial; He favours some with wealth and comfort, others He condemns to sweat and toil without any apparent reason; caprice and blind-will appear to be the distinctive characteristic of Godhead, and not mercy or justice.

This blasphemy naturally drew forth a long-winded discourse on divine grace from Yudhishtira, at the end of which, Draupadi in the style of the modern atheist who conforms to the standards of the herd with mental reservations, confessed to conviction.

After the term of exile was over, Yudhishtira, wishing to prevent a war with his cousins, sent Krishna to the court of Hastinapura as an envoy for negotiations; before his departure Krishna was called asked by Draupadi who showed him her dry, dishevelled hair, reminded him of her oath, and confided to him that negotiations should proceed only on those lines; the envoy assured her that her sentiments would be respected. No need to emphasise that the peace move failed.

On another occasion, when Yudhishtira, overburdened with a sense of the onerous responsibilities of kingship expressed a desire to renounce the world, Panchali, exasperated, told her other husbands: "If you are wise, you would lock up this brother of yours in a prison and take charge of the affairs of state. The man who, on account of a feeble intellect, acts thus never attains felicity."

Draupadi was jealous too. Though in theory she loved all her five husbands equally well, she had a lurking partiality for Arjuna; he was, after all, the man who won her in the Swayamvara; others became her husbands through an accident as it were. When Arjuna married Subhadra and brought this young lady to the house and introduced her to her co-wife, Draupadi's heart nearly broke. Though she did not show any signs of embarrassment or jealousy in Subhadra's presence, she told Arjuna when she was alone with him: "Why tarriest thou here, O son of Kunti? Go where the daughter of the Satwata race is. A second tie always relaxeth the first one upon a faggot!"

We are also told that for her partiality towards Arjuna, she was the first to drop off in the last journey of the Pandavas to the realms of the blessed.

Draupadi in Virata's Harem

The character of Panchali is perhaps best shown in the Virata Parva of the epic. Incidentally the Parva gives us an account of the life of a king's harem at the time of the *Mahabharata* and a detailed notice of her humiliation in the court of Virata and the destruction of her ravisher Kichaka will not be out of place here.

As we have seen, the condition of exile imposed by Duryodhana was that, after twelve years, the Pandavas should spend the thirteenth incognito. For this purpose they decided to enter the service of Virata, king of the Matsyas. So, dismissing their retinue, they together with Panchali left the forest in disguise and went to the kingdom of Virata.

Yudhishtira appeared before Virata as a Brahmin, proficient in secret arts and in gambling, and was appointed as an adviser; he gave his name as Jaya. Bhima got a situation in the harem as cook, and was known as Vallabha. Arjuna who, on account of a curse, had been turned into a eunuch, obtained a position in Virata's harem as a teacher of music and dancing; his assumed name was Vrihannala, "the son or daughter without a father or mother". The description of Vrihannala, give in the *Mahabharata* would show that this class has changed little in India through the centuries. "He was decked in the ornaments of women, wearing large earrings, and beautiful conch bracelets overlaid with gold. And that mighty-armed individual with long and abundant hair, floating about his neck, resembled an elephant in gait". His main duty was to coach princess Uttara in music and dancing, and generally supervise the dancing girls attached to the palace. Prince Sahadeva became the keeper of Virata's cattle, while Nakula was appointed the superintendent of the stables.

Draupadi applied to the queen for the post of a lady-in waiting (Sairandhri), whose chief duty was to prepare scents and unguents for the king and queen; she gave her name as Malini. Queen Sudeshna who knew something of Samudrika Sastra (science of auspicious marks), seeing the candidate, observed:

> You have none of the marks of the servile, but abundant signs of the queen. Your heels are not prominent, your thighs do not touch each other. Your navel is deep, your voice solemn and resonant. Your toes, bust, hips, dorsa, nails and palms are proportionate and well-developed. Your soles and face are ruddy. Your hair is glossy, breasts, round full and elevated. Your hips are plumb. Like a mare from Kashmire, you possess every auspicious mark of your sex. Your eye-lashes are beautifully arched, your neither lip is like the ruddy gourd. Your waist is slender and your neck bears the lines that mark the conch-shell. Your veins are scarcely visible, while your eyes resemble the lotus. Your face is like the full moon and your body has the fragrance of the blue lotus.

These, then, were the distinctive physical characteristics of the queen.

Sudeshna was very much impressed by the beauty and bearing of Malini but wondered whether or not it would be prudent to appoint such a glamorous woman as her Sairandhri, what with men being men and her husband not being an exception; she frankly expressed her apprehension to Malini herself. But this lady set at rest the queen's misgivings on this point by observing that she was quite capable of looking after herself as she was the wedded wife of five Gandharvas (celestial beings) who always guarded her and would not allow any one with an evil intent to approach her. On this assurance, the queen appointed her as her Sairandhri.

Though Virata was the crowned king, the real power in the kingdom was wielded by the unscrupulous and ambitious Kichaka, brother of the queen and commander-in-chief of the armed forces. It would appear that between Kichaka and his sister most of the important affairs of the state were settled and the king's sanction came as a matter of course. Now Kichaka, one day, happened to see Malini in his sister's mansion and was struck by her beauty. He wished to have her for his pleasure and told Sudeshna so. As a rule, women in the harem, especially in the lower ranks, were not much noted for their purity or chastity and Sudeshna thought that no harm could result from an interest developed by her brother in her Sairandhri; besides, in spite of Malini's assurances on the point, the queen was viewing with alarm certain tendencies in her husband who would not, for instance, use garlands or unguents made by any one but Malini. So, Sudeshna considered her brother's interest in Malini a lesser evil, and one day sent her to Kichaka on a trivial mission.

On seeing Malini, Kichaka did a vigorous piece of royal courting. In an impassioned address, he described her charms like a Sanskrit poet and his love like an infatuated youth. He told her too that he was the real ruler of the Matsyas, that he would marry her and make all the Matsyas slave for her. But Malini told him that she was the virtuous wife of five Gandharvas who always guarded her, and advised him in his own interest, to desist from making such sinful advances to her. After offering these excuses she beat a hasty retreat from the palace of Kichaka. The disappointed lover did not make any offer to stop her but thought time would soften her.

Time, however, did not soften Draupadi, and Kichaka again approached his sister to contrive some means by which he could obtain Malini. And it was agreed between the brother and sister that Malini should be sent to Kichaka's palace to fetch certain choice wines for the royal table. When Malini was selected for the job by Sudeshna, she naturally objected stating that she might be molested by Kichaka as his behaviour on the last occasion was not very correct. On this, Sudeshna assured her that, out of respect for her, his sister, he would refrain from objectionable activities even if inclined that way. On the strength of this assurance, Malini, once again went to Kichaka's palace conveying the queen's message.

On seeing Draupadi, Kichaka's passion was inflamed. He was, moreover, in a violent mood. When she resisted his overtures and made good her escape, the infuriated voluptuary chased her. She ran for life to the court of Virata where Yudhishtira and the king were sitting in council together with other dignitaries of the kingdom. Kichaka followed her, caught her by the clothes and on her falling down, kicked her in the presence of all; he was prevented from doing her further injury by the timely intervention of the councillors who sent her to her apartments.

This was an insult to be wiped out in blood. Draupadi sought out Bhima and recounted to him all her misfortunes, one by one; how she, a princess, wedded to five valiant princes, found herself the most miserable woman on earth, how she had to suffer humiliations and privations even poor women of the meanest class did not have to put up with, how she had to wander in wild forests as an exile, how she was insulted by Duryodhana and his gang who denuded her in public, how she was carried away by the villain Jayadratha, and how, now, she was kicked in the court of Virata by a reprobate when her eldest husband sat there unconcerned. She expressed disgust at Yudhishtira's pacifism under such provocations, and questioned the manliness of her other husbands. Indeed it was a pleasant sight for her, she said, to see her eldest husband chant, like a sycophant, the praises of the imbecile Virata, to see the redoubtable Bhima cooking like a drudge in his kitchen, and the nenowned bowman Arjuna clad in clownish clothes, leaping like a baboon for the amusement of the slave-girls of the harem!

Thus worked up, Bhima decided to kill Kichaka that very night. Draupadi was asked to keep a secret appointment with Kichaka, and Bhima undertook to do the rest.

Draupadi had no difficulty in arranging a secret meeting. For Kichaka, after the performance in the court, sought out Draupadi and came to apologise; he also pointed out to her his omnipotence, and assured her that in the whole kingdom there was none able to resist his will or whim, and if she would not acquiesce in his designs she would be courting further trouble. Draupadi feigned conviction and made a show of repentance. She was not aware of his power till then, she said, but was under the apprehension that her husbands might do her harm if she proved unfaithful, but that she was now convinced that none could prevail against Kichaka. In order to keep the matter a secret, however, she suggested that they should meet that night in the dancing hall of the palace as the place would be vacant after nightfall. The delighted Kichaka closed in with the proposal, and Draupadi duly informed Bhima of the secret appointment.

Bhima, under cover of night proceeded to the dancing hall well in advance of the appointed time, and hid himself under a bed. When Kichaka came, he fell upon him like a lion, strangled him, left his corpse a mangled mass of boneless flesh, and disappeared from the scene without any one coming to know of the incident.

When the body of Kichaka was discovered in the dancing hall, it was given out by Draupadi herself that her Gandharva husbands who had been guarding her, had done this to avenge her wrongs; the corpse of Kichaka which had been reduced to a lump, out of all recognition of its human shape, by the muscular strength of Bhima, compelled conviction. Anyway, it was plain to everyone that Draupadi was the original cause of the destruction of Kichaka, and his friends decided that she should die as a punishment. Some of them were for killing her on the spot, while others, more imaginative, wanted her to be burnt alive on his funeral pyre. This view finally prevailed, and the partisans of Kichaka obtained Virata's permission for the move. Accordingly, Draupadi was tied to a bier and taken out in procession, but when the *cortege* reached the cremation ground, Bhima appeared there disguised as a Gandharva, and uprooting a tree played the part of the celestial so well that the frightened Matsyas fled leaving the bier in the cremation ground; on this, Bhima released Draupadi.

Forms of Marriage

The eight kinds of marriage recognised in the *Grihya Sutras* are mentioned in the *Mahabharata* too. The Brahmins, it would appear, followed the first four. Among the Kshatriyas and in intercaste marriages, many variations were prevalent which were generally controlled by traditional usages and local customs. The Kshatriyas had a partially for the Swayamvara form of marriage, as this gave them splendid opportunities for organising pageants or displaying skill in arms.

Swayamvara

In Swayamvara, the procedure was not uniform in all cases. Though the name would indicate that the bride had her own choice in selecting her husband (Swayamvara means, 'own choice'), in actual practice it was not always her choice that prevailed. A few cases of Swayamvara mentioned in the *Mahabharata* will illustrate the point.

The Swayamvara of Draupadi, already mentioned would show that the princess was offered, more or less, as the prize in an archery contest. Anybody, however, was not allowed to take part in the contest; Pratiloma taboos were respected and we have seen how the princess herself disqualified Karna whom she considered of lower birth than hers.

In the story of the celestial marriage of Sati, a theme beloved of Puranic scriptures, it would appear her father invited for her Swayamvara all the people in the three worlds except the person she was in love with, namely Shiva. But Shiva appeared in the Swayamvara hall without invitation, at the right moment, and Sati placed the wedding garland on his neck, when Daksha, her father, was compelled to give her in marriage to Shiva according to the prescribed rites.

Uninvited guests to Swayamvara did not always fare so well. Usually what happened was that the aggrieved suitor appeared on the scene with a gang of desperadoes and carried away the bride by force, fighting and even killing those who resisted him.

The marriage of Damayanti, narrated in the *Mahabharata*, was, perhaps, the ideal Swayamvara. Though they had not seen each other, Nala and Damayanti fell in love by their reported greatness and beauty and decided to marry; the decision was conveyed through a trusted agent. Both belonged to the ruling royal clans and Bhimaka, Damayanti's father, invited all eligible suitors to the Swayamvara including Nala. The suitors arrived, and when they were assembled in the marriage hall, a lady-guide conducted Damayanti through the hall, introducing each suitor to her. She carried the wedding garland in her hand. When damayanti was introduced to Nala, she paused, bestowed the garland on him and thus accepted him as her husband. Though to be sure, there was some disappointment for the rejected suitors, all ended well, and the guests departed blessing the bride and the bridegroom.

This is, perhaps, what a Swayamvara ought to be, but many fell short of the ideal. In the Swayamvara of the princess of Kalinga, for instance, it was not the choice of the princess that prevailed but the will of the haughty Duryodhana who was determined to marry her whether she liked it or not. She when the guide introduced Duryodhana to the princess and she quietly moved on to the next suitor, he could see no point in her going farther, and promptly seized her and made off with her, Karna fighting a rear action with the pursuing column sent by Chitrangada, king of Kalinga.

There is no doubt that Swayamvara was a historic institution among the indo-Aryans. The greeks, as we have already seen, mention it. The institution was revived by the Rajputs who claimed to be the lineal descendents of the epic heroes, and the last recorded Swayamvara was of Samyogita, daughter of Rajah Jaichand of Kanauj, whom the hostile Prithwiraj Chawhan captured from the Swayamvara hall. Prithwiraj, it may be mentioned, was historical personage who lived in the twelfth century A.D.

Rakshasa or Marriage by Capture

In some of the Swayamvara, capture, as we have noticed, formed an important element. The spirit of the sword was considered highly becoming of a Kshatriya in the matter of marriage too. In fact it was almost a point of honour with a Kshatriya to capture the girl he loved, if the parents objected to her marriage with him, especially if the girl too loved him. Many famous captures were of this nature, and some, in actual practice, took the form of elopement.

In the case of Subhadra, Krishna's sister, who was captured by Arjuna with the connivance of Krishna, capture took the form of a farce, something like the mock fight and capture even now practised by some tribes in India and elsewhere. Arjuna during his one year's exile was staying with his cousin Krishna in the city of the Yadavas, when he happened to see the young and lovely Subhadra and wished to marry her. He broached the subject to Krishna who was delighted with the proposal. But there were certain difficulties that had to be overcome. Krishna's elder brother Balarama had his own ideas about the marriage of Subhadra, and in such cases it was always the will of the elder that prevailed. Nor was Krishna quite sure that Subhadra was particularly fond of Arjuna and, if a Swayamvara was arranged, Subhadra's choice would definitely fall on him. Further, begging for a wife of her guardians, as though he were a mendicant Brahmin, would be unbecoming in an independent Kshatriya. So Krishna was of opinion that, under the circumstances capture would be the most honourable as also the surest course of action open to Arjuna for winning Subhadra. Accordingly, a plot was hatched between the two. While Subhadra was attending a festival of the Yadavas on the mountain slope of Raivaka, Arjuna drove a pleasure chariot to the foot of the hill, and hid himself in a convenient spot for an opportune moment. The lively Subhadra, while sight-seeing, wandered away from the main body of her attendants and friends, when the lurking lover appeared suddenly, seized her and, placing her in the chariot, drove off towards Indraprastha.

There was an uproar, and when news of the abduction reached Balarama, the fierce warrior was thoroughly roused and ordered fleet horses to be harnessed for the pursuit of Arjuna; he also spoke harshly about the behaviour of Arjuna and his abuse of hospitality. But the cunning Krishna pacified Balarama by many a soothing word. Arjuna, he pointed out, was, in every way, a fit husband for Subhadra; he was young, brave, and came from the illustrious lunar race; they were related to him, as Kunti, his mother was one among them; as for the capture and the supposed abuse of hospitality, Krishna maintained, that it had been recognised throughout the world that the proper course of action for a Kshatriya who loved a girl was to capture her, as the results of any other method could be uncertain. "Who would, among Kshatriyas," asked Krishna, "accept the gift of a bride, as as though she were an animal of an inanimate object? What man, again, is there who would sell his offspring or buy his wife? Considering all these, I think Arjuna acted rightly and in accordance with the time-honoured law of the Kshatriyas." The persuasive Krishna thus pacified the Yadavas and Balarama who now sent a party of messengers who wooed the fleeing lovers, and brought them back and had them married.

It may be mentioned that Krishna himself captured Rukmini, one of his wives, from her father's house, though she was intended to be married to Shishupala, an enemy of Krishna.

According to the conventions of capture, it was not necessary for the lover himself to stage the capture, but his guardian could do it for him. King Sini is said to have captured Devaki and married her to his relative Vasudeva (Krishna's father). The capture of Amba, Ambika and Ambalika was actually effected by the venerable Bhishma for marriage to his ward and nephew, Vichitravirya. The marriage of these three princesses had been arranged by their father, the king of Banaras, but when the girls entered the marriage hall, Bhishma with a picked body of fighters forced his way into the palace, and in the resultant confusion, captured all the three young ladies and sped with them to Hastinapura, the king of Banaras making futile attempts to stop them.

When the marriage of the three princesses to Vichitravirya was being arranged, Ambika and Ambalika were willing, but Amba objected on the plea that she was in love with, and already betrothed to, the king of the Salvas. On this Bhishma released and sent her to her lover; the Salva king, however, refused to accept her on the ground that he was not the man to wed to woman captured by another, and turned her out. Thus abandoned, she repaired to a forest colony of hermits; she asked them for enlightenment as to the party responsible for her misery. After a thorough discussion, the hermits held Bhishma to blame in the affair; the sages held the rejection of Amba by the Salva king as valid, but the conduct of Bhishma as objectionable for capturing a betrothed girl. Amba is said to have committed suicide and re-born as a eunuch to kill Bhishma.

This would indicate that the capture of betrothed women was not permitted; in a regular war, however, it would appear that the women of the vanquished and killed were, at times, appropriated by the victor for marriage, pleasure or service. Of the 16,008 wives of Krishna, the odd eight were regularly married to him, but the 16,000 were mostly women of conquered kings. As we have already noticed, capture of married women after defeating their husbands and relatives seems to have been prevalent among the Indo-Aryans in days gone by, but by the time the epic came to be written, the practice had fallen into disrepute. As a rule, the epic would indicate that the capture of maidens was permissible, if other circumstances, such as caste taboos, Pratiloma, etc. did not stand in the way of a regular marriage.

Marriage by Contract

While marriage was generally considered sacramental and indissoluble among the Indo-Aryans, there is one highly respectable contract marriage mentioned in the *Mahabharata*. It was the marriage between king Shantanu, Bhishma's father, and the lady Ganga. It is related that king Shantanu (prior to his marriage with Satyavati) went out hunting into a forest where he saw a beautiful girl; Shantanu wished to marry her, and she agreed but put in a condition that she could do what she liked after marriage and her husband had no right of objection. In case he objected, it was stipulated, she was free to leave him.

Things went on well till the birth of a baby. As soon as a son was born to her. Ganga took the child into a river and drowned it. Shantanu was terribly upset over the unnatural behaviour of Ganga, but did not express disapproval because of the covenant he had made with her. This thing happened every time a child was born, and thus seven sons were drowned by Ganga. But when the mother took her eighth baby and proceeded towards the river. Shantanu stopped her. Ganga now left her husband, leaving her son with him.

This son was Bhishma. The conduct of Ganga is explained in the epic by the fable that she was the personification of the celestial Ganges and was cursed to be born on earth and bear the eight Vasus (an octad of godlings) as her sons.

Such contract marriages were rare among the Indo-Aryans themselves, though prevalent in inter-racial and inter-caste matrimonial alliances; in these marriages Indo-Aryan males generally married non-Aryan women and they often conceded to some of the customs of their wives' people. The marriage of Shantanu and Ganga can fall into this category since Ganga was considered a nymph and not a regular Indo-Aryan lady.

Gandharva Marriage

Gandharva marriage, as we have seen, was consummation of mutual love. Many Gandharva marriages were of an impermanent nature wherein no regular ceremony took place, like the union between Parasara and Satyavati, Bhima and Hidimbi; but in other cases, there were regular ceremonies and permanent marital relations, such as the marriages of Shantanu and Satyavati, of Yayati and Devayani. It would appear Gandharva was more popular among non-Aryan communities and in inter-caste marriage. One celebrated case of a Gandharva marriage which became a precedent down the centuries may be mentioned in some detail here; this was the marriage between Shakuntala and Dushyanta, the main theme of Kalidasa's celebrated play.

King Dushyanta, so goes the story in the epic, one day, while hunting in a forest, strayed into the hermitage of the sage Kanva, where he met the beautiful maiden Shakuntala. Though burning with love for her, he did not, at first, court her as he took her for the Brahmin hermit's daughter; but he came to know that she was actually the daughter of king Visvamitra born of an affair with the dancer Menaka; both her parents had disowned her, and she was brought up by the hermit Kanva. This knowledge emboldened Dushyanta who courted Shakuntala; the atmosphere of the hermitage was ideal for romance, especially as the hermit was away.

Dushyanta went away, promising to return and take Shakuntala to his palace. But what with his many royal cares and the fear of scandal, Dushyanta did not go back to the hermitage; the meantime the change in the physical condition of Shakuntala made it impossible for Kanva to keep her in the hermitage, and the sage sent her with an escort to the court of Dushyanta.

Dushyanta received Shakuntala and her escort with becoming courtesy, but when he found that she had come to stay with him expressed surprise and disowned all knowledge of her. Her escorts told the king that she had been brought up in the guileless atmosphere of a hermitage where she was not taught to tell lies like the children of kings in palaces; they believed her, they assured the king; they left her in the court, and returned to the hermitage. Poor Shakuntala, exasperated by the behaviour of Dushyanta, wept and recounted to him of their meeting in the hermitage, of his promise, and reminded him of his duty towards his wife and forthcoming child. The king was not moved by her plaints or sermons and persistently denied ever having met her, when a celestial voice proclaimed Shakuntala as his wife; on this, the king accepted her and declared that, in order to save her and himself from scandal, he was waiting for a sign which would convince the courtiers that Shakuntala was really his wife.

It is interesting to note here that though Hindu law-givers have declared that the progeny of Gandharva would be weak or wicked, the son born of this union between Dushyanta and Shakuntala was neither, but the great emperor Bharat from whom India took her Sanskrit name, Bharatam. Anyway, the dangers of Gandharva are well set forth in the story; when a man disowns a woman, she has no way of proving her case when married according to the

Gandharva rite, and truth in every instance is not proclaimed by miracles.

Asura Marriage

Asura form of marriage was prevalent among certain Indo-Aryan clans though it was looked down upon by others. Krishna, as we have seen referred to it contemptuously. The Aryans of the Middle Country too, it would appear, shared his views. It was, however, prevalent among some clans of the Punjab, but the custom was not so disreputable as to preclude marriage between clans who practised it and those who did not. In fact, Pandu married Madri, by paying a bride-price. When negotiations for this marriage was progressing, it is interesting to note the embarrassment with which the Madra king broached the subject of a bride-price. After accepting the proposal, he told Bhishma, guardian of Pandu: "But there is a custom in our clan, followed by us from ancestral times, which, be it for good or for evil, I am incapable of transgressing". Then he told Bhishma in detail the nature of the custom and the amount of the bride-price. Bhishma agreed to respect the sentiments of the Madra clan, paid the bride-price and took Madri to Hastinapura where she was married to Pandu according to the prescribed rites.

Marriage of Savitri

There is, in the *Mahabharata*, an isolated story of the marriage of a princess which has no precedent or parallel in Indian literature or history. This is the story of the marriage of Savitri. This princess, we are told, was the daughter of king Asvapati but such was her splendorous beauty that no man dared ask for her hand. In this predicament, Asvapati, desirous of getting her married, sent her with an escort to look for a bridegroom in the neighbouring countries. The princess wandered into many lands in search of a husband but found none to her liking. At last, while returning to her own kingdom, she came by way of a forest where she saw Satyavan, son of the exiled king Dyumatsena, and fell in love with him.

On coming back to her father, Savitri reported to him that she had chosen Satyavan for her husband. The sage Narada was present in the court of Asvapati at the time, and the all-knowing saint objected to her selection, as Satyavan was a doomed man whose death was to take place a hundred days hence. When the matter was disclosed to Savitri, she refused to alter her decision as she had already married him in her mind, and was not prepared to marry any other. Seeing her determination, Narada advised Asvapati to get Savitri married to Satyavan as she desired, and leave the rest to God.

Accordingly, Savitri married Satyavan, and the princess lived with her husband in the hermitage of Dyumatsena. By her virtue and devotion, Savitri not only reclaimed her husband from the grim hand of death, but restored her father-in-law to his kingdom and lived with her husband for many years.

Though, among the Indo-Aryans, the growth of an unmarried girl to an advanced age had always caused considerable anxiety to her parents, a young lady, whether princess or commoner, going in search of a husband, was something very undesirable, and unheard of. As such, the story does not seem to have any historicity; it is rather the figment of imagination of a writer who wished to create a unique heroine.

Women and the Rules of Hospitality

The ancient rule of Aryan hospitality by which the lady of the house had to 'attend' on an honoured guest had fallen into disuse by the time the *Mahabharata* was compiled. There is, however, a story narrated in the epic, of the lady Oghavati, wife of the good Brahmin Sudarsana, who entertained a guest in the ancient way. Sudarsana, we are told, wished to attain perfection by living the life of the ideal householder, and had instructed his wife that, as the greatest duty of the householder was hospitality, no Brahmin guest should go out of his house displeased either with his wife or himself. One day, while Sudarsana went out, a Brahmin came to the house, and Oghavati immediately proceeded to entertain him with the choicest of viands. The guest ate well, but was not quite satisfied with this, and wished to take the lady to bed; at first she showed reluctance, but at the persistent request of the guest decided to yield to his demand rather than send him away displeased.

While the guest and the hostess were thus in the bed-chamber, Sudarśana returned after his peregrinations. He called out his wife to open the door, but there was no response. This unusual silence made him shout the louder from the yard, when the guest in the bed-chamber enlightened him as to why Oghavati could not answer him just then or open the door. On this, Sudarsana apologised for his intrusion, and the inconvenience caused to his guest; on this, the guest transformed himself into the god Dharma who had come down to earth to test the virtue of Sudarsana.

The Brahmins by the time the *Mahabharata* came to be compiled in its present form, were claiming to be greater than gods, and some of them made extraordinary demands on the credulous, as the displeasure or curse of an offended Brahmin was feared to cause dreadful results. Anyway, while there might have been some stray case as that of Oghavati, the general trend of the *Mahabharata* would show that the ancient Indo-Aryan practice of wives attending on honoured guests had fallen into disuse.

Instead, young ladies of marriageable age usually saw to the comforts of distinguished Brahmin guests who were not, however, expected to develop anything more than a fatherly interest in them. Services rendered to holy personages were thought to ensure desirable husbands for young ladies. Kunti, as we have seen, was in charge of the arrangements made for the stay of the sage Durvasa in her house; the sage was a personage hard to please, but the princess did the impossible and the guest granted her the boon of communing with gods.

Such solicitude of young ladies for Brahmin guests did not always lead to happy results. The sage Narada, for instance, with his nephew Parvata, once visited King Srinjaya; the king's daughter Sukumari played the hostess so well that Narada fell in love with her. This was highly improper, and Parvata remonstrated with his romantic uncle; the latter would not give in, but asked Srinjaya for his daughter's hand. Narada did marry Sukumari, but Parvata got so disgusted with the old dotard that he cursed him to become a monkey and the laughing stock of the three worlds.

The Position of Women Generally

By marriage, a woman, in law, became the property of her husband but in practice, as we have seen in the case of Draupadi, she was often the equal and at times the superior of her husband. Gandhari, wife of the blind king Dhritarashtra, held a particularly high position in the royal household, and of all the men and women in Hastinapura, she alone could exert some influence on her self-willed son Duryodhana. Kunti, again, exercised almost the authority of their father on her sons.

Perhaps the best exposition of the status of the wife is given by Shakuntala while remonstrating with Dushyanta, and recalling him to a sense of his domestic duties, as distinct from his royal duties. Shakuntala said:

> The wife is half the man, and the best of friends. She is as a father to her husband in the performance of religious rites, and as a mother in sickness and times of distress. The wife is the constant companion of her husband; in exile, she follows him into the forest: in adversity, she always beside him. In death, the devoted woman joins him in the grim regions of Yama; if she precedes him, she waits for him...It is said by the wise that a man is born in his son hence the wife is the sacred field in which a man is born again. A man, scorched by grief or suffering bodily pain, feels as refreshed in the company of his wife as a sweating person by cool bath. Even Rishis cannot procreate off-spring without women....Hence no man, even in anger, should ever do anything that offends his wife.

The following sermon on the greatness and responsibilities of the wife was delivered by Uma, wife of god Shiva, when she was asked to set forth the duties of married women.

> A women becomes, by virtue of the nuptial fire, the associate of her lord in the performance of all righteous deeds. A wife who is blessed with a good disposition, sweet speech, good looks and a blameless character should derive as much joy

on beholding her husband as she does, her own child. A woman, who regulates her conduct by prescribed ordinances is truly chaste and religious; she should observe all the vows of her husband, should wait upon him and serve him as her god; surrendering his own will to that of her husband, she should always appear cheerful, and should not, even in thought, entertain any man except him. That wife who, even when treated harshly or indifferently, assumes a cheerful countenance, is indeed truly virtuous: that wife who does not cast her eyes on the sun or moon or on a tree that has a masculine name is regarded truly virtuous; that woman who treats her husband with the affection she shows her child, even when he happens to be poor or sickly, is truly virtuous; that woman who has self-control, who serves her husband with devotion and diligence is truly virtuous; that woman who supports her poor kith and kin, considers her needs less important than those of her husband, is indeed truly virtuous. That woman who takes pleasure in rising at dawn, attends to the sacred domestic fire and keeps her house clean, offers flowers to the deities, feeds guests before all, gives to dependents and servants their due share and takes her meals last, acquires great merit. That woman who dutifully serves her father-in-law and mother-in-law as her own parents, is reckoned as possessing the merit of ascetics. That woman who observes vows difficult to perform, and ever seeks the welfare of her husband, shares in the merits of her husband. Devotion to her husband is the greatest virtue of a married woman; it is her penance and salvation. The husband is the god a woman has. He is her friend and refuge. Women have no greater refuge, no greater gods than their husbands. The husband's grace and heaven are alike to a woman. If a husband, poor, diseased, distressed, fallen among foes or afflicted by the curse of a Brahmin, were to command his wife to do anything that is improper or unrighteous or any thing that might even lead to the loss of life itself, the wife should, without hesitation, accomplish it bearing in mind, the code of conduct sanctioned by the Law of Distress.

This was, no doubt, the ideal towards which every good woman had to strive, but Draupadi, has given, in the epic, a more balanced account of the duties of a wife, drawn mainly from her own practical experience. On one occasion, Satyabhama, wife of Krishna, asked her what was the secret of success in her domestic life, and wished to know if she, Draupadi, was resorting to any drugs or charms; for she, Satyabhama, always found her friend managing, with ease, five husbands while she herself found it extremely difficult to deal with one Draupadi replied :

> When a husband learns that his wife resorts to charms, spells and drugs from that moment he begins to dread her like a serpent ensconced in his bedchamber. And can a man, oppressed by fear, have peace or happiness? Further, we hear of dire diseases caused by drugs and potions; indeed enemies often send poisoned delicacies and food in order to cause the death of those whom they desire to slay, and unthinking women have often caused dropsy, leprosy, decrepitude, and importance in their husbands by ill-advised administration of drugs in love-charms........Hence, hear, my friend, how I control my husbands. Without vanity and egoism, without jealousy and malice, I always serve my husbands and my co-wives with devotion and kindness. I never bathe or eat till my husbands have eaten, nor do I take my meals before the servants are fed. when any of my husbands comes home, from the field, forest or the deliberations in the assembly, I hasten to receive him, bring water to bathe his feet, and lead him to the house. I keep the whole house and the utensils clean, and have wholesome food cooked for the family. I myself serve them food punctually at the proper time; I never indulge in angry or fretful speech, and never follow the ways of wicked women. Indolence is the besetting vice of many women, and I always keep myself busy doing useful work. I do not linger at the gate, go about sight-seeing in the street, or wander in pleasure parks. I never laugh except at a wholesome jest; separation from my husbands is painful to me and during periods of enforced

> separation, I renounce flowers and fragrant pastes, and practise vows and penances for the welfare of my husbands. Whatever my husbands drinketh not, eateth not, relisheth not, I too renounce.

I obey the behests of my mother-in-law and faithfully carry out all her instructions; I never speak ill of her, nor even in thought offend her.

These were her duties when she was living in exile. When Yudhishtira ruled in Indraprastha, Draupadi, as the chief queen, had much more onerous duties and responsibilities, such as managing the armies of slave-girls in the harem, general supervision over palace establishments, etc. into the details of which we need not go.

Whatever might have been the legal position of woman as the wife, as mother she held a high social status. We have seen that in Buddhist texts patricides are mentioned but no man is said to have ever killed his mother. Similar sentiments are expressed in the *Mahabharata* too. "A man's preceptor", we are told, "is greater than ten Acharyas (religious hierarchs), his father greater than ten preceptors and his mother greater than ten fathers."

With all this, a definite case of killing his mother by a son, on the orders of his father, is mentioned in the epic. This slayer of his mother was none other than the Brahmin saint Parasurama, worshipped as an incarnation of Vishnu. The story would illustrate the father's supreme position in the family. Renuka, we are told, was the devoted wife of the sage Jamadagni and by the power of her devotion to her husband she could mould clay without water and bake it without fire; hence when she went to the river to fetch water, she never took a pitcher, but picked up clay from the river bank, made pots and brought water in them. But one day while moulding clay, she happened to see a young man sporting in the water and entertained unholy thoughts; as a result, the clay would not bake and she had to go back to the hermitage empty-handed. The omniscient Jamadagni discovered what had gone wrong, and waxing wroth he ordered each of his sons to kill his mother as a punishment for her sin; the first four sons refused but the youngest Parasurama promptly took his axe and chopped off his mother's head. The sage, highly pleased with Parasurama, asked him to name a boon, and turned the first four sons into idiots for disobedience. parasurama now asked for the resurrection of his mother with no consciousness of having been killed, and the restoration of his brothers to normal intelligence.

The story was possibly invented for illustrating the absolute authority of the father. In another story of a similar nature, we are told that Ahalya was caught by her husband Gautama sinning with Indra; after cursing Indra with impotence, the sage asked his son Shiratkaru to kill his mother. Shiratkaru was less prompt than Parasurama, and he started weighing the pros and cons of the case. For one thing, he could not decide whether disobedience to his father or killing the mother was the greater sin; for another he maintained that a woman was not responsible for her actions. "A woman commits no offence", said he to himself, "only men can commit offences".... Indeed, on account of the natural weakness of the sex, as shown in every act, and their liability to solicitation, women cannot be considered offenders." The idea is linked with property rights in women and the responsibility of their owners for their good conduct. A woman, not properly controlled by her owner, might commit acts of folly for which she could be held responsible, just as, in the case of cattle straying into fields, their owners were to be blamed and not the cattle. The *Mahabharata,* in the style of the *Code of Manu*, observes: "In childhood the father looks after the girl, in youth her husband, in old age her sons; a woman is never free."

Reverting to Shiratkaru, it may be mentioned, that before he could decide on any definite course of action, his father repented of his rash order on the ground that his wrath was inspired by jealously, and jealousy was unbecoming of a sage; he congratulated his son for delaying action, and got reconciled to his wife.

There are references in the *Mahabharata* to seclusion of women. When Draupadi was dragged to Hastinapura from Indraprastha by Dussasana, it is lamented that, as a high born lady, she had not been seen by the sun and the wind, a favourite style of expression with ancient Indian poets when they wished to emphasise the nobility of their royal heroines. Purdah, if it existed, was, however, confined at the time to queens who wished to protect themselves from the gaze of the vulgar, and did not extend to the women of lower orders.

The Ideal of Pativrityam

The general behaviour of the heromes of the epic would indicate that Patrivrityam, devotion to husband to the exclusion of all other considerations, had not matured in the Mahabharata period; though it was enjoined in several passages, that a woman must worship her husband like a god, these injunctions appear to be later interpolations, as the actual behaviour of ladies like Draupadi, described in the epic, was quite different.

Anyway, the ideal of Pativrityam which found its fulfilment in the *Ramayana* and in the *Dharma Sastras,* had taken root in Hindu society from very early times as is seen from several references in the *Mahabharata.* Gandhari, we are told, who was married to the blind Dhritarashtra, always placed a bandage in her eyes so that she might not enjoy the pleasure of sight denied to her husband. Renuka, as we have seen, was ordered to be killed by her husband for the sin of thinking of another man.

The need for all-absorbing attention to the husband to the exclusion of every other duty of a woman is emphasised in the story of Kausika and the housewife narrated in the *Mahabharata.* Kausika was a sage of great ascetic merit; one day, while he was resting under a tree, a hen-crane, perched on a bough, happened to ease herself and the dropping fell on the head of the saint. The furious sage cursed the bird which, scorched by the power of the curse, fell down dead. After washing his dirty head, the sage went to a near by village to beg alms. In the house he went he saw the busy housewife engaged in her domestic duties; he asked for food, but the housewife told him to wait, as her husband was expected shortly and she was racing against time to be ready with his meals on arrival. On this, the face of the irascible sage flushed; he was the most mighty ascetic in the three worlds, knew the four *Vedas* and six *Vedanagas* by heart and was capable of scorching all creatures by his fire-dating look and here was a woman who asked him to wait because her silly husband was expected. The sage uttered a mighty curse which however had no effect on the woman. Smiling, she told him that she was no hen-crane to be scorched by his ire, but a Pativrata on whom none had any power except her husband and who was omniscient besides. If he was not quite convinced, Kausika was asked to go for instruction to a fowler in Mithila who knew more about Dharma. For a woman, she assured the sage, there was neither god nor saint greater than her husband. Never was Brahmin so badly humiliated as Kausika by the housewife!

This tale, no doubt, teaches a moral which is different from the story of Oghavati narrated elsewhere. But then consistency is not one of the strong points of the *Mahabharata.*

Sati, that extreme manifestation of Pativrityam, was not widely prevalent in the epic age, but some cases are mentioned in the *Mahabharata.* Madri, one of the two wives of Pandu, burnt herself on the funeral pyre of her husband, but this was something of a penance for having lured him to her embrace which caused his death; Pandu's other wife, Kunti survived him. The wives of Vasudeva, Krishna's father, died with him, but most of the wives of Krishna outlived him Satyavati, wife of Shantanu, her daughters-in-law, Ambika and Ambalika, and most of the wives of the heroes fallen in the Mahabharata battle lived long after the death of their husbands. The attitude of the *Mahabharata* towards the institution of Sati was, more or less neutral. While there was no undue praise showered on Sati, there was no condemnation either. If any widow loved her lord so well that she thought it impossible to live after him, she could very well follow her lord, but it was neither compulsory nor even generally recommended. It would appear that during the

Mahabharata period too, as already indicated, Sati was confined to certain royal clans only.

The Family

The *Mahabharata,* like most other Indian scriptures, is mainly concerned with the activities of gods, sages and kings, and seldom interests itself in the affairs of the common folk. Yet occasionally we come across references to the common man and his domestic life. We have already noticed some details of the family of Sudarsana and Oghavati, and the village household into which the sage Kausika went to beg alms. The joint family does not appear to have come into popularity by the Mahabharata time. In the family of Sudarsana there was obviously none other than the wife and husband, as the manner in which Oghavati entertained her guest would not have been possible in a joint family with its numerous members.

We have, however, a very detailed description of a delightful Brahmin family of the village of Ekachakra where the Pandavas and Kunti lived. As it is a rare instance of an intimate picture of family life found in ancient Indian literature, we may take some detailed notice of it.

The family consisted of a Brahmin, his wife, young daughter and little son, and the Pandavas with Kunti were living in their house as their guests in the guise of mendicant Brahmins. The Brahmin seems to have lived on the bounty of the villagers or by performing priestly offices for the community.

The king of the country lived far away from Ekachakra, and it would appear that he was an inefficient imbecile whose prestige counted for little and power less; the people of Ekachakra were more or less at the mercy of Baka, a Rakshasa, who relished human flesh and lived in a wild mountainous region not far from Ekachakra. He was the virtual ruler of Ekachakra and the people of the village, in order to restrain his wanton depredations, made a covenant with him by which they were to send him daily a cart-load of food, two buffaloes and one human being. Each family, in turn, had to send him one of its members, and the turn of the

Brahmin family came when the Pandavas were staying as its guests.

When the decision of the village was communicated to the family there was, naturally, panic. The pathetic scene opens with a futile expression of regret by the Brahmin for the folly of his having listened to his wife. It would appear that when the depredations of Baka had started, the Brahmin suggested that the family should migrate to a safer locality. The wife had turned down the proposal on the ground that she would live and die in the village she was born and brought up, and among her people. The Brahmin eventually had to accede to her request but now deplored his decision. Anyway, he had sufficient sense left to see that crying over past events was not going to help, and he suggested to his wife that he himself would go to Baka. Said he:

> I shall never be able to abandon one of my own to be devoured by Baka, as long as I am alive. You, my dear wife, are my helpmate in all my virtuous deeds, self-denying, always affectionate as a mother. The gods have given thee to me as a true friend, and you are my chief stay. You were, by my parents, made the participator in my domestic duties. Of pure lineage, of good disposition, fond mother of my children, ever devoted to me and innocent, are you. I am wedded to you by sacred rites, and can never abandon you to save my life. How, again, can I sacrifice my daughter whom I have begotten, who hath been placed as a sacred pledge with me by the creator?' I am to enjoy through her, the regions obtains by those only who have daughter's sons. Some people think that a man's affection for his son is greater, others that his affection for his daughter is greater; but mine is equal for both. How can I, further, abandon my little son upon whom rest my hopes of attaining regions of bliss and of perpetuating my name and lineage? But if I sacrifice myself I would scarcely know any peace in the next world, for indeed, without me, my whole family, unable to support itself will perish. Alas! What course am I to take? It is well that I should die with my whole family.

Here, there is no preference for son against daughter, and the affection of the head of the family comes forth as the most moving factor in domestic life. We must also note the reference to regions of bliss obtainable only through a daughter's son. In later Hinduism, the daughter and her son had no function in ensuring bliss to the departed.

The wife, then, offered to go to Baka and her defence of the decision was as under:

> You, my husband, should not grieve thus, You have learning and must know that all beings are born to die. No one should grieve for that which is inevitable. Wife, son and daughter, all these are for one's own self. I myself am the proper person to go to Baka. A woman should always seek the good of her husband; my sacrifice of myself will save you and our children, will bring me fame in this world and bliss hereafter. The object of a wife, has already been realised by you; I have borne thee a daughter and a son. You are well able to support your children whereas, bereft of you, I will be more of a burden to them. Widowed and masterless, with two children to support, how will I be able to feed and clothe them? Indeed, as birds seek meat that has been thrown away on the ground, do wicked men treat a widow, and how can I, rendered helpless by your death, retain my virtue and good name? If this daughter of ours is solicited in marriage by wicked, vain men, unworthy of alliance, how can I protect her? How shall I, in your absence, impart to our little son those accomplishments which have made you so noble? And when your son becomes so unlike you and your daughter placed under some unworthy wretch, I shall be despised even by the despicable, and, not knowing what to do, might die of disgrace and want. Then our children, bereft of our loving care, might perish like fish in a tank, when the water drieth. Thus, without you, all the three of us will perish; hence, give me leave to proceed to the Rakshasa. Moreover, law-givers have ordained that women should never be slaughtered, and Rakshasas cannot be ignorant of

> these ordinances. Therefore, while it is certain that Baka will kill you, it is doubtful if he would do any harm to me... Besides, if I am dead, you can marry another, and with her acquire religious merit. There is no sin in this, as men are permitted by law to marry many wives; but it is very sinful for a woman to marry a second husband after the death of the first.

The Brahmin would not abandon his wife; they embraced each other and started weeping.

Then the daughter offered herself to go to Baka. She maintained that a daughter, sooner or later, had to be abandoned by her parents and given over to a husband, and she could not think of a greater way of becoming useful than by sacrificing herself to save her parents and little brother. If the father died, she said, all the remaining three of them would perish for want of a protector and breadwinner; if the mother died, bereft of her loving care, the children will pine away. Further, she reminded the family on high authority "the son is one's own self, the wife is one's friend, but the daughter a source of trouble." So if she were to be sacrificed none would be the worse for it, she maintained.

Her argument was the most convincing, and if reason were to prevail, she should have been sent to Baka as a meal. But man does not live by reason alone; neither parent would let the sweetheart of the house go to the Rakshasa, and all started weeping and wailing.

The son now came to the rescue of the afflicted family, Plucking a blade of grass, the little fellow shouted; "I shall go to Baka, and kill him with this." Hearing this all of them burst out into laughter forgetting their misery.

It may be mentioned that the family was saved by Bhima who went to Baka with the meal cart and killed him in single combat.

There are certain important points to be noted in the story. The housewife does not talk of Sati; if the custom were prevalent among ordinary Brahmin householders, this was the place where she could have mentioned it; she merely mentions that in case of her husband's death, she would be reduced to misery and possibly become a prey to the designs of the wicked. Anyway, widow marriage had become censurable, which she plainly mentions.

Further the daughter appears to have been a young lady of mature age, and not a child. As such child-marriage was not prevalent among the general run of Brahmin householders. Again, as in the case of this family, most of the common folk were possibly monogamists; the middle classes, it is good to remember, in all civilisations which permitted polygyny, were generally monogamous, polygyny being a luxury of the wealthy and the powerful, and of learned sages who enjoyed royal patronage.

Rtu and Child-Marriage

One of the main reasons for child-marriage, advocated by later law-givers, was that the Rtu or fertile period of a woman should not be allowed to be wasted. The idea must have originated among the Indo-Aryans at a time when continuous wars were taking a heavy toll of the Aryan population and the fertility of women had to be pressed into the service of the community to raise the birth rate. In an earlier chapter we have seen that it was incumbent on parents to get their daughters married within seven menstrual months of their attaining puberty; later law-gives insisted that not one Rtu should go waste, and a girl should be married before reaching puberty so that her first Rtu might be availed of to replenish the race. The *Mahabharata* represents the age of transition between these two views.

Now this Rtu or so-called fertile period, formed the first ten nights from the start of the period, of which only those nights following the cessation of the menstrual flow were to be availed of. The woman was reckoned cleansed, ceremonially and physiologically, by the menstrual blood, and after the purificatory bath following the cessation of the flow, she was considered in an ideal spiritual and material state for the reception of the seed and the generation of the embryo. Intercourse during this period alone was believed to cause conception. Modern research, however, would indicate that this is the safe period and not the fertile period in a woman, but this discovery need not detain us here.

When her Rtu stood in danger of going waste due to the absence or negligence of her husband, a woman, in the epic time, seems to have had recourse to practices which were normally considered immoral. In this connection we are told the story of Uttanka in the *Mahabharata*. This young man was studying in the house of his Guru, and when, once, the Guru was away, his wife had her Rtu. There was no chance of the Guru coming back to fertilise her Rtu, and the attendants of the lady approached Uttanka with a request to go into the Guru's wife. Now, the Guru's wife, by the rules of conduct of a student, was to be treated as his mother, by a student, and any sexual intimacy between the two was reckoned a grievous sin for which there was no atonement. On the other hand, letting a woman's Rtu go waste was a sin tantamount to embryo-murder. In this predicament, Uttanka is said to have abstained and let the Rtu go waste, and his teacher, when the matter was later reported to him, approved of his conduct.

Another interesting story is that of king Uparichara. This monarch went out hunting and could not leave the forest in time to reach the palace to fertilise the Rtu of his wife. The king was, hence, compelled to send his seed to his wife by hawk-post; the bird, by accident dropped it in the Jumna, in the course of its flight. A fish swallowed the royal seed which grew into twins, one male and the other female, in the belly of the fish; the fish was caught by a fisherman who sold it to the cook of Uparichara. The fish being cut open, the human twins came out; the king took the male, who became the king of the Matsyas; the female was given over to the fisherman who brought her up as his own daughter. She was the famous Matsyagandhi or Satyavati. The myth was obviously invented to invest Matsyagandhi with a lineage worthy of her lovers, husbands, and sons all of whom were mighty Brahmins or Kshatriyas.

Further, the lady Saradandayani, we are told in the *Mahabharata,* was once reduced during her Rtu to such straits for a man that with the permission of her elders she went to the crossroads of the village, accosted a stranger and, after offering oblations to fire with him, got three sons.

Anyway, these stories would illustrate how fast the ideas of the need for intercourse during a woman's Rtu was developing. It is specifically stated in the *Mahabharata* that a man who restricted his sexual activity to the Rtu of a woman was as good as a celibate, just as "the man who eats meet always after offering it to the deities is to be considered a vegetarian." That is why sages like Parasara, Vyasa and Dirghatamas were not considered blameable when they fertilised that Rtu of women who were not their wives.

With all this, child-marriage had not become general in India in the early centuries of the Christian era. Bhishma in the Anusasana Parva of the *Mahabharata,* no doubt, mentions, in the style of later law-givers, that "a man of thirty years of age must marry a girl of ten, wearing a single piece of cloth, and a man of twenty-one years, a girl of seven." But this is obviously an interpolation by a later writer who lived in an age which practised the marriage of infants; for all the main feminine characters of the *Mahabharata* were married after reaching puberty. Panchali, Gandhari, Kunti Madri, Ambika, Ambalika, in fact, hundreds of princesses mentioned in the epic were-married after they were fully grown, and many of them selected their husbands. Nor was this late marriage confined to the Kshatriyas; we have seen that in the Brahmin family of Ekachakra, the unmarried daughter of the householder had already grown or was growing into maturity.

The Nature of Woman

There are, no doubt, several noble feminine characters in the *Mahabharata.* They seem to have attained to their honoured position not on account of their feminine nature but in spite of it. For like some of the Jain and Buddhist texts, the *Mahabharata* maintains that feminine nature is inherently base, much more base than masculine, and a good woman must always strive to overcome her essentially evil nature by piety and obedience to men.

In the Anusasana Parvá or didactic section of the *Mahabharata* we have lengthy discourses by the dying Bhishma on all conceivable subjects. The Anusasana Parva is something of a detached section which has nothing to do with the plot of the main story, and is obviously the work of later interpolators who wished to obtain the sanction of the epic for practices which were not prevalent when the book was originally compiled but later crept into Brahminism. The fully developed Brahminical ideals of religion, caste, morals and virtue are preached at length in this section, in addition to the omnipotence of the Brahmins, wickedness of women, Ahimsa, vegetarianism and many other ideals foreign or even opposed to the general spirit of the main story We may take some detailed notice of what the Anusasana Parva has to say about the nature of women.

Bhishma was in general agreement with the views of the later Hindu law-givers who enjoined on men the strictest control and supervision over their women. Though a celibate, Bhishma was well conversant with the nature of women through observation, hearsay, and study. Narada, that tireless enquirer after truth, had, according to Bhishma, ascertained the true nature of women from one of their own sex, the courtesan Panchachuda. At first, it would appear, Panchachuda showed reluctance to converse with Narada on the subject. "If I tell you the truth," said she, "I shall be doing a dis-service to my sex, but if I were to hide it, I will be telling a lie." Narada now lectured to the prostitute on the greatness of truth, and insisted on hearing the truth, the whole truth and nothing but the truth from her. On this Panchachuda, thus revealed to the saint the true nature of woman :

> Women, even if the high-born and blessed with beauty and efficient guardians, love to transgress the codes of society, and rebel against all restraints. None is more inclined to sin than women. Women are the root of all troubles. Even when married to noble, handsome, wealthy men, women are inclined

> to be faithless when opportunities arise. We, women, love to abandon modesty and court even reprobates when chances come our way. Women love those men who flatter them, who serve their whims. Among women, virtue is confined to those who have no access to men and to those who have a wholesome fear of their guardians. There is none whom they are incapable of admitting into their favour; they are never deterred by age or ugliness. Women of respectable families envy the freedom of the women of pleasure. Even those women who are loved by their husbands and treated with respect, bestow their favours on hunchbacks, idiots, dwarfs, the cock-eyed and the blind. Beauties lust after cripples and scarecrows. There are, in fact, no men, however, low or deformed, whom women consider unworthy of companion-ship. Women remain faithful and loyal to their husbands only when other men are inaccessible, or through fear of relatives or dread of punishments in this world and the next. They are by nature restless and hanker after new experience. Verily, women are like the word uttered by the learned (deep). Fire is never satisfied with fuel; the ocean is never filled by the rivers; death is never satiated with living things, and women, with men ... The destroyer, the deity of wind, death, the nether regions, the monsters that rove the ocean, fire vomitting ceaseless flames, the sharpness of the razor, virulent poison, the serpent—woman is all this in one.

It is not clear why Narada selected, of all women in the three worlds, a prostitute to enlighten him on the subject Possibly prostitutes best expressed uninhibited sex instincts.

Anyway, Yudhishtira, who was the main enquirer at the beside of the dying Bhishma, nodded assent and added:

> While men take pleasure in the company of women and sport with them, these, it seems to me, are constantly deceiving men. And if once a man falls into their trap, there is no escape for him. Like kine ever affecting new pastures, women

> seek men one after another. The illusion the Asura Samvara possessed, that power of delusion the Asura Namuchi possessed, that mastery of deception Asura Bali and Kumbhinasi practised, the sum total thereof is possessed by women ... That science of polity the preceptor of the Asuras, Sukra, and Brahaspati, the preceptor of the celestials, knew cannot be considered deeper or more distinguished for subtlety than what women's intelligence naturally brings forth. Methinks the masters of the science of polity learnt it from women. They make falsehood appear as truth, and truth, falsehood.

To Yudhishtira's question as to how to guard women, Bhishma replied that there was, in the universe, only one man who guarded women properly, and that too for a short while; he was Vipula, the disciple of the sage Devasarman. Once when the sage went to a distant place to perform a sacrifice, he asked Vipula to watch his wife, and Vipula, by the power of Yoga, possessed her and always remained with her. The god Indra, of whose interest in his wife the sage had particularly warned Vipula, appeared in Devasarman's house when the sage was away; on his approaching the lady, Vipula paralysed his charge. The passionate Indra still persisted when Vipula assumed his own form and rebuked the wicked god.

Vipula, because of his constant association with the lady, was himself suspected of intimacy with his preceptor's wife which led to the scandal; there was some serious talk of his going to hell, but Devasarman declared his innocence, and he eventually went to heaven.

Yudhishtira had one more pertinent point to clear before Bhishma died. Women being essentially evil, should a good man marry? Bhishma did not give a direct answer; his discourse would indicate that it was good to marry but better not to. And illustrated the point by narrating an ancient story.

In the good old days, said Bhishma, there lived a sage by name Ashtavakra, who approached the Brahmin Vadayana for the hand of his daughter. Vadayana felt that Ashtavakra was rushing into marriage without sufficient knowledge of women. So he asked his prospective son-in-law to undertake a journey to the sanctified regions of the north where dwelt a female ascetic and seek instruction in sex lore at the feet of the lady. Ashtavakra, accordingly proceeded to the north; after a long and perilous journey he reached the regions of Kubera, the regent of the north, and after a brief stay here proceeded farther and eventually reached his journey's end and saw a beautiful valley of many lakers surrounded by golden hills. In the valley was a splendid palace built of gold and precious stones, and as Ashtavakra stood at its gate wondering what it could be, there issued forth from the place of bevy of beautiful girls. Directed by them he entered the place in which he saw an old hag, worn, and decrepit, hardly able to walk or talk. From her appearance, he could make out that she was an ascetic; she discoursed to him on learned subjects, on duty and morals. As the night advanced, the edifying discourse was given up and Ashtavakra was conducted to a soft couch of downs, and the hostess slept in an adjoining room. But when the sage lay down to sleep, the old hag came out of her room and crept into his bed on the plea that it was getting cold and two would be warmer on a bed. The sage agreed, but when she started taking further liberties with him, he resented. When she found the Rishi cold to her advances, she lectured to him on the pleasures of sex and proclaimed her passion for him.

The hag's protestations of love, instead of attracting him, repelled Ashtavakra, when the old lady said:

The deities of wind and fire are not so agreeable to women as the deity of desire. Verily, women take the greatest pleasure in congress with men. Among a thousand, may be a hundred thousand women, sometimes one may be found who is devoted and true to her husband. When under the influence of Kama (passion) women care not for family, father or mother, brother or husband, sons or daughters, but pursue the way passion points out. Indeed, in the mad pursuit of their lust, they destroy the family they belong to by birth or marriage, even as rivers eat away the banks that contain them. The creator himself hath said this to be the nature of women.

Ashtavakra again rejected her appeal, stating that he was above all carnality, and only the need for getting offspring had made him seek matrimony. Thus foiled in her attempt, the lady requested the sage to stay in her palace for some time so that she might have the pleasure of serving him. The sage could find no harm in this, and he stayed with her for some time during which she made further ineffective blandishments to seduce him; finally she transformed herself into a beautiful young girl and requested him to marry her, which too Ashtavakra rejected.

On this the lady said that Ashtavakra had passed all the necessary tests of marriage and could return and wed Vadayana's daughter. The burden of the instruction which Bhishma wanted to impart was the essentially strong sex nature of women without a thorough knowledge of which no man was competent to marry.

Anyway, it appears from some passages in the *Mahabharata* that it was not necessary for all men to marry; a man with married brothers having sons to offer oblations to the manes could lead a celibate life. For a woman, however, marriage was becoming an obligatory sacrament without which her body was feared to remain impure. While there are indications in the Vedic literature that initiation for women was prevalent in ancient days, by the time the *Mahabharata* came to be compiled in its present form, marriage was considered the initiation ceremony for women, just as Upanayanam (investiture with the sacred thread) for boys. It was considered unnecessary for a woman to have a sacred thread when her husband had one.

The impossibility of women going to heaven unless their vile bodies were purified by the rite of marriage was stressed in the story of the lady Kunigarga narrated in the *Mahabharata*. This lady took to asceticism and penance though her father had asked her to get married. The lady acquired much merit by her austerities; when, however, old age over took her and she was about to die, the sage Narada appeared before her and assured her that she would not go to heaven as her body was not purified by the sacrament of marriage. On hearing this she immediately stopped her austerities and looked for a husband; being an old hag now, she found it difficult to obtain a husband but the sage Sringavat accepted her in marriage on being promised half her ascetic merit, and on condition that he would live with her only for a day. After the marriage, Kunigarga transformed herself into a beautiful young lady when Sringavat wished to prolong the contract for life. Kunigarga refused, and died after living with him for a day.

But these stories cannot be taken as the final authority in such matters. For we have also the story of the lady ascetic Santili who deprived Garuda, king of birds, of his power of flight by a mighty curse, warned him against speaking contemptuously of women and remained single to the end of her life. And if unmarried Kunigarga could not attain heaven, the sage Jaratkaru was held equally blameable for not marrying and begetting children; threatened with hell and charged with dereliction of duty to the departed, he was compelled to marry.

Licentious Indo-Aryan Tribes

In the *Mahabharata,* the Middle Country, i.e., the Jumna Gangetic region, was considered the pure land where sound Aryan laws were strictly followed. Of the main clans dominant in the land of the pure, "the Panchalas observe the *Vedas,* the Kauravas (in which both the Pandavas and the Kauravas are included because of their common progenitor Kuru) follow truth, and the Matsyas and Saurasenas perform the prescribed sacrifices." On the other hand, "the easterners follow the practice of Sudras, the southerners are fallen, and the Saurashtras are the progeny of mixed blood." So it is clear from the epic that there was no uniformity of custom and practice among the many Indo-Aryan tribes of the south and north, and some at least of the so-called Aryan tribes were of mixed blood while others were no better than Sudras.

In an argument between Karna and Salya, king of the Madra tribe, the former indulged in a tirade against all the clans who were inhabiting the Punjab, Sind and the north-western regions generally. Karna said:

> In the days of yore when the eternal religion was reverenced in all lands, the creator observing the practices of the people of the land of the five rivers, abandoned them. Even in the Krita Age (the golden age of the Hindus when all people were supposed to have been good) Brahma had censured the practice of these evil men begotten by Sudras on other people's women. What then would you say of these people in this age (Dwapara Yuga, third age of half evil)?

The reference is obviously to the age when the *Mahabharata* was written as the author seems to have had a good knowledge of the people of the north-western region; this region, at the time, was subject of periodical conquests from beyond the Khyber and many alien tribes had settled down in the country after bloody wars in which a good percentage of the indigenous male population was destroyed and women were seized by the victors for pleasure and marriage. Karna's pointed reference to Sudras having sown superior soil and begotten and adulterous generation would indicate such a situation. These alien conquerors, no doubt, were eventually admitted into the Indo-Aryan fold, but most of them continued to follow their ancestral marriage customs which were strange to the pure Aryans of the Middle Country.

The wicked habits of some of the tribes of this region were thus described by Karna:

> Among the Madras (this was the clan from which Madri, Pandu's wife hailed) the sire, the son, the mother, mother-in-law, grandson, and other kinsmen, friends, strangers and slaves, both male and female, mix indiscriminantely together. The Madra women seek the company of strangers and friends with equal eagerness. Of unrighteous conduct, subsisting on corn and beef, they drink liquor and laugh and cry aloud in their homes ... These women, when intoxicated with exhilarating drinks cast off their robes, sing and dance without any restraint, and copulate with any one they please. The young Madra maidens are shameless, hairy, Gluttonous and impure. How indeed would the Madras, and Sindhu-

> Sauviras know aught of duty, born as they are in a sinful land, and following the practices of Mlecchas ignorant of duty?"

This seems to have been inspired by authentic information Karna had gathered. He followed it up with what he had heard from travellers. He railed:

> There is a clan of Vahikas, by name Jartikas, they say, Jartika women, when well drink, throw away their clothes, laugh and dance outside the city walls, without ornaments or unguents, singing obscene songs; their voice is like the braying of asses, like the bleat of the camel. ... Then in that land where the Pilus thrive, the land of the five rivers with the Sindhu (Indus) for the sixth, is the country of the Arratas. In ancient days, a chaste woman was abducted by robbers hailing from among the Arratas and was done violence; upon which she cursed them saying : 'since you have violated a girl who has a husband, women of your clan shall become unchaste.' It is for this Salya, that the sister's sons, among the Arratas, and not their own sons are reckoned their heirs.

The last sentence is important. Descent through the sister's son is a distinctive feature of the matriarchate. The Arratas were probably matriarchs, and in matriarchates, as we have seen women enjoy greater sexual freedom than in patriarchal communities.

The Vahikas and Arratas formed the main target of Karna's attack. They were actually said to be the progeny of two Asuras Vahi and Hika though reckoned Indo-Aryans. Caste notions were poor among them, and good Brahmins were warned against staying too long among those tribes. A Brahmin who went to their country out of curiosity found that "one becomes a Brahmin, then a Kshatriya, then a Vaisya and finally, a barber." In the same family were found members following the occupations of these different castes. Further, according to Karna, there was an old saying that none who drank milk in the town called Yugandhara, bathed in the region called Bhuoilaya or resided in Achyutasthala could ever go to heaven."

Salya did not deny these charges of Karna, but defended himself by saying that the people of Anga, whose king was Karna, sold their daughters and that there were good and bad people in all countries.

There is no doubt that Karna was describing the existing practices of the Indo-Aryan tribes of the Punjab and north-western India, though the reasons he attributed to their origin were fictitious; even at present, it may be mentioned, we find strange practices among many peoples of the world but the legendary and miraculous accounts of the origin of such practices are often unconvincing.

A peculiarity of the people of Mahishmati, an Indo-Aryan principality that lay to the south of the kingdom of the Kurus, was that unmarried girls enjoyed complete sexual freedom and marriage was a restraining institution that limited a woman's sexual activity to her husband. The reason for this exceptional morality of the young ladies of Mahishmati is also given in the epic. King Nila of Mahishmati, we are told, had a pretty daughter with whom Agni, the god of fire, fell in love. From then on, "unless blown by the round, red lips of the princess, the household fire of the king's palace would not burn." One day, the god, disguised as a Brahmin, presented himself before king Nila and asked for the hand of the princess. The king refused, and Agni, enraged, started burning everything in Mahishmati; the king had enquiries made, discovered who the Brahmin suitor was, apologised to Agni and bestowed his daughter in marriage him with due rites. As a wedding gift, Agni bestowed two boons on Mahishmati: invincibility in war, and complete sexual freedom for her maidens.

In another version of the legend, we are told that the princess was found flirting with a Brahmin which led to a scandal in the town. The king, on making enquiries, discovered who his daughter's lover was, and gave her in marriage to Agni, and this deity, in order to free her from the scandal of pre-marital philandering, ordained that all unmarried women of Mahishmati should be free to flirt with any one they liked.

Whatever the actual reason for this promiscuity in Mahishmati, it is clear that in this kingdom child-marriage was not widely prevalent.

Mixed Picnics and Festivals

In several passages in the *Mahabharata* we read of feasts, festivals and picnics in which both men and women took part. Picnics into forests and river beds were favourite forms of outdoor sport both for men and women. We have already noticed how Devayani and Sharmishta went to a forest picnic and how they quarreled during sport.

In the *Mahabharata* there are several descriptions of mixed picnics. In one of these, we are told:

> Krishna and Arjuna, with the permission of Yudhishtira, set out with their friends and ladies. Reaching a delightful spot on the banks of the Jumna, which had been previously fitted out for the purpose, the party sported to their hearts' content. The place was full of stately trees and wild plants and flowers. The party had been well provided with flavoured viands, fruits, meat and drink in plenty, and the cottages constructed for the purpose were decorated with flowers and leaves and sprinkled with perfumes.

The party sported as they pleased. The women diverted themselves in the woodland groves, and in the rivers. "Partha and Krishna, Draupadi and Subhadra, exhilarated by wine, gave away to the ladies of the party, costly robes and ornaments. The women danced in joy; some sang, some jested and laughed. Some engaged themselves in water sport, in mock fights squirting water on one another, while the tried gossiped in the inner apartments of the mansions lying languidly on the couches."

The Yadavas, the race whose chief was Krishna, are described in the epic as a particularly convivial people, fond of wine, war and song. They often held grand functions in which men and women took part. Their main festival was held on the slope of Raivaka mountain. People thronged to the festival in thousands, and "the whole mountain side was converted into a sea of humanity. There came Ugrasena, the king, with his thousand wives accompanied by singing girls, and many other Vrishni chiefs, similarly attended. And among them roved the mighty Balabhadra (Balarama, Krishna's elder brother whose partiality to wine has become proverbial in India), well-drunk, his face flushed, accompanied by his wife Revati, followed by many singers and dancers".

From the *Mahabharata* it will be seen that Banaras had developed into a religious place of national importance to the Indo-Aryans, and the Pandavas with their mother Kunti are said to have gone all the way from Hastinapura to Banaras to participate in the annual festival held in the city in honour of Shiva. Most of the great festivals of India drew vast coglomerations of people from far and wide, and a good percentage of the pilgrims consisted of women of all ages, as the general restraints on women were generally released on these occasions on religious grounds. In these vast crowds, processions and pageants, individuality was often lost, each had his or her own pet diversion, and men often got detached from their women. The atmosphere was ideal for lovers to meet their sweethearts. Abductions and elopments at times took place in these festivals. It was, as we have seen, while Subhadra was roving in the hillside during the Raivaka festival that Arjuna abducted her.

In this respect India has changed little these two thousand years. Even now, religious festivals are occasions for romance. With the prohibition of child-marriage and the permission granted to young ladies of marriageable age to attend the feasts of deities, these provide excellent opportunities for lovers to meet each other without drawing undue public attention, as social intercourse between young men and women is even now discouraged among the orthodox.

4

Place of Women in Ramayana

Compared with the *Mahabharata,* the *Ramayana* is a more compact work, lesser in volume but more harmonious in plot and characterisation It deals with events supposed to have taken place in the Threta Yuga (the second of Hindu mythical ages). Rama, the hero of the *Ramayana,* is reckoned the seventh incarnation of vishnu, while Krishna, the eighth incarnation, appears in the *Mahabharata.* This precedence of events narrated in the *Ramayana* does not necessarily establish an earlier date for its compilation than that of the *Mahabharata,* as the ideals it advocates are definitely posterior to the *Mahabharata.*

It is impossible to fix the date of the epic from the internal evidence of its contents. While Rama is considered the seventh incarnation of Vishnu, Jabali, one of his courtiers, was a Buddhist, and the Buddha, as is well known, was the ninth incarnation of Vishnu. Further, by way of prediction, it foretells the birth of Krishna, the eighth incarnation of Vishnu and one of the main characters in the *Mahabharata.* This epic, again, contains, as we have seen, a summary of the *Ramayana.*

Unlike the *Mahabharata* with its liberal outlook, the *Ramayana,* as it stands at present, represents a later ideal, the ideal of a full-fledged Brahminism with its caste rigidity, moral inflexibility, extreme notions of Patrivrityam, and hostility to words and contempt of the non-Aryans and their institutions, a belated attempt, in fact, at establishing the supposed ideals of the Aryans married by the liberalism of the Mahabharata period.

Rama was, no doubt, a Kshatriya, but he had none of the gaiety of life, the Kshatriya spirit of the heroes of the *Mahabharata*. He was not a lover of life, but a sad, lonely spectator who viewed life with a philosophic calm. At best he was a competent executive of Brahminical ordinances and commands; from boyhood onwards, he cultivated the company of Brahmin sages and most of his martial exploits were undertaken at their behest. So zealous was he to please the Brahmins that on one occasion, at their request he promptly executed as we shall see later, a pious Sudra who had taken to the practice of austerities, an exclusive Brahmin prerogative at the time.

The original story of the *Ramayana,* like that of the *Mahabharata,* is very ancient. In the *Dasaratha Jataka* of the Buddhist Canon, we read the story of Rama and Lakshmana, sons of king Dasaratha, who together with their sister Sita went into voluntary exile for twelve years and then came back; from this tale, it would appear, Rama married on his return from exile. Different versions of the story were current in several parts of India, in some of which Ravana was depicted as a benign ruler and Sita as his daughter whom Rama married. The present Sanskrit version of the epic is attributed to Valmiki. Unlike the *Mahabharata* which is obviously the work of several authors, equally obscure, the *Ramayana* in its sound plot, harmony, diction and sense of proportion bears the stamp of a single genius, though some interpolations were made in certain sections by later writers. Valmiki was not only a great poet and story teller, but a philosopher, preacher and devotee of rare attainments. He drew freely from the current Rama-Ravana tales and developed an epic plot, investing his characters with the social and ethical ideals of his age and building round the hero a passionate, devotional halo.

The date of Valmiki's *Ramayana* has not been fixed. Though treating of an earlier epoch, it is in all probability a later work than the *Mahabharata,* a turning point towards Vaishnavism from the earlier Shaivism. Tamil literature would confirm this view. The *Ramayana* reached the south much later than the *Mahabharata,* and the Kuram grant of the Pallava king Paramesvara I (A.D. 660) made provision for the maintenance of the reader of the *Mahabharata* but none for reading the *Ramayana.*

With the spread of Vaishnavism in India, the *Ramayana* obtained wide popularity, and free renderings of Valmiki's Sanskrit version appeared in the main languages of India, all marked by an intense devotionalism. In many parts of India, this epic is now held in even greater esteem than the *Mahabharata;* no Hindu couple is held to be greater than Rama and Sita, and the ideal state is even now called Rama Rajya or the utopia of Rama, while Sita, the heroine of the *Ramayana* is the ideal towards which every orthodox Hindu lady strives.

Dasaratha and his Harem

The main story of the *Ramayana* begins with Dasaratha, Rama's father, and his three wives. Dasaratha, like many Hindu kings had no sons. It is significant that he did not have recourse to Niyoga; the institution was possibly becoming censurable in Valmiki's time. So Dasaratha made his wives swallow a magic potion which procured for him four sons; Rama, the eldest, was born of Kausalya, Bharata of Kaikeyi, and Lakshmana and Satrughna of Sumitra.

In no ancient Indo-Aryan palace did polygyny and the mutual jealousies of queens lead to such tragedy as in the harem of Dasaratha. Kausalya was the senior in age, but Dasaratha doted on Kaikeyi, a young and vivacious lady; these two were the chief rivals, and the other inmates of the harem were divided into their camps. Sumitra, it would appear, was more or less neutral Kausalya's perpetual complaint was neglect by her husband, and humiliation by Kaikeyi and her partisans. The rivalry between these two factions led to a crisis on the nomination of Rama as the heir to the throne by Dasaratha, who wished to retire from active rulership and install Rama as the king of Ayodhya.

Kaikeyi herself had taken the claim of Rama for granted, but her scheming old nurse Mandhara, who was an influential figure in the Kaikeyi faction, was bent upon securing the crown for Bharata,

Kaikeyi's son. So on the eve of the coronation of Rama Mandhara worked up Kaikeyi by enumerating the troubles and humiliations she would be put to, once the old king was superseded by Kausalya's son Rama. Kaikeyi now got convinced that she should prevent the coronation of Rama at any cost and secure the succession for her son Bharata. This prince was, at the time away in her own father's house; there was no time to consult him and she struck like lightning.

Kaikeyi now remembered that Dasaratha had once granted her a boon by which she could demand of him anything she desired. It would appear that in a military expedition the king had taken her with him, and in a difficult situation it was Kaikeyi's courage and presence of mind that saved his life; in gratitude. Dasaratha had granted this boon, and Kaikeyi decided to take advantage of it.

Accordingly, Kaikeyi wanted an immediate audience with Dasaratha and occupied the 'anger chamber,' and sent word to the king. He was busy making arrangements for Rama's coronation, but to find out what was gone wrong with his favourite wife. Dasaratha hurried to the 'anger chamber.' When the king came Kaikeyi reminded him of his old promise, and after he swore that he would do anything for his beloved, she asked him to crown her son Bharata and, in order to save him all embarrassment by the presence of Rama in the kingdom, to exile him (Rama) for twelve years. This dreadful demand paralysed Dasaratha. He could do nothing but wail, and Kaikeyi herself had to communicate to Rama his father's decision to cancel all preparations for his coronation and send him into exile.

When the decision was communicated to Kausalya she nearly collapsed. After the initial shock was got over, a conference was held between Kausalya, Rama and Lakshmana who was particularly attached to Rama. Kausalya considered this development as the meanest and cruellest blow Kaikeyi could deal her. There was a heated discussion among the three whether or not Rama was duty bound to abide by the decision of Dasaratha. Both Lakshmana and Kausalya were emphatically of the opinion that Rama was not to obey this unnatural father of his who ordered him into exile, incited by a jealous and wicked woman. Kausalya maintained that a son's duty was to stand by his mother even against his father. She said :

> It does not speak well for your sense of duty to abandon me and go into the forest to please that co-wife of mine. O, my son, if you wish to acquire religious merit, stay with me, serve me and be my support. The great ascetic Kasyapa lived in his house serving his mother constantly, and accumulating great merit obtained heaven on death. As your father is worshipful to you, so am I. I forbid you to repair to the forest. Without you, my beloved son, I do not wish for life or happiness.... If you depart, leaving me in sorrow, I shall fast myself to death and you will have to suffer the penalty for Brahminicide even as the god of waters did. (The aquarian deity is said to have gone to hell for causing grief to his mother, an act, according to Kausalya, as heinous as the murder of a Brahmin.)

The fiery Lakshmana, endorsing the opinion of Kausalya added:

> The king is uxorious, is in his dotage and given to worldly pleasures, and his judgement is perverted by his infatuation for Kaikeyi. ... I cannot find any fault in you, my brother, that you should be condemned to exile into a wild forest. By what law, does the old king abandon a son who is like a celestial, who is blameless, who is self-disciplined and loved even by his enemies? The king is in his second childhood and it is not obligatory on his son to carry out an order given by him under infatuation. I, for one, will fight all those who oppose your installation, and annihilate them. If our father, under the evil influence of Kaikeyi, turns out to be an enemy, my duty as a Kshatriya, is to fight him to death without hesitation. Even a spiritual leader deserves chastisement if he, puffed up with pride, goes astray. Tell me, my brother, by what law and by what cause does our father propose to disinherit you?

Turning to Kausalya he added :

> Whoever would confer the crown on Bharata is as much my enemy as yours. Verily I am attached to Rama, my brother, body and soul, and to you. By truth, by weapons, by gift and by everything dear to me, I swear I will enter fire before Rama enters the wood. Like the sun dispelling darkness shall I remove thy sorrow, O worshipful lady, and Rama and yourself shall witness it. I shall! even dispatch my father, a tool in the hands of the vile Kaikeyi, who contemptibly plays the child.

Rama pacified both his mother and fire-eating half-brother, by announcing his irrevocable decision to abide by his father's command which, he maintained, was his highest duty. He said :

> I am powerless to transgress the command of my father; I bend my head low to thee, my mother, but I must proceed to the forest as ordered by my father.:.. The learned Rishi Kandu, who lived in the forest as desired by his father, even killed a cow knowing it to be a sin. In our line, the sons of Sagara, at the command of their father, courted death; Rama, son of Jamadagni, decapitated his mother. These and other god-like personages obeyed heroically their fathers' orders.

And he concluded that implicit obedience to the father had been the duty of the kings of his line and that he was determined to follow their example.

Kausalya bewailed her fate thus:

> O my son, are you not born for my grief? A childless woman has but one cause of sorrow, i.e. : I have no child," and nothing else, but my afflictions are manifold. I have never, in my life, experienced that blessing and pleasure of women whose husbands are devoted to them. I looked forward to you as the one ray of hope in my gloomy life. Being the eldest of all the wives of the king, I had always to bear the

> cruel taunts of my co-wives who are all younger than I. There can be no greater grief for a woman than this. If, when you are with me, they have thus treated me, I do not know that they would do in your absence. O my darling, disregarded by my husband, I am, alas, like a maidservant of Kaikeyi or even worse. Those who serve me now and are obedient to me will turn against me once they see Kaikeyi's son installed.

Kausalya even insisted on her accompanying Rama into exile, and the prince had to sternly remind her of her duty to her husband, which poor Kausalya often forgot what with the neglect by her husband and the insolence of Kaikeyi.

In defence of Dasaratha, it must be mentioned that he himself was in favour of Rama's installation, but unable to retract the promise he had made to Kaikeyi was obliged to send Rama into exile. He was, perhaps, as pained as Kausalya at the turn affairs had taken and even suggested that Rama and his partisans should imprison him and formally usurp the throne, a suggestion Rama indignantly turned down.

Yet, it is, in a way difficult to understand Dasaratha's decision Hindu kings and gods had never been at a loss to quote the highest authority when they were bent upon doing something they wanted, even if it meant a departure from conventional morality, and it is not clear why Dasaratha, on the strength of a promise, consented to a palpably unjust act to please a wayward woman. Yudhistira and Krishna, we are told in the *Mahabharata,* had recourse to dubious methods, at times, to win the war. Rama himself killed Thadaka against the dictates of chivalry; further he slew the monkey chief Bali, by hiding himself behind a tree, an act considered blameable by all the laws of war at the time. Besides, we have the authority of great statesmen like Bharadwaja, Sukra, Kautilya and others, who maintained that kings were not bound to keep their word if the larger interests of the state were jeopardised by a strict adherence to truth, and even Manu and Bhishma were of the opinion that honest Aryans could break their pledge given to women.

As such Dasaratha could have easily availed himself of any of these sanctions and rejected Kaikeyi's cruel and manifestly perverse demand. Hence his acceding to her request betrayed his weakness and infatuation, and left room for suspicion that his decision involved more than a formal desire to keep his word. In fact, Lakshmana plainly declared that the king's grief was a pretext and his piety a fraud. When Rama, in reply, defended his father on the plea that destiny was at work, Lakshmana squarely upbraided him and declared that destiny was the refuge of imbeciles, and the duty of a Kshatriya was to fight out the issue and leave the result to fate.

Anyway, if Dasaratha had acted sensibly, there would be no *Ramayana* , and so we have to take the eipic as we find it. Rama was exiled, and he left Ayodhya with his wife Sita, and the devoted Lakshmana. The strain was too much for Dasaratha and he died soon after Rama left. Kausalya wanted to become Sati, but later changed her mind. In fact none of the wives of Dasaratha accompanied the old king.

Bharata returned from his maternal uncle's kingdom, and when he came to know all that had happened, he was almost as furious against his mother as Lakshmana was against his father. Instead of a grateful son, Kaikeyi found Bharata hostile and acrimonious; he reviled her for her cruelty and selfishness, and asserted he had no desire for a kingdom which by right belonged to Rama. He called her the slayer of her husband, the banisher of her son. And he announced his decision to go to the forest in search of Rama and bring him back to his palace and the throne.

Bharata was now joined by Satrughna, Sumitra's second son, and while the two were deliberating, the hunchback Mandhara came to congratulate them; she was dressed in superlative finery as befitting the occasion, expecting, no doubt, that the princes would be mighty pleased with the major part she had played in the drama; the sight of the prime mover of the tragedy infuriated the princes, and Satrughna hounded 'the monkey dressed in gold' out of the hall. He wanted to kill the hag but Bharata stopped him. "A woman," said he, "should not be slain. Do thou, therefore, excuse the wretch. I myself would have slain this wicked Kaikeyi of impious deads, were it not that Rama would be angry with me for killing my mother. If Raghava hears that the hunchback had been slain by us, he would not speak either with you or me."

Lakshmana, as we have seen, did not consider the slaying of an unrighteous father a sin, and Bharata, likewise, thought it right to slay a wicked mother. Here, it would appear, a love of justice and fraternal loyalties were more important than filial duties and obligations.

From the miserable Dasaratha and his conflicting crowd of sons and wives, it is a refreshing change to come to Rama and his wife. Having lived in this hellish harem atmosphere, it is no wonder that Rama preferred monogamy.

Sita

In Sita we get an ideal that leaves nothing for the moralist to be desired. She is a paragon of feminine perfections, and from the time the Brahminic ideal of wifehood was established, Sita has been held as an example to be followed by Hindu women, down the centuries to the present day. Sita's greatness is in the annihilation of her individuality. In Indian religions, it is good to remember, the annihilation of personality has been the general ideal of perfection; while men try to achieve this end by the practice of the various virtues or through asceticism and knowledge, for women absolute self-surrender to their husbands is recommended as the surest means of self-effacement. And in Sita this prime virtue of woman finds its fulfilment. Apart from her husband. Sita had no life. Never a harsh word escaped her lips even when treated almost inhumanly by her husband.

Whatever its shortcomings, the ideal has helped the Hindu woman suffer her lot bravely and patiently when the behaviour of her husband would otherwise have led to the break-up of the home. In fact, throughout the long and eventful history of Indian womanhood, largely writ in tears, the story of Sita has been the mainstay of many a Hindu woman whose lot has been as hard as Sita's and at times, even harder; and many have borne it as ungrudgingly as Sita. Sita's sufferings began with the exile of her husband, and ended only with her death, and the pathos of the whole epic is dominated by the tears of Sita.

Yet it must be stated that Sita lacks the human touch of Draupadi. She is more of a symbol, a conception, an ideal than a character or personality. And what is important, unlike Kausalya, Sita has no co-wives to share her husband's love, and Valmiki has not tested Sita on this important touchstone of feminine sensitivity.

Marriage of Sita

Sita was not born of human parents. When king Janaka of Mithila did the ceremonial ploughing of the sacrificial ground, the baby Sita, we are told, was found in the field; she was picked up by Janaka and brought up as his own daughter. Hence, she was known as the daughter of the earth.

She was given in marriage at the age of six. There is dispute among scholars about the age of Sita at the time of her marriage, and some are inclined to treat the verses indicating her age as interpolations. Anyway, it is clear that she had no choice in her marriage. She was to be given in marriage to any one who had the necessary skill in arms to bend a mighty bow kept in Janaka's court; when the boys Rama and Lakshmana were living in the forest under the protection of Rishi Visvamitra, this sage took the princes to the court of Janaka where the prodigy Rama bent and broke the bow and won Sita.

The formalities of marriage were gone through. The news of Rama's breaking the bow was conveyed to Dasaratha, and king Janaka sent a polite invitation to Dasaratha to go to Mithila, with Bharata and Satrughna on whom Janaka wished to bestow his two nieces. Lakshmana was to be married to Janaka's own daughter Urmila. Thus, though Rama himself won his bride by his skill in arms, in keeping with Kshatriya tradition, the marriage of the other princes was arranged by their parents.

Dasaratha with the princes and brilliant retinue went to Mithila. Here, one of the formalities was the repetition of genealogies of each of the royal house, by competent persons. In the case of Dasaratha's line, Vasishta, the family priest, repeated the genealogy; according to Vasishta's account, the race of Dasaratha was descended from Brahma, the creator, Maricha sprang from Brahma, Kasyapa from Maricha, Vivasvat from Kasyapa, Manu from Vivasvat and Ikshvaku from Manu; this Ikshvaku was the first king of Ayodhya, and hence Dasaratha was known as the Ikshvaku dynasty; this was also called Raghu's line, as Raghu was one of the most important king of the race.

The genealogy of Janaka's house was repeated by Janaka himself. His line does not appear to have been as illustrious as that of Dasaratha, and he started his lineage from the celebrated emperor Nimi but not from the creator Brahma. Anyway, his house was worthy of alliance with the race of Ikshvakus.

After the necessary formalities, marriage ceremonies were performed in conventional style in the house of the brides, and the party eventually returned to Ayodhya.

Sita in Exile

At the time of Rama's exile, Sita was eighteen years of age. Rama asked her to remain in Ayodhya with his parents. The surprised Sita expressed sorrow that her husband, well-versed in scriptures, should be reminded of the duties of a wife. She said :

> A woman's place is with her husband and not with his or her parents; when you are exiled, myself no less than yourself, has been exiled. I shall follow you wherever you go. Father, mother, son, brother, daughter-in-law, all abide by the rule of Karma, each one in his or her individual right. But the wife shares with her husband his fortunes and Karma. Neither father, mother, son nor friends, not even her own self, is the stay of a woman in this life or the next. The husband alone in her stay and support; for a woman the shade of the feet of her husband is greater than all palaces.

Rama now described to her, in vivid detail, the hardships of forest life :

> Life in the forest, my dear one, is fraught with many dangers, and it is for your own welfare that I advise you to stay back in the palace. The roar of the lion roving the hills and the thunder of tearing waterfalls pierce the ears of the forest dweller. The trackless forest is full of thorny brambles, and wild beasts attack man at sight. The rivers and lakes of the forest are infested with crocodiles, sharks and other fearsome creatures, and wild elephants sport in them. Then there are vast arid regions devoid of water. The wild notes of jungle fowl and other unfamiliar creatures rent the welkin. Nor are the labours of the toilsome day lightened at night; the forest dweller has to sleep in the open, on leaves and grass spread on the ground, exposed to attack by wild animals. Unable to comb or crop his hair, or to shave, his locks get glued and his beard teem with lice. Wild berries and roots are the only food procurable, and for clothes he has to put on rough barks of trees. There is no light or lamp of dispel darkness, no protection against lightning, thunder and storms, Reptiles, venomous and of forbidding size, creep in every direction watching for prey, while scorpions, blood-sucking leeches and pests infest the forest. Wild trees, untamed by the hand of man, throw forth their mighty branches, and in roaring storms swing frightfully, cracking and breaking, spreading terror far and wide.... All this is the lot of the forest dweller, and only men brought up to bear it can live in the forest, and not a tender lady like you brought up in a palace and in the lap of luxury.

Sita's reply was characteristic:

> All this I shall bear cheerfully, my lord, but not separation from you. In my childhood I have been taught by my worthy parents to follow my husband in all his misfortunes. And it had been predicted when I was born, by men learned in secret lore, that I will be condemned to live long in the

> woods, and I have trained my mind for it. I shall go with you, my lord, and learn to love the forest with all its terrors. Besides, the forest is not without charm. The woodlands abound in wild flowers that shed their fragrance for miles around; roving these delightful regions, we shall watch lofty peaks soaring into the sky, drink of gurgling brooks, walk round lakes filled with lotuses and water lilies, among which wild swans swim and sport. I shall be no burden to you, but shall always be a helpful companion; I shall walk before you as a guide and take my repast after you; I shall gather berries and dig up roots for our fare; and we shall live in the woods as though we are living in our palace.

There were some more arguments, but in the end Rama yielded. Hence, Rama and Sita with the ever-devoted Lakshmana left Ayodhya for the forest; Kausalya, however, stayed back in the palace.

It would appear Sita too shared with other women their essentially base nature but had overcome it by training. For in her farewell address to Sita, Kausalya said:

> Women, as a rule, are fickle, and have regard for their husbands only during the days of their good fortune. Though attached to them in prosperity, women, in adversity, reprimand their husbands for their thoughtlessness, take them to task and abandon them—such is the nature of women. Neither benefits received, nor learning nor gifts, can secure the heart of a woman; surely, women are unstable. But you have overcome the weakness of your sex by abiding and delighting in truth, acting according to the precepts of superiors, maintaining the dignity of your family and compassing the spiritual welfare of your husband. Therefore, although my son is banished and is in adversity, do not disregard or abandon him. Whether he is wealthy or poor, he is, to you like a god.

This had also been the opinion of sages and their wives whom Sita and Rama happened to meet in the course of their wanderings in the forests. The sage Agastya whom they visited, for instance, said to Sita: "Indeed in following your husband to the forest, you have done something doubly noble. For from the commencement of creation, it has been the nature of women to seek him who is rich and powerful and forsake him who has fallen on evil days. Women, in their instability is like lightning in their sharpness like weapons, and in celerity like the wind-god."

On another occasion, Anasuya, wife of the sage Atri, thus instructed Sita, on her duties to the husband: "They that love their husbands, whether living in the city or in the woods, whether well or ill, attain to great felicity. Wicked, immoral or indigent, a husband is the supreme deity to his wife. Than a husband, a greater friend a woman has none in this world and the next. The greatest virtue of a woman is ministering to his needs." And Sita agreed: "I know a woman's spiritual guide is her husband; even if the husband is poor, of a disreputable character, he should be ungrudgingly obeyed by the like of me."

Throughout the long years of wandering in the forests, Sita had done nothing to offend her husband in deed, word or thought but had always been a most devoted and dutiful wife. Once this over-attachment to Rama expressed itself in such bad from that she even accused Lakshmana of treachery towards his brother and dishonourable intentions towards her. The context may be described in some detail here. Ravana, after the mutilation of his sister by the princes, decided to abduct Sita. Not sure of success in a straight fight with the princes, he sent his stooge Maricha to the place where Sita lived with Rama and Lakshmana. Maricha, by his magic, transformed himself into a beautiful fawn of golden colour, and started gambolling in the vicinity of the cottage; Sita saw the sprightly animal, and asked Rama to capture it for her. Rama chased the fawn which, when caught, cried out in Rama's voice, "help, O, Lakshmana, O Sita," as though Rama's life was in danger. The ruse worked. Hearing Rama's agonised voice, Sita asked Lakshmana to rush to his help. But Rama had specially instructed Lakshmana not to leave Sita alone in the cottage under any condition whatsoever lest danger threaten her. As such,

Lakshmana told Sita that nothing in the world could ever endanger the life of Rama and he was quite safe wherever he went; on the other hand, it would be very unwise, he said, to leave Sita alone there as the place was in the domain of the Rakshasa Khara whose minions would be prowling about the forests to do her harm. No argument of Sita would make Lakshmana leave Sita and her anxiety about Rama's safety growing, she levelled a very unkind charge against Lakshmana. She cried:

> O, cruel man, you are the vile destroyer of your line! It is a disgrace that you pretend to protect me and wish for the death of your brother! It is clear to me that your intentions are dishonourable; donning the garb of honour, you hide, within you, an evil heart. Verily you are a monster of wickedness, and you have guilefully followed Rama in order to obtain me! Or are you an agent of Bharata, ordered to act in this manner? But your evil desire will never be gratified. How shall I desire another man, forgetting my dear husband? Certainly I shall not survive my husband.

This speech was indeed a revelation to Lakshmana. During all their wanderings in the forest, he had not by thought, word or deed entertained any dishonourable intentions against Sita, and it is even related in the *Ramayana* that he had never seen her face as he had conscientiously avoided looking at her. As such the speech of his sister-in-law cut Lakshmana to the heart. He said: "What you have uttered, ought to have never been spoken. Perhaps it is in the nature of women to be fickle, crooked and devoid of true knowledge; they bring about dissension between father and son, brother and brother. Your words pierce my ear as a heated rod; but the gods that range these woods are my witnesses and they know what I have said is true." After this protest, Lakshmana went in search of Rama, leaving Sita to the protection of the deities of the woods. And he never saw her again till the battle of Lanka was won.

Abduction of Sita

As soon as Lakshmana left, Ravana, who was hiding nearby,

came to Sita disguised as a wandering ascetic. Entertainment of ascetics and mendicant Brahmins, as we have seen, was one of the duties of a housewife, and the *Ramayana* has recorded an interesting conversation between Ravana and Sita. The first thing to strike Ravana, a connoisseur of women, was the physical perfection of Sita. She surpassed, we are told, all beings of the three worlds. Her complexion was of gold, and she wore a garland of lotus petals. Her teeth were all even with the tips resembling Kunda flowers. She had clear expansive eyes of a pinkish tint, with black pupils. Her hips were large and rounded, and things tapering like the trunk of an elephant. She had full, elevated breasts with pointed nipples, which captivated like plumb, luscious fruits. Her hair was exquisitely fine, and waist so thin that it could be measured by the thumb and index finger.

This is, however, the usual description of their heroines by Sanskrit poets and does not give us any distinctive picture of Sita. The guileful Ravana dragged the unsuspecting Sita into conversation, and she told him many details of her life and of Rama. Among other things, Sita said: "On the thirteenth year of my marriage, Kaikeyi ordered by husband into exile. My husband was then twenty-five years of age and myself eighteen." This would make the marriage of Sita at her sixth year and Rama's thirteenth year or so.

This passage is believed to be an interpolation by a later writer who wished to hold up Sita's marriage as an authority for child-marriage. It is highly improbable that Ravana, who wanted to abduct Sita before the return of Rama and Lakshmana, would have wasted any time in gossip with Sita.

Though Ravana abducted Sita and took her to Lanka, his treatment of her in his palace was strictly honourable. He kept her in a beautiful Asoka grove guarded by the women of his harem. He wooed her persistently, and Sita as persistently rejected his suit. But he never forced her. It is said a curse prevented him from forcing her. On an overall estimate however, the Rakshasas would appear to have had as sound a code of chivalry as the Aryans, if not better. Rama and Lakshmana, as we have seen mutilated Surpanakha and killed Thadaka. In the *Ramayana* again, we are told the story of Vishnu himself having killed a virtuous lady for her hospitality to the distressed; during a war between the gods and the Asuras, some Asuras took asylum in the hermitage of the sage Bhrigu and the lady of the house gave protection to the refugees; the enraged Vishnu, on this, is said to have cut off the lady's head with his discuss.

There is, further, an interesting episode in the *Ramayana,* in which. Indrajit, Ravana's son, hard-pressed by the monkey hosts wanted to dishearten the surging horde by a ruse. He made an exact image of Sita, infused life into it by his magic, and bringing it before the contending hosts loudly declared his intention of killing Sita in order to put an end to the general carnage. The monkeys, naturally took the image for Sita, and Hanuman, revolted by the threatened outrage railed: "Have you no pity, you monster? What harm has Sita done to you or any one else? To kill a woman is a heinous sin; to kill an innocent women is the deadliest of sins, and not even a demon would do it."

Indrajit promptly asked Hanuman why then his highly virtuous and chivalrous master killed Thadaka.

To the credit of the Rakshasas, it must be mentioned that none of them ever injured or forced Sita. On the death of his great son Indrajit, Ravana, maddened with grief for him, and taking Sita to be the root of all the trouble, rushed at her with drawn sword; but his counsellers pacified him and pointed out to him the enormity of the sin of killing a woman, and he recoiled from the base act. In this respect, the Rakshasas often showed a better sense of chivalry than the Aryan heroes and gods.

Reunion of Rama and Sita

Ravana and his generals were killed, and the battle of Lanka was over. Vibhishana, Ravana's brother who had deserted his people and gone over to Rama, was appointed king in place of Ravana, and the new vassal now dutifully brought Sita from Ravana's harem to Rama's camp. On the way all the monkeys lined up to have a look at Sita, but Vibhishana's men cleared the road in accordance with the practice of kings in those days who did not wish to have their women seen by the common people. Rama, however, asked Vibhishana to desist, and observed that royal ladies were not bound to observe Purdah on ceremonial occasions when they had to make public appearance.

At last, Sita met her husband after a year's eventful separation. The term of exile was over, and the two could now return to Ayodhya and rule over the kingdom. For Sita, however, the prospect of the glory of rulership was nothing when compared with the pleasure of meeting her husband. But Rama was set in a different mould. As soon as he met Sita, he locked at her sternly and told her severely:

> As the inaccessible southern region was conquered by the self-controlled ascetic Agastya, have I vanquished Ravana and reached Lanka; but in reclaiming you I have but vindicated my honour and the good name of my dynasty. It was to uphold the dignity of my royal house, and to wipe out in blood, the disgrace brought about by your abduction that I accomplished the conquest of Lanka and the destruction of Ravana. But as far as you are concerned, I have my own misgivings; in fact, the sight of you, to me, is like a bright lamp to one who has the sore eye. Which man of honour born in a royal line, take back his wife who had lived months in a stranger's house? You were held by Ravana and taken in his lap, drunk in by his lustful eyes, how can I, then, taking you to my palace, bring ignominy to my royal house? The object for which I reclaimed you, has been achieved; for the rest, you are free to go wherever fancy takes you. I have no more any love for you; what I have done is out of duty. You may now accept, for a husband, whomsoever you like; if you so desire, you may marry Lakshmana, Bharata, Satrughna, Sugriva or Vibhishana. For my part, I am not sure that you are pure, having lived in the palace of Ravana, notorious for his weakness for women;

> it should, indeed, be strange if Ravana had not availed himself of the opportunity, seeing how charming and lovely you are!

Poor Sita could hardly believe her ears. Nor could she bear this public humiliation. Neither her protestations of innocence nor her lamentations were of any avail, and in the end, Sita decided to go through the fire-ordeal to prove her innocence. Accordingly, she jumped into a fire-pit, made for the purpose by Lakshmana, and came out unscathed to the accompaniment of celestial voices proclaiming her purity.

It would appear that the solar race had higher notions of purity and honour than the lunar line to which the Pandavas belonged. In the case of Draupadi, public denudation by Duryodhana, rape by Jayadratha and kicking by Kichaka in an open assembly did not bring about her ostracism, whereas in Sita's case a single abduction led to her rejection, though from all accounts in the epic it is clear that Rama and all others concerned were fully aware that Sita had persistently resisted all attempts of Ravana to win her and had ever remained devoted to Rama.

Nor can we treat Sita's rejection as pure fiction. In the middle ages, when rigorous social codes gave rise to many superstitions concerning feminine purity and family honour among the Hindus, innocent women of the higher castes, when abducted or raped, were invariably ostracised and sent out of their homestead; in certain cases even their families were mercilessly excommunicated on the broad principle that abduction or rape of women was only possible through lack of vigilance on the part of their guardians. The earlier law-givers permitted the taking back of such women after their menses, as the menstrual flow was considered Nature's purification of a woman, but later moralists objected to this and abandoned for good women who were abducted or raped.

The End of Sita

The saddest part of the sad tale Sita is yet to be told. Rama, after the fire-ordeal, took her to Ayodhya and a coronation ceremony was held in grand style in the capital. Then followed an ideal reign which for prosperity, plenty and justice, has no parallel in history or fiction. As an example of Rama's love of justice and caste regulations, we have been regaled with the story of the death of a Brahmin's baby through the dereliction of another man's caste duty. One day, we are told, at the gate of the palace in Ayodhya appeared a Brahmin and his wife bearing the dead body of their son, and the wailling Brahmin accused Rama of misgovernment as in the reign of the ideal monarch premature death was unheard of Rama immediately consulted pious Brahmins who found out that this infant mortality was caused by a Sudra who arrogated to himself the Brahmin privilege of asceticism. According to the orthodox conceptions of the time, the duty of a Sudra was to serve his superiors by the diligent practice of which, he could get re-born in a higher caste after which he could think of asceticism and salvation. But now, instead of going through this proper channel, some Sudra somewhere was practising austerities as a short cut to salvation. An immediate search was made to find out the offender, and he was discovered in the southern region, the place of all evil. The man was a Sudra named Sambuka who was practising penances with his head down and feet up, and he confessed to an unholy desire for a race with the Brahmins for heaven. On this Rama killed him, and the Brahmin's child immediately revived.

Rama was extremely solicitous about the welfare of his subjects and kept himself well informed of all that happened in his kingdom. One day, some spies reported a strange rumour current in the city. It would appear a washerman, who suspected his wife of adultery, beat her, and on her protesting her innocence, drove home the point by a remark that he was not a fool, like his king, to believe that a woman kept by another man in his house for months was pure.

"Ravana did forcibly place Sita in his lap; how then can Rama find delight in her company? Having taken her to Lanka, Ravana made Sita live in his pleasure grove with his other women. Still Rama sees nothing wrong in this. From now on, we too shall have to put up with the vagaries of our women, for subjects invariably follow their king.' Thus, O king," said the spies, "your subjects talk of many things in the city and the provinces."

The sensitive Rama now decided to abandon Sita in order to placate public opinion, cultivate virtue among his subjects and raise the fallen prestige of his house. Sita was then in a delicate state of health and had, incidentally, expressed a desire to visit certain hermits dwelling in the forests, and Rama took advantage of the opportunity to abandon her in the woods. So Sita was sent to the forest with Lakshmana who had secret instructions to abandon her and come away. The prince took Sita to the hermitage of the sage Valmiki, and broke to her the cruel news. Poor Sita could hardly believe that her husband was capable of consigning her to the mercy of the woods in that condition, and told Lakshmana so. "When I lived in the forests of the south," said she, "the exile was a pleasure because my husband was with me; but here, myself big with child and Rama away, I am really forsaken, and do not know what to think of my husband's orders." On this Lakshmana told her of the gossip in the town, and that Rama was compelled to resort to this action for the good of his kingdom. Sita appreciated the force of this argument, reconciled herself to her fate and lived in the hermitage of Valmiki.

In Valmiki's hermitage Sita gave birth to the twins, Lava and Kusa. When the little ones grew to boyhood, Sita sent them to Rama. On seeing the young princes, Rama was so overcome with emotion that he sent for his wife. And gladly did Sita come. But on seeing her, he was again troubled by strange misgivings, and asked her for proof of loyalty during her stay away from him. Even Sita could not bear this. She cried to mother earth, who had given her birth, to take her back, and the earth, it is said, gaped and took her into her bowels.

Thus the tale of Sita is a beautiful illustration of how no woman, however devoted, could live up to the ideals of Pativrityam set by impossible masculine standards. The story, in its end, is more of a warning than an example.

General Remarks

The *Ramayana,* when compared with the earlier *Mahabharata* tradition, shows a general degeneration of the freedom of women. The Swayamvara, which was the pride of the Kshatriyas in the bigger epic; was going out of fashion and child-marriage was becoming popular. According to the existing version of the *Ramayana,* Sita, as we have seen, was six years of age at the time of her marriage, and later writers like Bhavabhuti accepted it.

The authority of the father over that of the mother has been well established in the *Ramayana.* Rama, as already noticed, rejected his mother's plea that a mother's order were as binding on the son as his father's.

Purdah was prevalent in royal households, though it was not very strict. Among the misfortunes of anarchy mentioned in the *Ramayana,* one was that "maidens decked with ornaments do not walk about in groups in public gardens, and pleasure lovers do not resort to groves and river-sides for sport with their ladies."

Some cases of Sati are mentioned in the *Ramayana* but it was not general even among kings. None of the wives of Dasaratha died with him. Wife of Kusodwaja, son of Brihaspati, is said to have died on the death of her husband.

A king's establishment, as in the time of the *Mahabharata,* had its army of courtesans, and one of the duties of these ladies was to anoint princes with oil and perfume and give them ceremonial baths. When preparations were made for the coronation of Rama, Vasishta, we find, gave orders to decorate and water the highways, and asked "courtesans proficient in music and dancing, adorning themselves, to occupy the second storey of the palace."

It would appear from the *Ramayana* that the joint family was coming into vogue. A story is narrated in the epic illustrating the onerous responsibilities of the head of a family and the difficulty of keeping peace among its many members. One day, we are told, Lakshmana brought to Rama, a dog that was found barking at the palace gates, which indicated that the animal had some complaint to make to the king. Rama enquired of the animal what its grievance was, and the animal told the monarch that a Brahmin had struck it without cause. The Brahmin was sent for and his guilt was proved. But neither Rama nor the counsellors could think of a suitable punishment for the Brahmin. According to the strict religious traditions which Rama wished to follow, a Brahmin was generally above the law of the land and any punishment was likely to infringe this tradition.. On the other hand, the dog was barking for justice, and if the guilty were not punished there would be a flagrant violation of justice. In this predicament, the dog itself found a solution; it asked Rama to appoint the Brahmin head of a family.

The king and the counsellors were surprised at this curious demand of the dog, and pointed out to the animal that the appointment of the Brahmin to be the head of a family was something of an honour and not a punishment. On this the dog told Rama that he, the dog, was once a pious and virtuous man; he was the head of a big family and in spite of all his efforts he could not discharge the onerous duties connected with his position to the satisfaction of all the numerous members of the household, nor even as justice and fairplay demanded, on account of which he was reborn as a god; the guilty Brahmin, the dog told the king, was, unlike him, an irascible man and if he was made the head of a family he was sure to fail in his duty and go to hell or get reborn in a state worse that a dog's.

5

The Kama Sutra and Sex

While most of the works so far mentioned are of religious character, in this chapter we may deal with two ancient Sanskrit works of a secular nature, i.e., Vatsyayana's *Kama Sutra* and Sudraka's *Mricchakatika.*

Unlike the epics which mainly treat of the activities of celestials and demi-gods, Vatsyayana's *Kama Sutra* deals solely with mundane affairs, especially with the pleasures of sex. There are, according to orthodox Hindu conceptions, four legitimate objects of life, namely, Dharma or duty (religious as well as social), Artha or acquisition of wealth and material property, Kama or the pleasures of life, and Moksha or liberation. For the good life, all the four are reckoned essential.

As the *Artha Sastra* of Kautilya treats of Artha, the *Kama Sutra* deals with the department of pleasure. Pleasure, in its wider sense, includes everything that pleases the senses but according to the stricter view the most important domain of pleasure is sex, and as such, the *Kama Sutra* is mainly concerned with sexual pleasure and only incidentally treats of other subjects.

The Kama Sutra

The date of Vatsyayana is not definitely fixed, and anything between the Mauryan and Guptan periods has been advanced as the possible date of the *Kama Sutra.* The first or second century is the more probable date, though some scholars are of the opinion that the prosperity of the Guptan age best indicates the leisured class mentioned in the *Kama Sutra;* but we have had the leisured class in India from very early times, and the poverty and want of the generality of the population have never been a serious handicap for the enjoyment of the good things of life by the favoured.

The Nagarika

Vatsyayana wrote for the leisured upper class who had plenty of money and time to devote themselves to the pursuit of pleasure. Unlike the gods, demons, sages and kings we generally meet in Hindu religious works, Vatsyayana's hero is the Nagarika or man-about-town who vigorously pursues the pleasures of life and is but remotely interested in things concerning the hereafter. He has but profound contempt for those ascetics and moralists who never tire telling us that woman is a snare. Vatsyayana holds the view that of all the pleasures in the world, there is none better than those sex affords. Though the sage of pleasure is mainly concerned with the methods of enjoying life, his work gives us a fairly good picture of society in his time.

The ideal Nagarika had his house in the suburb of a city, in a spacious, well-watered estate with pleasure gardens, canals and fountains. His mansion had two well-demarcated portions, somewhat like the Zenana and Mardana of Muslim India. In the Zenana, or women's apartments, lived the wife or wives of the Nagarika with children and domestic servants; the kitchen was naturally attached to this portion of the house. The Mardana was meant for the exclusive use of the master of the house and his guests. These guests were not necessarily males. The Nagarika used the Mardana for business or pleasure; he could, if he felt that way, invite courtesans to the Mardana and entertain them here, especially as it had a well-furnished bedroom to which he could retire with his sweetheart. At times, male guests brought their mistresses with them, and a convivial party was held in the Mardana. It was considered bad taste for courtesans and mistresses to enter the sacred precincts of the Zenana; similarly, the wife of the Nagarika and other respectable women of the household were prohibited entry to the Mardana when men and strange lady guests were being entertained.

Detailed descriptions of the Nagarika's daily life are found in the *Kama Sutra.* He got up in the morning, and after the inevitable ablutions, took his breakfast. Then he attended to the day's business, if he had any. The first meal, was taken just before noon; then he had a nap or spent his time going around his art-gallery or aviary, accompanied by his minlons who regaled him with their wit and wisdom. If he had no outdoor engagements, and if it happened to be a rainy day, he invited entertainers to his house and watched their performance. At night he took his dinner and enjoyed the company of his mistress in the bedroom attached to the Mardana, or repaired to the Zenana for more prosaic pleasures.

The Nagarika was a social figure too, and his pleasures included attendance at social functions in which men of his position took part. Twice a month were held, in the presence of many Nagarikas, musical and dancing competitions in the temple of the Muse, Sarasvati, in which singing girls and dancers performed for connoisseurs, and the deserving were awarded prizes. Any distinguished singer, dancer or poet from a foreign country was to be suitably honoured and the Nagarika was to be liberal with his cash on such occasions.

A more intimate social function was the Goshti Samavayam. This function was held, on a fixed date every month, in the house of Nagarika. The participants were all Nagarikas who attended with their mistresses, and it took place in a garden or spacious hall as the weather indicated; the entertainments consisted of light music and dancing, soft drinks, brilliant conversation and recitation of amorous verses.

Once or twice a month was held the Samapanakam or drinking party; in this, guests and their sweethearts were treated to intoxicating drinks. It was, for obvious reasons, more hilarious than the Goshti Samavayam, and we can be sure that a good deal of communal undressing took place in these functions.

The *Kama Sutra* also mentions mixed picnics at reverside or forests, moon-light revelries in woodlands where the usual dissipations were enhanced by drinking and gambling.

From this gay life of the Nagarika we may now divert our attention to his wife. She was strictly to confine her activities to the Zenana and her domestic duties; she was not· to enter the Mardana, nor appear at the gate of the house or talk to strangers. When her husband went out on his pleasure trips with his mistresses, she was to pray for his safe return. She could, however, go out to the temple or attend religious festivals with the permission of her husband. She could also go to the houses of relatives, especially on occassions of marriage, sickness or death. She had to remain loyal to her husband like Sita, no matter what his nature or activities were.

The Heroine of the Kama Sutra

From the foregoing it is clear that the partner of the Nagarika in his pleasures was not his wife, but his mistress. We have seen that the courtesan, from Rig Vedic times, had held an important position in Indian society, and in the *Kama Sutra* we see her as the ruler of high life.

Women; in the *Kama Sutra,* are grouped into two well-marked divisions each with its own functions and spheres of activities. The duty of the wedded wife was to bear children, preferably sons, to remain strictly faithful to her husband, to do nothing that might offend him and do everything in her power to enhance his pleasure and prosperity.

The *Kama Sutra* deals with pleasure and not duty, and as such, its heroine is not the dutiful wedded wife, but the Ganika or the woman of pleasure. Unlike the wife, the Ganika was a free courtesan who cultivated the sixty-four arts that please men; she ran palatial establishments for the entertainments of men, in which young girls proficient in music, dancing and blandishments captivated the heart of the pleasure-hunter. The Ganika attracted to her establishment poets, wits and wise men of the age, as well as wealthy merchants and high ranking nobles of the realm; even kings lavished their favours on her. Several chapters of the *Kama Sutra* are allotted to the Ganika and the techniques of her trade.

The greatest virtue of the Ganika was freedom from moral bonds. Profit and pleasure were the main objects of her life, and her duty the sale of her person; to shirk this duty was something of a sin in a Ganika.

This curious morality is, again, linked with caste notions. In an earlier chapter we have seen that for a Sudra to indulge in Vedic study or the practice of asceticism was a sin; similarly, the duty of a prostitute was to practise her profession well, and not to hanker after the virtue of the wedded wife of the higher castes. Most of the prostitutes were drawn from the lower castes whose traditional occupation was prostitution; for them to take to any others trade was a definite dereliction of duty.

As far as the Nagarika was concerned, once he had co-habited with his wife, during her Rtu, he had discharged his duty towards her, and was free to seek the courtesan for his pleasure.

Vatsyayana classified the courtesans of his time into nine beginning with the Kumbhadasi (street women, cheap as Kumbha or spittoons) and ending with the Ganika, the jewel of her class. The great men of the city vied with one another for her favours; to be seen with her in public was a rare privilege that enhanced a wealthy man's reputation as a man of substance and culture. Man's reputation as a man of substance and culture. A man's wife too shared his glory, and she too often encouraged him to secure for himself the coveted honour. Only the very wealthy could afford the luxury, as the Ganika often charged fabulous sums for such honours shown in public.

Eunuchs

In ancient literature, as we have seen, the main function of eunuchs was to guard the harems of kings, nobles and the wealthy, as males, for obvious reasons, could not be entrusted with this work.

From the *Kama Sutra,* it would appear that they had certain services to render other than the mere guarding of women's quarters.

They were widely used in perverted pleasures. In the harems of kings and nobles, there was a number of idle women in the full vigour of their sex life, who could not get all the attention they wanted from their husbands, and eunuchs. It would appear, gave these women what solace they could. Vatsyayana classified eunuchs into two: male and female. In the former male characteristics predominated and in the later, female.

Nor were they used only in the harems of the great. According to Vatsyayana, in sexual matters the tastes of men and women showed considerable variation, and some of the most innocent looking persons harboured in their hearts, grotesque perversions which could burst forth only in the secrecy of the bedroom. For the benefit of his readers, Vatsyayana has described some of these perversions, in which eunuchs played a prominent part. It is significant that Vatsyayana did not recommend it to any one but merely maintained that there were cases bordering on the pathological in sexual matters; in defence of his detailed descriptions of them, he stated, with the detachment of a modern scientist, that "a physician may describe the appearance and qualities of the flesh of the dog without any intention of recommending it as an article of food."

But in spite of the condemnation it has received from sages down the ages, perversion has been a permanent feature of brothels, and even now eunuchs are largely employed in Indian brothels mainly for the satisfaction of perverted pleasures of the clients.

Forms of Marriage

Vatsyayana, following the epics and the *Grihya Sutras,* classified marriage into eight. According to him the first four Brahma. Prajapatya, Daiva and Arsha were Dharmic (of duty), and the remaining four, i.e., Gandharva, Asura, Paisacha and Rakshasa, Kamya (of pleasure).

In the first four, marriage was generally arranged by parents or guardians, who sent intermediaries to see the girl, note certain auspicious and inauspicious marks on her person, to study omens on meeting her and consult the horoscopes, and then fix the marriage.

Certain broad hints were given for the guidance of the people who went to see the girl and conduct negotiations, and for parents. A marriage was to be between members of families of equal .or almost equal social standing; a girl who had both her parents living was to be preferred to one who had but one parent or none. Similarly, the girl who had living brothers was to be preferred to one who had only sisters. For the girl, physical beauty was more important than intellectual attainments, and for a boy the later and spiritual lustre in addition.

As a rule, the bride had to be a least three years younger than the groom. Marriages usually took place when the girl was about to mature though no blame rested with the parents if a girl actually matured before marriage. A girl was free to look for a husband, if her parents or guadians did not get her married three years after menstruation; this was the opinion of the law-giver Manu too, as we shall see later.

The *Kama Sutra* would indicate that early marriage was considered desirable; Child-marriage was coming into fashion, though there were many cases of late marriages.

It is clear from the *Kama Sutra* that a good number of girls remained unmarried even after three years of their menstruation, for various reasons. To a Hindu, marriage has been, all along the history of the race, an expensive affair. Before a marriage proposal took definite shape, there were protracted negotiations between several parties and go-betweens, and more often than not, a dozen or more proposals were actually considered before one was finally accepted. This meant continuous feasting of gentlemen who came to see the girl, in addition to presents and fees to intermediaries who practically lived on their victims. Then there was the question of finding money for costly garments and ornaments for the girl and for the expensive marriage feast, to say nothing of the major item which was the dowry to be given to the father of the bridegroom. People of middling income who often found it difficult to make ends meets, inevitably postponed the marriage of girls as long as they could, and very often girls remained unmarried for many years after menstruation in spite of the best intentions of their parents. Then there were girls who had no living male parents but stayed with relatives, who found them a burden, and were often careless about their marriage.

To such girls Vatsyayana recommended Gandharva or love marriage with desirable men whom they were asked to net in with all the cunning natural to the sex. Some of the methods they could employ with advantage were given in detail by Vatsyayana. A girl could, for instance, try to cultivate the friendship of a man who had been her friend and playmate in childhood, and whose desirability as a husband was well known to her. If such a man was not available, she could influence a man who could be counted to be loyal to her, to do her bidding and could be induced to interest himself in her. The girls was to avoid a man already married, however rich or well-placed he might be, as much-married, however rich or well-placed he might be, as much-married men were given to habitual falsehood. Another common sense advice was that a girl would be happier if she married, not the man she loved, but the man who was in love with her. Further she was discouraged an affair with an old man, a man of caste lower than hers, and a man whose business frequently took him to foreign countries. Other undesirable husbands were a vain man, a chronic celibate suddenly wanting to marry, a gambler and a drunkard.

Having selected her man, the girl was advised to ascertain trough reliable friends or through intermediaries like washer-women, flower-girls and fortune-tellers who had access to him, his inclinations. She was asked to appear in places like the temple, and attend feasts and religious functions, well-dressed, in order to attract his attention. She could meet him, as if by accident, in lanes or some out-of-the-way place he frequented. In these meetings she was to be careful not to give herself away; a winning smile or a courteous reply to what questions he might ask, was all that was permitted on the king's highway. Moreover, while encouraging him, the girl was not to take the initiative in love, as men do not prize high what they get easily.

After a few such meetings, the man was bound to ask for a secret appointment, to which she could agree after a show of reluctance and revolted modesty. After a few such secret sessions, the man was allowed to take liberties with the girl, and the relatives would be confronted with a *fait accompli* from which there was no escape for anybody.

In fact, the object of Gandharva, Rakshasa and Paisacha forms of marriage, according to Vatsyayana, was to present the relatives with a *fait accompli.*

There were men too who found it difficult to get married in conventional style. A young man without near relatives, at times, found that there was none to arrange his match. A newly rich man often found it difficult to marry into high circles. Further, a man who sincerely loved a girl could be prevented marriage with her by the perversity of her guardians who had other plans about her marriage. Again, according to the custom of certain communities, the maternal uncle's daughter was the legitimate bride of a man, but if he happened to be poor the parents of the girl at times tried to overlook his claim and find a more suitable husband for her.

In such cases, Gandharva, Rakshasa or Paisacha forms of marriage could be availed of by the man. Of the three the least objectionable was Gandharva. But it was difficult to establish direct contact with the girl due to the many restrictions imposed on girls of marriageable age in India, and the man had to employ intermediaries in the initial stages; these were either paid agents or trusted friends. The paid agents were usually menials or hawkers of trinkets or fortune-tellers who could visit the girl and talk to her without raising suspicion. Old midwives and female matrimonial agents could also be used for the purpose. After the agent had initiated the girl and worked her up with tales of the desirable qualities of the man as a possible husband, secret meetings were arranged which led to the defloration of the girl, when the lover calmly announced that the two were married according to the Gandharva rite, and the relatives were left with no choice.

Paisacha was resorted to when the girl showed no response. In this form of marriage, the girl was cunningly led to the house of an accomplice of the lover or to an out-of-the-way place by an agent; she was then drugged and raped and the Paisacha marriage was formally announced by her lover.

The Rakshasa, as we have seen, was abduction pure and simple.

In these objectionable forms of marriage, there were certain conventions to be observed. For a marriage of this type to be recognised, there were to be no circumstances which would have otherwise made it null and void. For instance, a man could not marry a married woman, living with her husband, in the Paisacha, Rakshasa or Gandharva rite. Nor were caste regulations to be infringed; a Chandala, for example, could not capture or rape a Brahmin girl and ask for its recognition as valid marriage; in such a case, the Chandala, instead of getting married to the girl, would be executed and the girl ostracised. Only if other things permitted, and the sanction of the parents or guardians was alone not forthcoming, could these forms of marriage be recognised; but when there were no valid objections, a Gandharva or Paisacha, when announced, had to be accepted by the guardians or parents of the girl.

General Remarks

Valid reasons for polygyny in Vatsyayana's time were : (1) Sterility in the first wife, (2) her giving birth to daughters only, (3) excessive libido in the husband, Wealthy men usually had an excess of libido, and these, as well as nobles and kings, were generally polygynous.

The senior wife in a polygynous household was enjoined to treat her junior co-wives as her younger sisters, and to hold her superior status by efficient management of the household and by giving sound advice to her husband in domestic matters. The futility of trying to hold her position by her charms was particularly emphasised. She could, however, play the younger wives, one against the other, by inciting their jealousies, and hold the balance of power between them.

The yonger wives, on the other hand, were advised to hold their position by their charms and ingratiate themselves into their husband's favour; they were not, however, to parade their powers before the senior wife who was to be shown deference even by the most favoured of the younger wives.

Widow marriages were prevalent in Vatsyayana's time, though rare. Remarried widows, who were generally looked down upon, fell into two divisions: those who were remarried before consummation of the first marriage, and those, after. The latter were again subdivided into four: (1) a woman who was, after the death of her husband, unable to contain herself and got remarried, (2) a woman who divorced her husband because of his vices or impotence and got remarried, (3) a woman divorced by her husband and remarried and, (4) a woman who left several husbands, one after another (she was reckoned no better than a prostitute).

The position of the remarried widow was never very high in the household of her husband; usually it was the beauty of the widow that led to her remarriage, and her husband was a wealthy man with several wives. She was advised, in her own interest, not to put on airs even when her husband doted on her as her social position was precarious and antagonism of co-wives could lead to her ruin. The best she could do was to play second fiddle to one of the legitimate wives of her husband, and hold her position along with her ally. She was not to aspire for a high independent status, as neither society nor the harem was likely to put up with it.

In is interesting to note certain points in the general standards of sexual morality in Vatsyayanas time. While adultery was generally deprecated, the Nagarika was permitted to seduce other men's wives under certain conditions. These were classified into eight. A good part of the *Kama Sutra* deals with the art of seduction.

Vatsyayana, however, is impartial, and in the same breath

teaches the art of seduction and that of defence against design and that of defence against designing men; the need for keeping strict vigilance over women and giving them no cause for discontent which would facilitate the sinister work of the seducer is emphasised.

Sati or Anumarana is mentioned in the *Kama Sutra.*

Sudraka's Mricchakatika

The *Mricchakatika* (Clay Cart) is a drama written in the first or second century of the Christian era by a king named Sudraka. Little is known about Sudraka except that he wrote this play; he was possibly of low birth, as the name indicates, and a Buddhist.

The *Mricchakatika* is one of the few ancient secular works in Sanskrit that have come down to us, and it gives us an inkling into the social life of the time. The play shows Buddhism and Brahminism as living side by side without much antagonism; the temper of the drama, unlike that of most other Sanskrit works, is thoroughly secular, and there is no supernatural intervention in the triumph of good over evil.

The heroine of the play was a courtesan by name Vasantasena. She was not the thoroughly commercial, unscrupulous Ganika mentioned in the *Kama Sutra,* but rather the virtuous, high souled type of the Buddhist tradition, the courtesan who was competent to instruct learned Brahmins in the Dharma. Other characters were, Charudatta, the hero, a Brahmin merchant improverished by his generosity, Samsthanaka, the villain, in love with Vasantasena who was in love with Charudatta.

The scenes were laid in the streets of the famed city of Ujjain; Brahminical pretensions were coming into contempt under the aegis of Buddhism and many scenes in the play would indicate the prevailing fashions of the time. Besides Charudatta, there were two other Brahmin characters in the play, a clown and a thief. Many acts made fun of the Brahmins; the Brahmin thief Sarvilaka, for instance, while effecting a breach in a wall, was made to exclaim: "I have forgotten my measuring line! Never mind, my sacred thread will serve the purpose. This thread is a most useful appendage to a Brahmin, especially to one of my complexion; it serves to measure the depth and height of walls, and to withdraw ornaments from their position; it opens a latch in the door as well as a key, and is an excellent ligature for the bite of a snake." It must be stated that the play was meant for public performance; the audience was obviously prepared to laugh at such jokes cracked at the expense of the sacerdotal hierarchy.

The Establishment of a Courtesan

In the *Mricchakatika* is a detailed description of the palatial establishment of Vasantasena, and it is, no doubt, based on the factual way of life of the powerful courtesans of ancient India. Maitreya, Charudatta's messenger thus described it, form the gateway to the living rooms:

> A very pretty entrance, indeed! The threshold is very neatly coloured, well-swept and watered. The floor is beautified with strings of sweet flowers; the top of the gate is lofty and gives one the pleasure of looking up to the clouds while the jasmine festoon hangs tremblingly down as if it is now tossing on the trunk of Indra's elephant. Over the doorway is a lofty arch of ivory; above it, again, wave, flags dyed with saffron, their fringes curling in the wind like fingers that beckon me. On either side, the capitals of the door-posts support elegant crystal flower-pots in which young mango trees are springing up. The door panels are of gold, stuck, like the stout breast of a demon, with studs of adamant.

By this gate Maitreya entered the first court. He said:

> Bless me, here is a line of palaces, as white as the moon, as the conch, as the stalk of the water-lily—the stucco has been laid on by handfuls; golden steps, embellished with various stones, lead to the upper apartments whence the crystal windows, festooned with pearls, and bright as the eyes of a moon-faced maid, look down upon Ujjain. The porter dozes on an easy chair as stately as a Brahmin deep

> in the *Vedas;* and the very crows crammed with rice and curds, disdain the fragments of sacrifices, as if they were no more than scattered plaster.

In the second court were the stables.

> The carriage oxen are in good case, pampered with Javasa, I declare; and straw and oil-cakes are ready for them; their horns are bright with grease; here we have a buffalo snorting indignantly like a lofty Brahmin whom some one has affronted; here the ram stands to have his neck well rubbed, like a wrestler after a match; here they dress the manes of the horses; here is a monkey tied as fast as a thief; and here are mahouts playing the elephants with balls of rice and ghee.

The third court was meant for visitors to wait. "Here the young bucks of Ujjain assemble. These are their seats, I suppose—the half-read books are lying on the gaming table, the pieces of which are made of jewels. Oh! yonder are some old hangers-on, lounging about with many coloured pictures in their hands and skilled in the peace and war of love."

The fourth court was something of a music hall.

> Here, the drums, whilst beaten by taper fingers, emit, like clouds, a murmuring tone; there, the cymbals beating time flash as they descend like the unlucky stars that fall from heaven; the flute here breathes the soft hum of the bee, whilst here, a damsel holds the Vina in her lap, and frets its wires with her finger nails like some wild minx that sets her mark on the face of her offending swain; some damsels are singing like so many bees intoxicated with flowery nectar; others are practising the graceful dance, and still others are employed in reading plays and poems. The place is hung with water jars suspended to catch the cooling breeze.

The fifth court was the kitchen establishment where many maids and men were employed in the culinary art. "Ah! How my mouth waters!" exclaimed the hungary Maitreya, "what a savoury scent of oil and asafoetida! The kitchen sighs softly forth its fragrant and abundant smoke—the odours are delicious—they fill me with rapture. The butcher's boy is washing the skin of an animal just slain, like so much foul linen; the cook is surrounded with dishes; the sweetmeats are mixing, the cakes are baking! ... This is certainly Indra's heaven; the damsels are Apsaras."

The sixth was the jewellers' court.

> Here skilled artists are examining pearls, topazes, saphires, emeralds, rubies, lapis-lazuli, coral and other jewels; some set rubies in gold, some work on gold ornaments on coloured thread, some string pearls; some grind the lapis lazuli, some pierce shells, and some cut coral. Here we have perfumers drying the saffron bags, shaking the musk bags, expressing the sandal juices and mixing essences. Whom have we here? Fair damsels and their gallants, laughing, talking, chewing musk and betel, and drinking wine. Here are the male and female attendants, and here the miserable hangers-on, men who neglected their own families, spent their all upon the harlot, and are now glad to quaff the draining of her wine cup.

In the seventh court was the aviary.

> The doves bill and coo in comfort. The pampered parrot croaks like a Brahmin Pundit, stuffed with curds and rice chanting a hymn from the *Vedas;* the Maina chatters as glibly as a housemaid issuing her mistress' command to her fellow-servants, while the Koil, crammed with juicy fruit, whines like a water carrier. The quails fight, the partridges cry; the domestic peacock dances about delighted, and fans the place with his gem-emblazoned tail, as if to cool its heated walls; the swans, like balls of moon-light, roll about in pairs, and follow each graceful maid as if to learn to imitate her gait, while the long-legged cranes stalk about the court like eunuchs on guard. I declare the lady lives here amongst the winged race as if she tenented Indra's garden.

The living rooms of Vasantasena, her mother and brother were built round the eighth court and each of the appartments were luxuriously furnished. Attached to the living room of the courtesan was a pleasure garden.

> A very lovely scene! The numerous trees bow down with delicious fruit, and between them are silken swings constructed for the light form of the youthful beauty. The yellow jasmine, the graceful Malati, the full-blossomed Mallika and the blue clitoria, shed their flowers, and strew the ground with a carpet more lovely than any in the groves of Indra; the reservoir glows with the red lotus blossoms like the dawn with the fiery beams of the rising sun; and here the Asoka tree with its rich crimson blossoms, shines like a young warrior bathed with the sanguine shower of the furious fight.

Vasantasena and Charudatta's Wife

The *Micchakatika* like the *Kama Sutra* confirms the two-fold division of women into the wife and the courtesan. The play, incidentally, shows how this double morality, so very conflicting to our modern notions, worked harmoniously in ancient India. The spheres of activities of the wife and the courtesan were clearly defined, and as long as each confined herself to her own sphere, there was understanding, appreciation and harmony; so at least the *Micchakatika* would show.

To understand this, it is necessary for us to note some details of the play. Vasantasena, one day, while going out, was pursued by the villain and his minions, and she ran for refuge to Charudatta's house. The malefactors lost sight of her, and as she took leave of Charudatta, Vasantasena left the jewel casket with him for safe custody lest the villain, who was the king's brother-in-law, should lie in wait for her and rob her of her ornaments. The ornaments were, unfortunately, stolen that very night from Charudatta's house by the thief Sarvilaka. This person was in love with Madanika, a maid-servant of Vasantasena; he gave the jewels as a present to his sweetheart and Madanika recognised the jewels and gave them to her mistress, the rightful owner.

In the meantime, finding Vasantasena's casket stolen, Charudatta was at a loss what to do, he had fallen on evil days, and neither Vasantasena nor the public was likely to believe him if he were to give out that the jewels were stolen, especially as he was impoverished and needy. Charudatta's wife now came to his aid; with his permission, she decided to send her own jewellery to Vasantasena with a story that the jewellery, left with her husband, was lost in gambling and she was sending, in lieu, her own ornaments.

When Charudatta's messenger came to her with the jewellery and the story, the amused Vasantasena showed apparent concern and accepted the jewellery. In the evening, however, she visited Charudatta and spent the night with him; Charudatta got up very early and proceeded to a site of picnic leaving word with his servant to take Vasantasena to the site, later, in his own pleasure cart.

After Vasantasena got up, she sauntered about the spacious house of Charudatta, and entered, without knowing it, those apartments meant for Charudatta's wife. She met a maid servant here and felt embarrassed as she had intruded into the Zenana.

Vasantasena exclaimed : What ! Did I find my way into the inner apartments?

Servant: Not only that Madam, but into every one's heart!

Vasantasena: I fear his family are vexed.

Servant : They will be vexed then only, when —

Vasantasena : When?

Servant : When you depart.

Vasantasena : Then is it my place to be afflicted ? Here, girl, take this necklace to my respected sister (giving her the necklace and other ornaments sent to her in place of the stolen casket), and say from me, 'I am Charudatta's handmaid, and your slave, let this necklace be once again the ornament of the neck to which, it, of right, belongs.'

Servant : But, lady, Charudatta will be displeased.

Vasantasena : Go, do as I bid you; he will not be offended.

Servant : As you command. (She goes and returns presently)

Madam, thus says the lady : 'You are favoured by the son of my lord; it is not proper for me to accept this necklace. Know that the only ornament I value is my husband.'

At this point, Radanika, Charudatta's maid-servant enters with his little son leading a toy cart.

Radanika : Come, my child, let us ride in your cart.

Child : I do not want this cart. It is of clay — I went one of the gold.

Radanika : And where are we to get gold, my little man ?

Wait till your father is rich again, and then he will buy you one. Now this will do. Come, let us go and see Vasantasena. Lady, I salute thee.

Vasantasena : Welcome, Radanika. Whose charming boy is this? Although so ill-attired, his lovely face fascinates me.

Radanika: This is Rohasena, the son of Charudatta.

Vasantasena : (Stretching out her arms) Come here, my little dear, and kiss me. (Takes him on her lap) How like his father!

Radanika : He is like him too in his disposition. Charudatta dotes on him.

Vasantasena : Why does he weep?

Radanika : The child of our neighbour had a golden cart which this little fellow wanted. I made him this of clay, but he is not pleased with it, and is crying for the other.

Vasantasena : Alas ! Alas ! The child is already mortified by another's prosperity. O Fate ! Thou sportest with the fortunes of the kind, like water drops trembling on the lotus leaf. Don't cry, my good boy, and you shall have a golden cart.

Child : Radanika, who is this ?

Vasantasena : A handmaid purchased by your father's merits.

Radanika : This is your lady-mother, child.

Child : You speak an untruth, Radanika; how can she be my mother when she wears such fine things?

Vasantasena : How piteous a speech, for so soft a tongue ! (Takes off her ornaments in tears.) Now I am your mother. Here, take this trinket, and go but a gold cart.

Child : Away, I will not take it; you cry at parting with it.

Vasantasena : (Wiping her eyes) I weep no more. Go, love, and play (fills his cart with her jweles). There, go, get you a golden cart.

A few points in the scene may be noted. While good relations between a man's wife and his mistress were possible, it was bad taste for them to mix. The dealings between Vasantasena and Charudatta's wife were through a servant. Vasantasena did not enter the wife's apartment; further, the name of Charudatta's wife was never mentioned. It was bad form in ancient India to mention the name of a respectably married woman, and Sudraka had kept this convention.

With all the splendour attached to the life of a courtesan (Vasantasena is often mentioned in the play as the pride of the city of Ujjain), there was a certain public contempt for her profession which often showed itself with particular vehemence in certain scenes. For instance when Vasantasena rejected the advances of the worthless, drunken Samsthanaka, his clown said:

> Why, Vasantasena, you act quite out of character. The dwelling of a harlot is the free resort of youth. A courtesan is like a creeper that grows by the roadside. Her person is for public sale, her love a thing money will buy, and her welcome is equally bestowed on the amiable and the disgusting. The sage and the idiot, the Brahmin and the outcaste, all bathe in the same stream, and the crow and the peacock perch on the same bough. ... The Brahmin, the Kshatriya, the Vaisya, and all of every caste are ferried over in the same boat; and like the boat, the creeper, the bough and the stream, the courtesan is accessible to all.

It would appear the courtesan envied the respectability of the housewife, and the later the freedom and splendour of the courtesan.

The concluding scenes in the play throw certain interesting side-lights on the social conditions of the time.

Vasantasena, who persistently rejected the advances of the villain Samsthanaka, was assaulted and robbed of her ornaments by him, and was left for dead in a deserted place near Buddhist nunnery. Samsthanaka accused Charudatta of the murder, and by circumstantial evidence furnished by a strange combination of coincidences, the court found Charudatta guilty and condemned him to exile, as Charudatta was a Brahmin and Brahmins could not be punished by death. The king, however, overruled this objection and condemned him to death.

Charudatta made no effort to defend himself. On hearing of Vasantasena's death, he lost all interest in life, and almost courted death. At the same time, he had a kind thought for his wife and son. On the way to the block, he wailed:

> My good Maitreya, what will be thy grief
> To hear of my grief ? And thine, dear wife,

The daughter of a pure and pious race?
Alas! My boy, amidst thy youthful sports,
How little thinkst thou of thy father's shame!

Hearing of Charudatta's condemnation, his wife, dutifully decided to put an end to her life and enter the pyre. Here an objection was raised by a friend. A Brahmin lady was not allowed to enter a separate pyre from that of her husband.

Anyway, she was saved from death by the timely arrival of Charudatta and Vasantasena with a crowd of admirers. Vasantasena was not really dead; she was taken to a convent by a Buddhist monk who found her unconscious at the site of the crime, and nursed back to health by the nuns. Vasantasena reached the place of execution just in time to save Charudatta; the two hurried, with the crowd, to Charudatta's house, where the wife and the mistress embraced each other as two devoted co-wives would.

6

Lagitimisation of Feminity

We now come to the most tragic period in the history of India not only in respect of her women but of the race as a whole. For some reason not yet fully explained, India that had the cultural leadership of Asia from the time of Asoka, suddenly sank into an age of bigotry and seclusion which not only deprived her of her leadership of Asia but practically isolated her from the civilisations of Asia for the building up of which she had done so much. Foreign travel became taboo to Indians, and shut up in its own shell like a snail, the country produced institutions which became a reproach to civilisation in general and her own glorious traditions in particular.

Perhaps the decay of Buddhism had something to do with it. As we have seen in an earlier chapter, Buddhism was the dominant religion of India from the time of Asoka onwards, but under the Imperial Guptas (fifth-sixth century A.D.) there was a Hindu revival and a gradual decline of Buddhism. Though Harsha leaned towards Buddhism, from Huien Tsang's writings it is clear that Buddhism was steadily losing ground to Braminism. The eighth century sounded the death-knell of Buddhism in India. Two names are generally associated with its disappearance, those of Sankara and Kumarila Bhatta, and both these celebrities lived in the eighth century. They literally disputed Buddhism out of India. The favourite method of settling a religious dispute, at the time, was for the leader of one faction to challenge the other to a wordy duel; the defeated disputant had the choice of either killing himself or accepting, along with his followers, the religion of the victor. Between Sankara and Kumarila Bhatta, practically all the Buddhists are said to have been defeated and made to become Hindus with all their followers and shrines.

Whatever truth there may be in this legend, it is a historical fact that Buddhism ceased to be an active force in India after the eighth century; it lingered in East India for some time, but with the onslaught of Islam it had a complete collapse from which it never recovered.

On the defeat of Buddhism, Brahmins came out with extraordinary powers. They now regained the monopoly of religion in India, and their power grew greater than during the sixth century B.C. when the Buddha and Mahavira revolted against them. The Kshatriyas more or less degenerated into mere executives of Brahmin hierarchs. Practically all over India the rulers were Hindus; Brahmins legislated for the country, and the Kshatriyas enforced the laws. The caste system was rigidly enforced, almost as zealously as in Rama's time. Great temples rose all over the country, and the wealth of the temples were even greater than that of kings so much so, invaders like Mahmud of Ghazni were content to plunder temples and leave kings alone.

In a priest-ridden country, values, as is well known, are upside down, the needs of the life-to-come having precedence over the exigencies of the present life. The generality of men and women lived for the pleasures of the next world and made light of the problems of this life; the only exceptions were the priests themselves who were competent to enjoy the good things of both the worlds. The love of life characteristic of the Mahabharata tradition, and even the pleasures of a decadent society as depicted in the *Kama Sutra* were gone for good; instead, came a love of the hereafter. Life was held cheap, and it mattered little how many men and women died in the service or caprice of gods and their visible representatives of earth, the Brahmins, as long as these were kept in good humour.

We need not pause here to discuss the social injustice involved in the iniquitous caste laws, rigidly preached and enforced during this period, which condemned the majority of the population of the country as untouchables and unapproachables, but would rather pass on to those injunctions of jurists which tended to treat woman as a sort of perverse animal, in an attempt to elevate the soul at the expense of the body. For in those days of pseudo-spiritual values, woman, as the perpetuator and bearer of life, was particularly censured and dreaded; her freedom was curtailed, knowledge of not only the scriptures but even letters was denied her and her status was reduced to that of an appendage on man. We shall now go into the details of this subjection and degeneration of women in India, from the ill effects of which they have not yet fully recovered.

General Spirit of Later Codes and Puranas

The age of the later codes and *Puranas,* the darkest period in Indian history, falls roughly between the seventh and twelfth centuries, the period between the decline of Buddhism and the spread of Islam in India; this was a period of secret, exotic cults, of reaction against the liberal, international traditions of Buddhism and the shutting out of all outside influences, which ended in the degeneration of the race and the devastation of the country by foreign conquerors.

The literature of the period was worthy of the age. It produced little of importance except some law books and commentaries; the main output was some puerile *Puranas* and *Taxtras* which sanctified and extolled the new trends in isolation and secrecy; for the rest, the writers of the period were content to interpolate ancient texts in order to bring them into conformity with the sins of the age.

The more ancient of the *Dharma Sastras* (the law books of the Hindus), like the codes of Yajnavalkya and Manu, date from the early centuries of the Christian era and the writers drew mainly from the *Grihya Sutras* and other post-Vedic literature. Later jurists wrote on the basis of earlier law-givers, but added their own laws to meet the requirements of the times; when they could, they interpolated the earlier texts to yield sanction for the new codes; when interpolation was not possible and the earlier texts were in contradiction with the new laws, the discrepancy was explained away by the fiction that ancient authorities were not valid in Kali Yuga.

There are many law books among the Hindus of which twenty are considered the more important. Of all the law books, the Code of Manu is considered the most authoritative. Manu was one of the earliest of law-givers and the legends that have collected round him make him a semi-mythical figure. But so great, so exclusive in fact, was his authority as a law-giver in India, that medieval law books in Burma, Indonesia and other countries of South-East Asia to which Indian civilisation spread formulated their laws on the pattern of the Code of Manu, and in most of these countries, as in India, the origin of law is ascribed to Manu.

Yajnavalkya comes next in importance to Manu and his code is considered by certain authorities as anterior to even Manu's. The extant works of both these law-givers abound in contradictions, due, no doubt, to the hidden hand of later interpolators who wished to obtain ancient authority for new legislation.

Further, most of the ancient texts now extant are obscure, and would be unintelligible without later commentaries. For all practical purposes, the commentary known as *Mitakshara,* written on the code of Yajnavalkya by a South Indian Brahmin named Vijanesvara who lived in the twelfth century, was since then, the basis of Hindu law for practically the whole of India except Bengal, where *Daya Bhaga* of Jimuta Vahana, another commentary, was followed.

We are here concerned not so much with medieval Hindu law in general as with those portions of it which deal with woman. In this respect, the burden of all the codes, earlier or later, has been to establish the abject dependence of woman on man. "In childhood," says practically every law-giver including the venerable Manu. "a woman is to be dependent upon her father, in youth on her husband, and in old age on her son; a woman is never fit for independence."

In ancient days, the marriage ceremony, it would appear, was meant for uniting two souls into one, but according to the *Dharma*

Sastras there was no union but only a merging of the woman into man, as a river merging into the ocean. "Akshamala, a woman of the lowest birth, being united to Vasistha, and Sarangi being united to Mandapala, became worthy of honour. These and other females of low birth have attained eminence in this world by the respective good qualities of their husbands." The rights of women in practically all law books are identified with those of Sudras, slaves and children.

The right of physical correction of women was conceded to husbands, though dangerous assaults were condemned.

The earlier law-givers permitted both widow marriage and levirate, but certain passages in the same texts prohibit both, and the hand of the interpolator is clearly discernible in these. All later law-givers, without exception, severely condemned both. The main objection to widow marriage was that the woman was already given away by her guardian to her husband, and "no gift of the same thing could be made twice over."

Manu was in perfect agreement with the epic and post-Vedic writers as regards the base nature of women.

> Women do not care for beauty, nor is their attention fixed on age; thinking it is enough he is a man, they give themselves to the handsome and the ugly.
>
> Through their passion for men, through their mutable temper, through their natural heartlessness, they become disloyal towards their husbands, however carefully they may be guarded in this world.
>
> Knowing their disposition which the Lord of Creatures laid in them to be such, every man should most strenuously exert himself to guard them.
>
> When creating them, the Lord of Creatures, allotted to women a love of their bed, of their seat and of ornaments, impure desires, wrath, dishonesty, malice and bad conduct.

> For women no sacramental rite is performed with sacred texts, thus the law is settled; women (who are) destitute of strength and destitute of the knowledge of Vedic texts, are as impure as falsehood itself, that is the fixed rule.

Further, "three persons, a wife, a son and a slave, are declared by law to have no wealth exclusively their own; the wealth they may earn is regularly acquired for the man to whom they belong."

In marriage while a man's eligibility was judged by his intellectual and spiritual accomplishments, the girl's desirability was solely dependent upon her physical attractions. She was to be "free from bodily defects, should have an aggreable name, should be of graceful gait like a swan or an elephant, should have a moderate quantity of hair on the body and on the head, small teeth and soft limbs."

A man was not to marry "a maiden with reddish hair, nor one who has a redundant member, nor one who is sickly, nor one either with no hair (on the body) or too much, nor one who is garrulous or has red eyes." An Aryan was not to eat with his wife; "nor look at her while eating, sneezing, yawning or sitting at her ease."

This was what Manu thought of women. Later law-givers were even more harsh. A good wife, according to the law-giver Daksha, was not born but made. A wife was always to be taught her place; if, out of misplaced affection, she was allowed to have her own way, "she becomes uncontrollable like a disease neglected; all wives are like leeches; even if daily gratified with ornaments, dresses and food, they never cease to extort a man.

"The small leech merely sucks the blood while the other draws the wealth, property, flesh, energy, strength and the happiness of a man."

Another law-giver, Atri, was of the opinion that "a man shall not take food in the house of a barren woman even if she is his own daughter; he who takes food out of love, goes to hell." Further, "a woman, who, during the lifetime of her husband fasts while performing a religious rite, robs the longevity of her husband. Such a woman goes to hell."

According to Atri, there was no need for a woman to hazard a long journey when she wanted to obtain merit by bathing in sacred streams. All that she had to do to obtain equal or better merit was "to wash the feet of her husband and drink the water".

And most law-givers, both earlier and later, were of the opinion that a woman was bound to worship her husband as a god, even if he were a drunkard, gambler or debauchee.

This may be said to be the general attitude of most of the codes towards women of the higher castes. As a rule, they were not to own property, not to be given freedom or the benefits of literacy, and were to be kept constantly under male surveillance. But in several of the codes, even in the most severe, we find stray passages which directly contradict this general tone and even confer on women a status higher than that enjoyed by men. At first sight, this might appear the varying moods of the same writer, a piece of masculine irrationality, common to all ages and races, by which, at times a man surrenders all, life itself, for his sweetheart, but at other times feels like murdering her; Othello's attitude towards Desdemona, to quote a western example.

But there is more than caprice in these contradictions found in the Hindu codes. A good many of the passages, favourable to women, in the codes as well as in certain other Hindu texts, can be traced to the secret hand of the Tantric interpolator. The Tantrics, in private, held a very high opinion of women though in public they professed, like the others, a contempt for women. The influence of this sect will be given in some detail in a later chapter, but here we may note the passages which can be reasonably attributed to Tantric sources.

In both Manu and Yajnavalkya we find passages exhorting men to honour women and keep them contented and happy, lest misfortune should overtake the household through the sorrows of neglected women.

A woman, according to some passages was always pure. "The moon has conferred on women purity, the Gandharvas sweet speech, fire the most exalted state of holiness; therefore women are most holy. If a woman commits adultery, she gets purified by her menses."

> Again, according to Angiras........ a woman is purified by her menses, and a river by its current.
>
> There is no Sastra superior to the Veda; and no elderly person superior to the mother.
>
> A woman is not sullied by being known by another; nor a Brahmin by (harmful) Vedic rites; nor water (of a river) by urine and excreta; nor fire by burning impure things.
>
> Women were first enjoyed by celestials; then by the moon, the Gandharvas and fire. Afterwards men came to enjoy them. They are never affected by any sin.
>
> When a woman conceives by being known by an Asavarna (a Sudra) she remains impure as long as she does not give birth to her child.
>
> When, after delivery, the menstrual blood is seen, the woman becomes purified like pure gold.
>
> If, despite her unwillingness, a woman is known deceitfully forcibly or stealthily, that woman, unaffected by any sin, should not be renounced.

It must be mentioned here that throughout the middle ages, the question had been raised in Hindu society as to what was to be done with women abducted or forced during war and reclaimed; the more humane of the law-givers maintained that the woman could be taken back after her menses or delivery. During the partition of India in 1947, there were widespread riots and rape of women in many places in the country and the question came up with particular force as to what was to be done with women who had been forced or abducted and later reclaimed; the desirability of taking them back was then universally accepted by all the Hindus, including the orthodox sections, and the main authority for this move was the sanction of law-givers like Atri who seem to have had to deal with similar situations.

While the period of menses itself was feared to throw a woman out of caste, because of her ceremonial impurity, throughout the middle ages in India, the physiological phenomenon was generally held to be a cleansing process. Her social degradation on the first three days of the menstrual flow was thus described by the law-giver Angiras: "On the first day of the menses, the woman (of whatever high caste she may otherwise be) becomes a Chandala, on the second, the murderess of a Brahmin and on the third, a washerwoman; on the fourth day, she is purified." In keeping with these notions, a woman was usually isolated during her period, and was allowed to use only rags, torn mats and broken pots as befitting her degradation.

Child-Marriage

In post-Vedic literature and in the earlier codes, there is no insistence on pre-puberty marriage and as such modern scholars are divided in their opinion about the antiquity of child-marriage in India; the later law-givers, however, have left us in no doubt on this point. A girl had to be married before she menstruated.

While Manu did not consider post-puberty marriage as sinful, Yajnavalkya was of the opinion that the parents of a girl who did not give her away in marriage before puberty "will be visited by the sin of the destruction of the foetus at every time of her menses." Yama, another law-giver, thought that "by beholding a maiden in her menses (before marriage) her mother, father and her eldest brother—these three—go to hell." According to the law-giver Marichi, "a father who gives in marriage a girl of eight goes to heaven, the giver of a girl of nine, Vaikunta; one who gives his daughter in marriage before she attains the age of ten attains the heaven of Brahma. But the father of a girl married after puberty goes to hell". The imprecation of Parasara, the self-styled law-specialist of Kali Yuga, on negligent parents, was even more harsh. "If a father", he wrote, "fails to give away his daughter in marriage when she has reached the twelfth year, her ancestors drink her menstrual flow every month. The father, mother and eldest brother of a maiden seeing her in her menstrual course, go to hell. The Brahmin who, blinded by ignorance, marries her, is unfit to converse or dine with; he is the husband of a Sudra woman."

While the ceiling on marriageable age was thus fixed, there was no minimum mentioned, and even infants were married, among the orthodox, in medieval India. There also arose an added incentive to infant marriage in the ancient Hindu belief that the human husband of a girl was actually her fourth; when the public hair began to appear, the god Soma was thought to enjoy a maiden, when breasts grew, a Gandharva or celestial quirister, and at menstruation, the god Agni. Such behaviour of the celestials—came to be considered highly objectionable in later times, though considered proper in the earlier ages. Hence later law-givers insisted that girls were to be married before the appearance of the public hair and the breasts, and before the celestials developed interest in them.

Though marriages were performed in infancy, consummation, as a rule, took place only after the girl's menstruation. But some later commentators were of the opinion that in the interest of higher morality, it were better if premature girls were carnally known by their husbands, "for it does happen that sexual desire establishes itself before puberty, and if the husband fails to gratify it, she might do something improper".

At first, it would appear, these injunctions were enforced only among the Brahmins, but slowly other castes, who aspired for spiritual merit and respectability, followed the lead of the Brahmins. Of the race suicide caused by child-marriage, an eminent modern authority may be quoted.

> Woman was allowed no choice in the selection of her husband, and she was married at an age when she was incapable of understanding the real significance of marriage and exercising her own judgement and discretion. Womanhood was sacrified at the altar of supposed social convenience and purity, and out of its ashes rose a race of cabined, cribbed and delicate creatures too fragile for the propagation of life, too ethereal to be of any earthly use. With women's degeneration began the degeneration of the people which has continued to the present time with rapid and disastrous acceleration.

This was, no doubt, the main reason for the physical decline of the Hindus as a race, and the ease with which the Muslims conquered India. It must, however, be noted that the Sudras, who formed the bulk of the population of the country and supplied the main fighting forces, as well as certain sections of the Rajputs, did not strictly follow the injunctions of the codes, and it is this that prevented complete race suicide through child-marriage.

The *Brahma Purana* recommended marriage of girls between the age of four and ten; in her eighth year a girl was known as Gauri and this came to be looked upon as the ideal age of marriage for a girl, and we can take it as a general rule that marriages of girls, in the later Puranic and Dhama Sastra period, were performed between the ages of four and ten, though there were exceptions.

By this time marriage was also made compulsory for a woman without which she could not hope to go to heaven. For a girl, it became the equivalent of the Upanayanam (initiation) for boys, and the age of eight was considered the ideal for both marriage (for the girl) and Upanayanam.

As marriage became a religious obligation for the salvation of girls, law-givers naturally toed the line, and maintained that it was better for parents to get their daughters married even to unworthy persons than to let them remain unmarried. As a result economic incentives were freely employed to get unwanted girls married; the lot of defective or deformed girls was particularly pitiable; they were married to persons who were given large dowries but in practically every case the girl was superseded by a more desirable co-wife.

The joint family, which now became the unit of Hindu society, also facilitated child-marriage. From the description of families in the *Mahabharata, Kama Sutra, Mricchakatika* and other ancient works, as we have seen, men usually set up their families after they were able to make a living. But such hiving off became censurable in later times, and a married person normally lived with his father, mother, brothers and sister-in-law, in the same household; the family property was held in common trust, each member bringing to it what he earned and each getting out of it what he needed or rather what the head of the family thought he needed.

From earlier law books, it would appear, the sons of a man usually divided his wealth among themselves on his demise, and Yajnavalkya and certain other law-givers definitely laid down what each should get, including daughters and female relatives. There was also provision for the separation of the eldest son, while the father was living, if he wished to set up house after marriage; those who were independent earners were given little from the ancestral wealth but set up and maintained their families with their earned income.

All this changed towards the later Puranic period. A normal Hindu family, the joint family as it was called, became an unwieldy, unmanageable affair with the eldest male member as the head, and his younger brothers and sons, with their wives and children, often running into several dozen. The ancestral property was enjoyed in common. Just as the male members were under the discipline of the eldest male, the women were under the mother-in-law who was usually the oldest female member; the tortuous sway of this individual over the younger women of the household, especially over her daughters-in-law has become a byword for petty tyranny in India.

The economic structure of the joint family was ideally suited for early, irresponsible marriage. There was no need for a man to be economically independent to get married. As a matter of fact, marriage was not an individual responsibility but rather the joint responsibility of the family. A boy often married at the age of ten or twelve, and his child-wife lived in the house till she reached puberty when the marriage was consummated. Both the boy and the girl, as members of the joint household, were entitled to live under the ancestral roof and share, with others, board and lodging. When the young man entered the ancestral occupation which did not entail his departure from his home he stayed with his wife in the family; when service or business necessitated his leaving his native village or town, he usually went alone, leaving his wife in the household and sending his savings to the head of the family which went to the common pool.

Child-marriage also produced a good many other evils. When married at the age of seven or eight, girls had precious little time for education. Initiation into Vedic literature was, of course, prohibited for women from very early times, but girls in later India had no time for secular education even if they wanted it, not at any rate for learning the art of reading and writing. And as literacy became difficult, conventions arose which made illiteracy holy and knowledge of letters sinful; in medieval India, feminine literacy was considered the accomplishments of prostitutes, and a girl who knew how to read or write was reckoned a menace to society as the art was feared to facilitate intrigue by correspondence with forbidden friends and paramours.

All told, in the later Puranic period, the respectable wife was the most uninteresting companion a virile man could possibly have. Condemned to domestic drudgery, ignorance and premature motherhood, developing, in most cases, physical infirmities or deformities due to early and continued child-bearing, the married woman in respectable households was no fit company for a normal healthy man; and this was in no small measure responsible for the extraordinary high position prostitutes gained in later India and for the hold they obtained even in temples and places of pilgrimage.

The Widow and Sati

Worse than the fate of the child-wife was that of the widow. In the earlier periods in Hindu history, widows, as we have seen, had the right of levirate, divorce, separation and remarriage under certain conditions. But all these were prohibited in the later Puranic period. Manu permitted widow marriage in certain passages and prohibited it in others; apart from the possibility of interpolation, the contradiction might also indicate, as in the *Artha Sastra,* that divorce and remarriage were permissible in the case of Gandharva, Rakshasa and Paisacha forms of marriage and objectionable in the case of the other desirable forms.' Manu's objection to widow marriage as we have seen was that a gift could be given away only once; but in the case of the 'blameable' forms of marriage there was no giving away, and the rites, if any, could not be so binding as a conventional marriage ceremony performed with the mystifying and immutable Mantras.

Anyway, during the period with which we deal, widow marriage came to be strictly prohibited for the three higher castes. The earlier law-givers advised the widow to lead a holy life in memory of her dead husband, to eschew all worldly pleasures, and drudge in the household of her husband for her mother-in-law or sisters-in-law. In certain regions her head was shaved, a custom possibly enforced in imitation of Jain and Buddhist nuns who were not to interest themselves in worldly affairs.

Perhaps the most reprehensible Hindu custom which made India a reproach to contemporary civilisations the world over, was Sati, known to early Europeans as Suttee, and some detailed reference to its origin, development and wide prevalence in later Puranic times will not be out of place here.

In practically all primitive communities, which believed in the survival of personality after death, it was customary to bury, with a dead chief, victuals, cooking utensils, horses, dogs, servants, slaves and wives, for his use or company in the journey to the mysterious unknown regions. The custom of burying live spouses with the dead bodies of important persons was not confined to kings alone. In certain places where women had higher status than men, it was customary to bury with the dead body of a royal lady her live husbands and lovers. The incident narrated in the seventh voyage of Sindbad the Sailor was based on actual facts of history; in Ashanti, for instance, when a king's sister died, handsome youths among her lovers were compelled to commit suicide so that their spirits could accompany the lady.

The practice of sacrificing women on the death of their husbands were prevalent among Gauls, Goths, Celts, Slavs, Thracians and Scythians and others. India developed her social pattern out of the customs of many races who settled down in the country and were admitted into the Hindu fold, and, as we have seen, Sati was prevalent in India among certain clans from the very dawn of history. It would appear that the custom was prevalent among primitive Aryans, but by the Rig Vedic times, it had been given up, possibly because of the need for pressing into service the maximum bearing capacity of women against depopulation through constant wars. Practices reminiscent of Sati were prevalent in Rig Vedic period. In hymn xviii, 8, of the *Rig Veda* we read, the widow was taken to the grave of her husband where she lay with the body but was raised by the hand and led to her house by her brother-in-law.

Though the custom had fallen into disuse among the Rig Vedic Aryans, reports of its prevalence among some tribe or other in India have persisted in Indian literature and in the accounts of foreigners from very early times. We have seen that the Greeks have mentioned the custom as prevailing among the Kathai as early as 317 B.C. Diodorus, who lived in the first century B.C. has not only reported the prevalence of Sati in India, but has left us the following interesting account of its origin.

> Now it was an ancient law among the Indians that when young men and maidens were minded to wed, they did not marry according to the judgement of the parents, but by mutual consent. But when espousals were made between persons of immature age,, mistakes of judgement were of frequent occurrence, and when both sides repented their

> union, many of the women became depraved, and through incontinence fell in love with other men, and when at last they wished to leave the husbands they had first chosen, but could not in decency do so openly, they got rid of them by poison, a means of destroying life which they could readily procure in their country which produces in great quantity and variety drugs of fatal potency some of which cause death if merely introduced as powder into food and drink. But when this nefarious practice had become quite prevalent, and many lives had been sacrificed, and when it was found that the punishment of the guilty had no effect in deterring other wives from their career of iniquity, they passed a law ordaining that a wife, unless she was pregnant or had already borne children, should be burnt along with her husband, and that if she did not choose to obey the law, she should remain a widow to the end of her life, and be for ever excommunicated from the sacrifices and other solemnities as being an impious person.

Whatever the reasons ascribed to Sati by Diodorus, his testimony as to the prevalence of the institution of Sati in ancient India is valid. Earlier Indian literature, as we have seen, just mentioned the institution without praising or condemning it, but from about the eighth century of the Christian era fiery advocates of Sati began to appear.

> Angiras argued that the only course religion had prescribed for a widow is that of Sati. Harita maintains that a wife can purify her husband from the deadliest of sins if she burns herself with his remains; the two will then reside in heaven happily for three and a half crores of years. A passage, interpolated in *Parasara Smriti* observes that just as a snake charmer drags out a snake from a hole by force, in the same manner the Sati takes out her husband from hell and enjoys heaven with him for three and a half crores of years. Even if the wife had led a dissolute life, it would not matter; her immolation, even if not voluntary, will ensure a permanent seat in heaven both in her and her husband.

At first, it would appear, the custom was more prevalent among the Kshatriyas. The *Padma Purana* speaks very highly of Sati, but prohibits it to the Brahmins, and declares that any one helping a Brahmin widow to become Sati would be guilty of the sin of Brahminicide. This would appear to be a reforming attempt, as the *Mricchakatika* seems to approve of Sati for Brahmin women; the objection to Charudatta's wife burning herself, as we have seen, was not against Sati as such but to burning in a pyre separate from her husband's.

The impetus Sati received after the decline of Buddhism in India must be studied against the background of the pseudo-spiritualism that was rising in the country under the aegis of Brahminism. Under the New Dispensation, life was becoming cheap, and certain sections of Hindus were beginning to consider suicide and head-offering as the highest fulfilment of life. While the fighting classes considered it an honour to perish in.the battlefield which ensured Vira-Swargam, (the heaven of heroes), the religious considered it highly meritorious to die in places of pilgrimages, and if nature did not oblige, the pious were anxious to court death by drowning themselves in sacred streams or throwing themselves under the wheels of the charlots of riding gods. Nor were such superstitions confined to the ignorant. Indian philosophers, as we have seen, as a rule offered their heads as the price of defeat in wordy duels. Huien Tsang tells us that a philosopher of the Lokayata sect hung up a written challenge at the gate of Nalanda University for any Buddhist to come and claim his head in a philosophic debate; the Chinese philosopher himself, following the Indian convention, had to offer his head for a stake in a polemic combat, but he saved his head by winning. It can be easily seen hat there was greater merit in a woman's offering her life to accompany her husband to the other world than a philosopher staking his head in metaphysical debates which carry the combatants nowhere.

The spirit of the times also demanded that loyalty and love should be sealed in blood. It was customary among certain royal clans of South India, to burn not only his wives but a large number of his nobles at the time of the death of a king; on a king's accession to the throne, some three or four hundred select adherents were initiated into an order known as 'King's Companions' by eating the rice cooked for the king himself; these devoted men had to burn themselves to death to the last man when the king died or was slain. The institution had the double advantage of promoting loyalty and preventing assassination of kings by his close associates. Sati had possibly its origin among royalty in such a need; the king's harem, as we have seen, was a perpetual source of danger to a king, and when all the women of the royal household had to be burnt with a dead king, chances of plots against his life in the harem were remote.

The Muslim invasion too led to the spread of Sati among the Hindus. Till the Muslim conquest, invaders who settled down in India usually accepted the religious hegemony of India and were assimilated into Indian society; but Islam had clear-cut dogmas which would not easily compromise with Hinduism, and the struggle between the Hindus and Muslims in the initial stages of the Muslim invasion was particularly bitter and violent, as each community considered the other as unredeemed barbarians. The Hindus who were suffering defeat after defeat began to feel, as the Muslims penetrated into the heart of their homeland, that it was better for their women to perish in the flames rather than fall into the hands of the enemy. It was usual among the Rajputs, who had to bear the brunt of the Muslim onslaught, for women to build up pyramids of firewood, the moment their men-folk left for the battlefield, in order to set fire to them and perish in the flames if victory went against them. Thousands of Hindu women died in this terrible rite known as Jawhar, during the bitter days of the Muslim invasion of India.

Such large-scale immolations of women and the devastation the Muslim invasion caused, added not a little to the development of morbid notions about the fleeting and undesirable state of life, and of tendencies that looked for more permanent joys in the life-to-come.

Even after the bitterness caused by the Muslim conquest died down, the institution of Sati came to stay, and throughout the length and breadth of the country rose Sati stones or monuments, erected at the ground made holy by the Sati, with inscriptions that extolled the sainted souls; the earliest of these stones, now extant, dates from the ninth century of the Christian era.

Whatever might have been the general attitude of the Hindus towards Sati during the unhappy days of Muslim conquest, there had been protests against it from many quarters, especially during normal times, and the fact that there was no Vedic sanction for the practice considerably strengthened the position of those who opposed it. But an enterprising Pundit produced the needed Vedic sanction. In the Rig Vedic hymn xviii, 7, which mentions the taking of the widow to the grave of her husband, the word 'agre' meaning end, was altered into 'Agne' (into fire) which yielded the required sanction. Of this perversion of the text, the eminent orientalist Max Muller wrote: This is perhaps the most flagrant instance of what can be done by an unscrupulous priesthood. Here have thousands of lives been sacrificed, and a practical rebellion threatened on the authority of a passage which was mangled, mistranslated, and misapplied."

After the custom was well established in India, it became, more or less, a point of honour with the Hindu widow to mount her husband's funeral pyre, and all sorts of persuasion and subtle coercion were often brought to bear upon a reluctant widow. Sati, moreover, offered a cheap way to sainthood. Not only was she supposed to bring about the salvation of her husband and herself, but she even elevated the spiritual condition of her household and relatives, and every effort was made, by all concerned, to persuade her to take the fatal decision except when pregnancy, babe-in-arms, old age or some other disqualification prevented it.

The institution of Sati became so popular in the later Puranic period and the centuries that followed it that even communities to which it was expressly forbidden adopted it. The ruling chiefs among the Sikhs were partial to it, though it was expressly forbidden by Guru Amardas. In the *Carnatic Inscriptions,* two cases of Sati by Jain women are recorded.

There were certain interesting side-lights to the formal decision of widows to become Sati, out of convention rather than conviction. A Kashmiri historian has recorded two cases of queens who publicly announced their decision to become Satis but privately arranged with their ministers to save them from the cremation ground, and bribed them for the purpose. The arrangement was that the queen should proceed to the burning ground in procession with the avowed intention of burning herself, but the minister should appear at the last moment with a strong body of supporters and forcibly take her away on the plea that her life was indispensible to the good of the state. In the case of queen Didda, we are told, her minister Naravahana saved her as arranged; but in the case of queen Jayamati, her minister Garga took the bride but did not turn up at this burning ground, as he held very privately the view that his country would be better without the queen.

Once Sati was well established, the treatment meted out to those unfortunate women who survived their husbands was such as to condemn them to life-long misery, and many widows left their homes for the comparatively better atmosphere of the street. A thirteenth century Tamil inscription narrating the miseries a widow would be subjected to if she survived her husband, adds: "Those who do not bind her and throw her into fire and kill her, would get the sin of prostituting their wives."

The Muslim scholar Alberuni, a keen observer of the Hindus and their institutions, thus summarised their marriage conventions, in his book on India, written in the eleventh century :

The Hindus marry at a very young age; therefore, the parents arrange the marriage for their sons...Husband and wife can only be separated by death, as they have no divorce.

If a wife loses her husband by death, she cannot marry

> another man. She has only to choose between two things—either to remain a widow as long as she lives, or to burn herself; and the latter eventuality is considered the preferable, because as a widow she is ill treated as long as she lives. As regards the wives of kings, they are in the habit of burning them, whether they wish it or not, by which they desire to prevent any of them, by chance, committing something unworthy of their illustrious husband. They make an exception of only women of advanced years, and for those who have children; for the son is the responsible protector of the mother.

It must, however, be mentioned, that the *Dharma Sastras* were applicable only to the three higher castes, and even among these, traditional customs had as much validity as the laws if not more; the Sudras and other lower castes, among whom marriage was not sacramental, did not, as a rule, observe the laws respecting Sati, though the wealthier among them at times imitated the higher castes. And as the vast majority of Hindus were of non-Aryan castes, Sati even at worst periods, claimed but a small percentage of the total widows in the country.

Devadasis

Another undesirable institution that gained considerable popularity during the later Puranic period was that of temple dancers. These were known as Devadasis or 'slaves of gods' and every temple in medieval India had a large number of them in its service.

In all archaic religions, especially those of ancient Babylon, Egypt and Greece, prostitution held an honoured place, and it was generally pressed into the service of religion mainly to enhance the attractions and profits of well-known shrines. Prostitution itself was not always considered an evil in the ancient world, and priests could find no harm in employing courtesans in the sanctuaries of their pampered gods.

In regions where Greek religion flourished there were numerous temples dedicated to venus the Courtesan, and in keeping with the reputation of the goddess of free love these shrines were the haunts of courtesans and their clients; in the temple of Corinth, we are told, hundreds of prostitutes lived in the precincts of the temple and the main income of the shrine was from these gay women. In ancient Babylon, it was obligatory for every woman of the great city to live, at least once in her life, in the precincts of the temple of Mylitta, the goddess of fertility, and hire herself out to strangers and offer the fees thus collected to the goddess; the young and pretty, we are told, got clients immediately they occupied their quarters, while the elderly and ugly had to wait for days before they could discharge their debt to the goddess. In Egypt, the temples of Isis and Osiris were well known for their orgies, and dancing by professional courtesans formed the main attractions of the great feasts and festivals of these shrines. Moloch, Baal, Astarte and other gods of the ancient world had their orgiac feasts too. The prohibition in *Leviticus* "not to do after the doings of the land of Egypt, nor after the land of Canaan" mainly referred to these practices. In fact, till the Hebraic ideals, expressed through the media of Christianity and Islam, spread to the Mediterranean world, sex was not, in these regions, considered incompatible with religion.

In India, however, prostitution was not associated with the pre-Buddhist Vedic religion, though courtesans are mentioned in Vedic literature. This was not due to any religious antagonism towards prostitution as such, but rather due to the simplicity of Vedic religion and the martial character of vedic Aryans and their gods. The Rig Vedic Aryans were semi-nomads, most of the time on the march, and they had no great temples and pompous rituals. Even in the later Vedic religion with its emphasis on sacrifices, the need for temples had not risen, as sacrifices were usually performed on temporary altars, constructed for each occasion, with attached sheds or halls for the accommodation of priests and the people.

But with the development of the Puranic religion and the regular worship of Shiva, Vishnu and their spouses,. there arose great temples of all over India. These gods had replaced the ancient, hard-riding, Soma-drinking, flesh-eating Indra and his warlike associates. The pleasures of the new gods were of a different nature; they loved ablutions, ornaments, flowers, soft couches of downs, fruits, milk and above all, music and dancing. It was for the pleasure of these gods, to amuse them with song and dance, that courtesans were first employed in Indian temples.

We have seen that the Buddhist scripture and the *Artha Sastra* contain detailed accounts of the high position and wide prevalence of courtesans in ancient India, but neither text mentions their use in the temples. Temples were, at that time, only beginning to come into prominence in India; in the Mauryan period Buddhist shrines were austere institutions where a few monks lived in cells round a simple or ornate stupa, and there were hardly any Hindu temples of importance.

In the *Mahabharata,* however, we find mention of Deva Vesyas or harlots of the gods. It is not clear whether they were actually attached to temples or were merely variations of the Thirthagas (harlots of the sacred waters) who vamped on pilgrims.

By the time of Huien Tsang (seventh century A.D.) the institution of temple-dancers had been well established in India. The sun temples became particularly famous for eroticism, and the Chinese pilgrim saw a large number of dancing girls in the sun temple of Multan. According to the *Bhavishya Purana,* the best way for a man to obtain Surya Loka (heaven of the sun-god) was to dedicate a bevy of dancing girls to a temple of the sun. And many were the plous who sought heaven by this meritorious act.

As a rule, temple-dancers were drawn from the classes of prostitutes every city and town in India had in abundance. But there were other sources of recruitment too. In times of famines, in ancient and medieval India, poor parents often sold their children and temple authorities bought good looking girls and brought them up as devadasis. At times, pious parents who had no children offered their first-born, in case the child happened to be a girl, to the temple in keeping with some special vow. In certain regions in

India, again, unlucky girls were abandoned by superstitious parents and given to temples; a fifth girl was generally considered a bringer of evil to the family, as was also one born at an inauspicious conjunction of stars or with certain mystic marks portending evil, and parents who did not wish such girls to ruin them gave them to the gods who were capable of counteracting their evil influences.

The Abbe Dubois who visited India in the nineteenth century mentioned a peculiar custom prevalent in a South India temple; when the idol was taken out in procession, the priests went among the pilgrims and demanded of their guardians any good looking girls they found; while some of the pilgrims acceded to their request, others, we are told, indignantly turned down the proposal.

All accounts indicate that the institution of the Devadasi was borrowed by the priest from the king. Just as kings employed armies of prostitutes for enhancing their pleasure and pomp, the temples engaged them for singing and dancing before idols, for fanning them during processions, and generally adding to the attraction of temple rituals and feasts. Their sacred duties did not, however, occupy the full time of the Devadasis. Their remuneration from the temple was nominal, and when not engaged in their legitimate duties, they were allowed private practice. They acted in stage shows, danced and sang in social functions held in well-to-do households, and the more accomplished were paid highly. Their wages for granting favours of a more intimate nature were even higher, and the better classes of Devadasis of the later Puranic period were noted for their wealth and liberality like the Ganikas of Vatsyayana's time.

Though, in the earlier stages, the sun temples seem to have specialised in Devadasis, later, temples of all sects had their full complement of singing and dancing girls. As a rule, the number of Devadasis in a temple was in direct proportion to the wealth and prestige of the shrine. The famous temple of Somnath which Mahmud of Ghazni destroyed in the year 1026 A.D. (this temple was dedicated to Shiva) had five hundred Devadasis in its service in order "to provide music before the deity throughout day and night." According to a medieval account, Gujarat had some twenty thousand dancing girls distributed among four thousand temples and their chief function was "to sing twice daily while offering food to the deities and while presenting flowers".

The Tanjore temple built by king Rajaraja in the tenth century had an initial endowment of four hundred Devadasis from the king who gave gifts of land for the maintenance of each. The number, however, did not remain steady; when Sir Monier Williams visited the shrine in the nineteenth century, he found only fifteen Devadasis in the temple, ten of whom performed for him in the temple court-yard.

The general effect of the institution of Devadasis was undesirable, as the more refined among the Hindu population could easily see; it often happened that the fame of a shrine was identified, not with the greatness of the deity of whom it was dedicated, but rather with the charm of his voluptuous attendants who attracted more pilgrims than the deity. And right-minded Hindus often protested against the institution. Alberuni noticed that certain sections of Hindus resented it, but kings, who were patrons of many shrines and had their own parallel institution of court dancers, combined with vested interests, were too powerful for dissenting factions, and the institution of Devadasis flourished in spite of active opposition. Alberuni's statement is supported by internal evidence too. We read in an inscription of the tenth century A.D. by a Rajput chieftain that if the arrangement he had made about the "employment of dancing girls in the temples were interefered with by ascetics and Brahmins, they should at once be stopped".

Throughout the later Puranic period, the institution of Devadasis flourished with unabated vigour. Only with the onslaught of Islam and the destruction of the great temples of the north did it show any sign of decline. In the Vijayanagar kingdom of the south, they flourished with the same vigour as in pre-Muslim India. The European traveller Paes who visited the kingdom wrote about the temple-dancers and courtesans of Vijayanagar.

> They (the Hindus) feed the idol every day, for they say that he eats; and when he eats women dance before him who belong to that Pagoda; all girls born of these women belong to the temple. These women are of loose character and they live in the best streets; it is the same in all their cities; their streets have the best rows of houses. They are very much esteemed and are classed among those honoured ones who are the mistresses of captains; any respectable man may go to their houses without any blame attaching, thereto. These women are allowed even to enter the presence of the wives of the king, and they stay with them and eat betel with them a thing which no other person may do, no matter what their ranks may be.

7

Feminists in India

In all ages, even during the worst periods of the subjection of women in India, there have been spirited women who have exerted their individuality and risen over the times, just as there have been hen-pecked husbands, dominated by their wives. Panchali, as we have seen, though legally the property of her husbands, virtually ruled over them. Similarly, there have been Hindu queens; throughout the historic period, who have influenced their husbands, and the names of some of them appear, jointly with those of their husbands, on coins and charters. For instance, "Kumaradevi, wife of Chandra Gupta, the founder of the illustrious dynasty of the Guptas, was termed Mahadevi—the great queen—and even coins were minted in her name, a privilege accorded only to kings." Again, "Minaldevi, mother of the great Sidharaj Jayasingh ruled over Gujarat at the end of the eleventh century. Rani Durgavati, the Rathod queen of Jodhpur, had not only to rule the state for her infant son but had to defend it against the great Moghul Aurangazeb. Comming to more recent times, Ahalyabai Holkar of Indore was an illustrious woman who ruled on behalf of her adopted son. Rani of Jhansi took part in the Great Mutiny for the injustice the British had done in depriving her of her estate."

In a philosophic dispute held between Sankara and Madanmishra, in the eighth century, the wife of the latter is said to have presided; and what is more important, she gave the decision in favour of Sankara and not her husband.

Nor shall we fail to take note of the celebrated ecstatic Mira, a Rajput princess who left her husband and relatives and, fired with a rare devotion to Krishna, literally sang and danced her way to Mathura, the centre of the Krishna cult. She lived at the time of Akbar when both Hindu and Muslim conventions had fixed the yoke well on the neck of woman.

These, however, are the exceptions that prove the rule. But there were also some organised attempts to raise the position of women in India, with which we may now deal.

The Tantrics

In the scriptures of the Hindus, as we have already noticed, the reader often comes across unexpected passages, usually out of context, which extol women. After pouring calumny on women we are, at times, told immediately after, that women are as good as goddesses. In such contradictions we detect the hidden hand of the Tantric interpolator. The Tantric held the secret view that woman was superior to man while in public he professed the popular opinion about the inferiority of women.

Tantric concepts had existed in India from time immemorial and some scholars are of opinion that the religion of the Indus Valley people was Tantric. Though the *Rig Veda* does not appear to have been favourably disposed towards the Tantric cult, the *Atharva Veda* was considerable Tantric leanings. In the Puranic religion there was an undercurrent of Tantricism, but with the decay of Buddhism in India, the cult came up with extraordinary vigour, and not only Puranic Hinduism but even decadent Buddhism was permeated with its precepts and practices.

The Tantric cult is dominated by sex-magic rites, and as such the more important rituals are practised at night by a select circle of worshippers. The central doctrine of the cult is that the male principle in the universe is inert, and that all active virtues are inspired by the female principle which should be the main object of worship.

> The Yonijas (worshippers of the Yoni or female principle) maintain that the feminine principle is anterior and superior to the male. It is said that Shiva and his wife Parvati had a dispute between them as to the superiority of the sexes, and each one created a race of men. Those who were created by Shiva devoted themselves to the exclusive worship of the male deity; and their 'intellects became dull, their bodies feeble, their limbs distorted and their complexions of different hues'. The race created by Parvati, on the other hand, worshipped the female principle and they 'became powerful, virile and handsome'.

Tantric secret rituals, called Chakrapuja (Circle-Worship), often took the form of the worship of a living woman by a number of men, and indulgence in certain communal sex activities which other sects considered objectionable. As such a Tantric, on initiation, was foresworn not to divulge his true religious affiliation but was to pose in public as a practising Vaishnava or Shaiva.

This double morality of the Tantrics made it difficult for them to openly oppose any practices of Vaishnavas or Shaivas, however much they might have despised them. As the upholders of the superiority of women, the Tantrics held, in private contempt, practices that were injurious to the freedom and status of women, but had to conform to most of these in public, and pay lip-service to the scriptures of Puranic Hinduism and to the *Dharma Sastras*. Their own scriptures, known as *Tantras*, taught different doctrines; these texts were for private circulation only, and could not be published as they contained many magical formulae which were feared to lose their potency if published.

In spite of such secrecy and reticence, some of the less esoteric literature of the Tantrics, that has fallen into the hands of the impious, has been published, and the *Mahanirvana Tantra* is one of these published texts. This Tantra, no doubt is one of the milder ones, but it is sufficiently informative to give us a clear conception of the Tantric attitude towards women.

The *Mahanirvana Tantra* does not condemn older texts that are in conflict with its teachings but merely states that the ancient texts were good enough for a bygone age but not for the current age, a line of argument, as we have seen favoured of all later Hindu legislators.

The duties of a householder are thus enumerated in the *Mahanirvana Tantra*:

> The householder should cherish his wife, educate his children, and support his kinsmen and friends; this is the eternal duty.... The householder should never punish his wife... The wise man whilst his own wife is living, should never, with wicked intent, touch another woman, otherwise, he is sure to go to hell. By riches, clothes, love, respect and sweet words should one's wife be pleased. The husband should never do anything that is unpleasant to her.

Sati is condemned in the *Mahanirvana Tantra* in no unmistakable terms. "A wife should not be burnt with her husband. Every woman is the image of the goddess-she resides concealed in the forms of all women in the world. Hence that woman, who, in her delusion, ascends the funeral pyre of her husband shall go to hell."

Rape of women, according to *Mahaniravana Tantra*, is punishable with death. "A man who ravishes a woman, even if she is a Chandala (outcaste) should be punished with death, and should never be pardoned." Further, "the punishment for those wicked men who have unnatural intercourse with a woman is death."

Even rudeness to women has to be expiated.

> The man who uses offensive language towards a woman who sees the private parts of a woman who is another man's wife or laughs mockingly at a woman, should fast for two days.
>
> If a man talks rudely to his wife, he must fast for a day, if he beats her, he must go without food for three days, and if he causes bloodshed, then he must fast for seven days.

> If a man in his anger or folly calls his wife his mother (meaning she is not his wife) his sister or daughter, then he should purify himself by fasting for seven days.

Further, "he who unjustly forsakes his wife, shall put on ass's skin and beg in seven houses with the words `give alms to one who has left his wife'." A wife so forsaken is even permitted to consort with another man without being considered an adulteress.

The *Mahanirvana Tantra* permits widow marriage and divorce on certain conditions. "If a girl becomes a widow before consummation of marriage, she ought to be married again by her father. This is the command of Shiva." A woman married to an impotent man has the right of divorce and remarriage. Giving away daughters in marriage for money is condemned in the *Tantra* as a heinous sin.

In addition to the eight forms of marriage recognised by the law-givers, Tantric texts mention a form of marriage known as 'Shiva'. This marriage ceremony, a very short one, is generally performed for enabling a Tantric to take part in the secret Circle-Worship when, for any reason, the wedded wife of the worshipper is not admitted into the Circle. The relation between the man and his Shaiva wife is known only to those initiated into the Circle, and the woman, for all practical purposes, is the man's wife, though not living with him. The Shaiva wife and her children have right of maintenance though not of inheritance.

Killing of female victims in animal sacrifices is prohibited to the Tantrics.

Tantric practices were confined to their own sects and there was no attempt on their part to popularise their views, though they interpolated certain ancient texts which showed an inordinate love of running down women. They did not start any campaign against Sati, but among themselves they refrained from burning widows, and many cases of inexplicable refusal of widows to mount the funeral pyres of their husbands must be ascribed to this secret Tantric horror of Sati.

Outspoken Critics of Injustice Against Women

There were, apart from the Tantrics, certain champions of women's right who openly protested against the treatment meted out to women in India. Of these, Varahmihira may be considered the most important and ancient. He lived in the sixth century of the Christian era. He was a great astronomer who wrote many treatises on his special subject. His views on the social problems of the day were not considered authoritative, but some of his writings on sex inequality have come down to us as curiosities of literature. His bitter criticism of the treatment of women in his time has a modern ring in it, and shows that the spirit of chivalry was never dead in India. In the *Brihad Samhita,* he says:

> It is women who adorn jewels, not women who are adorned by jewels. In fact, women are the jewels; there are no greater jewels created by God than the jewel that is woman, that is capable of giving delight to man by sight, by hearing, by speech, by thought and touch. With her, Dharma, Artha and Kama are possible; a son is also possible only through her. Hence the fair sex should be considered the main-stay of society, the home of the goddess of prosperity, and should be held in honour and respect.... Those men, who, without regarding these qualities of women, perpetually rail against them, in ascetic rage, are themselves wicked; their loose talk has no basis. For what fault have women, which is not shared by man? If anything, women have been driven to wickedness by men; women are superior to men in virtue. What does Manu say in this connection? Soma has given them beauty, the Gandharvas, sweet speech, and Agni purity. Hence they are pure as gold. The Brahmins are pure in their feet, the cow on her back, the goat and the dog in the mouth; but women are pure in their whole body. Women are incomparably pure; they are never defiled; their menstrual periods destroy all their impurities. The households in which virtuous women are disrespected are accursed, and are destroyed as if struck by the goddess of destruction. Man is born of woman; hence, O ungrateful ones who slander women,

to whom you owe your very existence, how can you ever be happy? Conjugal fidelity is enjoined on both husband and wife, and its violation by either is censured equally by the *Sastras,* but men disregard this, while women do not; hence women are superior to men. The man who becomes faithless to his wife can only be purified of his sin if he wears the donkey's skin with the hair outside, and beg alms for six months with the announcement: 'I have been faithless to my wife; pray give me alms.' man's sex desire is not abated even when he is a hundred years old; it abates in him only with the loss of virility whereas in women it is controlled by their will. What impudence of those wicked men who indulge in slandering women, which is like the impudence of the thief who accosts the very person he has robbed crying out to him: 'Stop! You thief!' The sweet words a man utters to a woman in privacy, he soon forgets; on the contrary, the woman, out of fidelity, embraces even the corpse of her husband and enters his funeral pyre.

Another fiery advocate of women's rights was the poet Bana who lived in the seventh century. His views on Sati are of particular interest to us. He writes :

> To die after one's beloved is most fruitless. It is a custom followed by the foolish. It is a mistake committed by infatuation. It is a reckless course followed on account of hot haste. It is a mistake of stupendous magnitude. It does no good whatsoever to the dead person; it does not help him in ascending to heaven nor prevent him from falling into hell. It does not at all ensure union with the departed; the person who has died goes to the place determined by his own actions, and the person who immolates on the funeral pyre goes to the hell reserved for those who are guilty of the sin of suicide. On the other hand, by surviving the deceased, one can do much good to oneself and the departed, by offering prescribed oblations for his happiness in the other world. By dying with him one can do good to neither.

Other opponents of Sati were Medhatithi who observed that the custom of Sati, though mentioned by the *Angiras Smriti,* had no authoritative value since it was opposed to a Vedic text which forbade suicide to all, and Virata who pointed out that the widow could do some good to her husband if she survived and offered him the prescribed oblations at the Sharaddha (rites for the departed). "Devanbhatta, a 12th century writer from South India, maintains that the custom of Sati is but a very inferior variety of Dharma and is not recommended at all."

Thus, it can be seen that, from very early times, there were enlightened Hindus who held the view that there was considerable social injustice against women and Sati was an objectionable institution. We have already noticed alberuni's observation that many Brahmins disapproved of the presence of prostitutes in the temples, and kings, who had vested interest in temple revenues, were the main patrons of Devadasis.

With all this, it must be emphasised that, after the collapse of Buddhism, there was no effective organised public opinion in India against Sati and similar institutions, and the general trend of popular feelings was in favour of the subjection of women. The views of those enlightened Hindus who held contrary opinions were generally confined to stray writings and expressions of personal disapproval in private and had very little effect on the population as a whole. For this, the general lack of missionary zeal among the Hindus was mainly responsible. The Hindus, as a people, seldom took the trouble of improving others or converting them to their way of thinking, and the tolerance of a good many superstitions and even human sacrifice, which all right-minded Hindus held to be objectionable, must be explained in this light. If the sage considered Sati as bad, his duty ceased once he gave expression to his views; for the rest he left it to those who had ears to hear and eyes to see to follow him. It was not for him to grant sight to the blind or hearing to the deaf; true these benighted souls might die in their ignorance, but one death did not put an end to life and the ignorant might receive enlightenment in several subsequent births and eventually attain perfection. In the light of this philosophy of patience, reformist and missionary zeal was reckoned vulgar.

Hence for those movement which started the real emancipation of Indian women, we have to look for inspiration, not in the Indian social background, but elsewhere. Here we may take note of a reform movement which made some organised effort to divest medieval Hinduism of many of its undesirable accretions and incidentally worked towards the emancipation of Hindu women. This was the Lingayat movement of southern India.

The Lingayats

The Lingayats sect was founded by Basava, a South Indian Brahmin who lived in the twelfth century A.D. He maintained that Hinduism had fallen from its pristine purity through the ignorance of its teachers, and wished to restore it to its ancient glory. Basava rejected most of the cherished beliefs of the Hindus of his time. He taught monotheism and condemned idolatry and polytheism; the only symbol of godhead his followers were allowed to recognise was the Jangama Lingam, a small soapstone representing the formless Deity, which every Lingayat had to wear on his person. Basava rejected caste and its distinguishing mark, the sacred thread, and every one was free to join his sect and get invested with the Lingam. His most revolutionary religious innovation was the rejection of the doctrine of metempsychosis which even Buddhism and Jainism, the main heterodox persuasions of India, had accepted. The Lingayats rejected cremation and practised burial.

Many scholars have found in Basava's teachings Christian influences. Christianity had been established in southern India from the very beginning of the Christian era and it is possible that Basava came in contact with it; Basava's nephew Channa Basava, who was even a greater zealot than his uncle, is believed to have been immaculately conceived in Basava's sister through the working of the Holy Spirit, a dogma held by the Lingayats. Such similarities between the Christian and the Lingayat conceptions cannot be purely accidental. Anyway, these speculations are not quite relevant to our subject, and we shall see what the Lingayat attitude towards women was.

According to Basava, men are not superior to women; the fair sex is to be treated with respect and kindness; child-marriage and widow-burning are objectionable. While marriages may be arranged by parents, the opinion of the contracting parties is to be ascertained, and no marriage is to be forced on either a girl or boy. Widows should be allowed to be remarried, even when they have children who may be made over to the relatives of the husband. Divorces are permitted on certain conditions.

These teachings, advocated in the twelfth century when the subjection of woman had been complete in India, naturally brought upon Basava and his nephew the ire of the orthodox, and the two and their disciples had to suffer much at the hands of orthodox Brahmins and of Jains who had considerable hold in southern India at the time.

Thé Lingayats started well. The early converts to the faith were inspired by much missionary zeal, propagated their faith among all sections of the Hindu and Jain communities and practised what they preached. Old Brahminism, for some time lay low. But gradually it spread its painless tentacles, and as the zeal of the early teachers died down. Brahminical usages slowly crept into the sect. Caste, that despair of all reformers in India even in the present day, reasserted itself and the better classes of Lingayats began to claim nobler blood than their less fortunate brethren. Conversion was discouraged, especially from lower castes, child-marriages became fashionable among the upper classes and the well-to-do, and even Brahmin priests were invited to fix auspicious days and time for ceremonies most of which had been rejected by the earlier teachers. All told, the Lingayats, for all practical purpose, are, at present, just another sect of the vast conglomeration of peoples who constitute orthodox Hindus.

8

Hindu Women and Society

In regard to the question of the relations of men and women it is wise to be less solemn and more sincere. We tend to fake a part to the world in these deepest matters of life. Where truthfulness and inward integrity should prevail, pretence and artificiality pervade. It is better to face the facts honestly and devise plans which are not too ideals. The pattern of goodness, the code of moral action we set before men, must be such as they can follow. It must be relevant to the world in which we live, where the structure of social habit and behaviour is being undermined, and society is being dissolved and shaped anew.

Men, who are responsible for many of the views about women, have indulged in fantastic stories about their nature and men's superiority to them. They have nearly exhausted their ingenuity in portraying the mystery and sanctity of women, as well as their glamour and instability.

Women in Ancient India

When it is said that the male and the female are like purusa and prakrti, it is meant that they are complementary. The bisexuality of the human race conditions a division of labour. There are certain functions which man cannot undertake. This specialisation does not rob women of their femininity; nor does it spoil the natural relationships of men and women. Man is the creator and woman the lover. Her special qualities are grace and tenderness, peace and affection, surrender and sacrifice. Brutality, violence, anger, rights to spiritual life and discipline. Even when unmarried, men and women have the same claim for spiritual growth.

There was no religious obligation that every girl should be married. To be a wife and a mother is undoubtedly the most important, highly skilled and difficult task that a woman can perform, but one is not to be compelled to do it. Democracy is not so much a form of government as the recognition of the value of the individual, whether he be man or woman, outcaste or criminal. There is right through the realisation that, for some spirits, it is possible to achieve their aims when they lead a single life, and that the pleasures of love and marriage, like those of social life, are distractions from the life of spirit. If there are persons who are content with celibacy, if they are inclined to it by nature, if they wish to be left alone and undisturbed, there is no reason why society should not let them have their single freedom. It is unfair to force them to a domesticity for which they are not suited. The whole tradition of school and society, small talk and the selfishness of parents who wish to see themselves perpetuated, the fear of not having any successor to pray for one's soul, the so-called 'dharma', force even unwilling individuals into marriage. Latterly, however, on account of economic and other conditions, unmarried people are on the increase.

There are, however, a few women who are of a 'masculine' type, energetic and ambitious. They fight for the prizes of life, and are interested in sports and politics. They try to avoid all relations of love and marriage. If by accident they enter into such relationships, they strive to be superior to their husbands and disturb the harmony of married life. They take pride in proving that they never developed a talent for domesticity. Though these cases are few, society will have to allow for them. Such 'masculine' women do not reach the highest of which womanhood is capable.

Seclusion of women was unknown. Young girls led free lives, and had a decisive voice in the selection of their husbands. On festive occasions and at tournaments (samana) girls appeared in all their gaiety. Women had a share in the property of the father, and they were sometimes allowed to remain unmarried, with their parents and brothers. The *Atharva Veda* refers to daughters remaining with their parents until the end of their lives. A part of the ancestral property is given to them as dowry, which becomes their own property, and is called stridhana in later writings.

In the Epic period, women did not suffer from any special disabilities. They practised austerities and wore garments (valkala). Dhritavrata, Srutavati, Sulabha remained unmarried and pursued the life of spirit.

Under the shadow of the great ideal of sannyasa, the weaknesses of women were exaggerated as a warning to monks. To encourage renunciation, women were despised as the source of worldliness. Hemacandra looks upon them as "the torch lighting the way to hell." According to a great religious tradition, scarcely had woman been created than she was accused in the revealing sentence : "The woman tempted me." Christian Europe has been brought up on the belief that death would have been unknown but for the unkindness of women. She was accused of treachery, backbiting and tempting men to their doom. But Varahamihara (sixth century (A.D.) urges that the pursuit of the ends of dharma (righteousness), and artha (wealth), depends on women, and that they are essential for human progress. He complains against the other-worldly, who overlook the good qualities of women and emphasise their weaknesses. The faults of women are the faults of men also. To speak the truth, they have more virtues than men can claim.

Left to themselves, without the guidance of any tradition, women are neither more not less constant than men. Their sexual tendencies are no less variational than those of men. Woman is hatred are not her typical features. Masculine dominance is not natural. There were ears and forms of society in which masculine domination was not nearly so certain as we ignorantly assume. The fruits of grace will save woman more effectively than the masculine virtues. The differences are essential and are meant for mutual education. The Zulu dictionary defines man as an animal trained by women. She is essentially the educator of man, both when he is a child and an adult. The *Aitareya Brahmana* says: "because the father is born again of his wife (jayate punah) she is called jaya. She is his second mother." *Gitagovinda* opens with a verse where Radha is enjoined to lead Krsna home, to further the fulfilment of his nature, as he is a timid child. When the sky is overcast with clouds, the path of the future lies through a thick forest, and when we are utterly alone in darkness without a single ray of light, when all around are difficulties, we place ourselves in the hands of a loving woman.

The female child is called by the name duhitr, which is the English daughter, and the term indicates the prominent duty of milking the cow. Weaving and needlework, household duties and watching the crops, are her main duties. Education was regarded as quite important. While Brahmin girls were taught Vedic wisdom, girls of the Ksatriya community were taught the use of the bow and arrow. The Barhut sculptures represent skillful horsewomen in the army. Patanjali mentions the spearbears (saktikis). Megasthenes speaks of Chandragupta's bodyguard of Amazonian women. Kautilya mentions women archers (striganaih dhanvibhih). In the houses as well as in the forest Universities of India, boys and girls were educated together. Atreyi studies under Valmiki along with Lava and Kusa, the sons of Rama. Fine arts like music, dancing and painting were specially encouraged in the case of girls. Till recently, women proved themselves capable of performing efficiently work which is generally assigned to men. Yet till today the view persists that women are inferior to men in intellectual competence. A Chinese proverb says: "A man thinks he knows, but a woman knows better."

In the Vedic age the highest expression of religion is the sacrifice. Husband and wife both took part in it. Prayers and sacrifices were offered jointly by them. Girls had upanayana performed for them and carried out the sandhya rites. "A young daughter who has observed brahmacarya should be married to a bridegroom who is learned like her." Sita is mentioned as performing sandhya rites. Harita holds that women are of two classes, brahmavadini and sadyovadhu. The former do not get married and so study the Vedas and perform the prescribed rites, and the latter have the upanayana performed about the time of marriage. Yama is quoted to show that girls in past ages had the girdle, studied the Veda and recited the hymns. Manu holds that marriage should be regarded as the substitute for upanayana for girls, but in view of the past practice, and the spirit that husband and wife are complementary halves of one whole, the two should have the same not an innocent lamb, nor is man a devouring monster. In early times promiscuity was the fashion, and it was not regarded as sinful. Women used to go about as they liked. Whenever conditions permitted, they rejected the monogamous relationship. Among the natives of Victoria, the women have so many lovers that it is almost impossible to tell the true paternity of the children. In Arabia and Madagascar women of rank, despite a marital connection with only one man, have many lovers. The burden of child-bearing inclines woman to the monogamous life. If freed from economic subservience, she is not likely to be more monogamous than man. A monogamy which is interrupted by frequent divorces is only nominal. There are references in the *Mahabharata* to regions where promiscuity prevailed, the land of the Uttarakurus and the city of Mahismati. It is sanctioned by precedents and praised by great sages. The *Mahabharata* says that Svetaketu felt mortally wounded when his mother was taken in hand by another Brahmin in the presence of his father, who quietly declared that this was ancient usage. He said: "The women of all classes on earth are free, O son; men in this matter, as regards their respective classes, act as kine." Svetaketu is given the credit for supplanting promiscuity by regular marriage. A single standard for both men and women was then laid down. "The wife who does not adhere to her husband will be sinful from this date; she will commit as great and heinous a sin as the killing of an embryo. The men who will go to other women, neglecting a chaste and loving wife who has observed from her youth the vow of chastity, will commit the same sin." Monogamous marriage is not a natural condition, but a cultural state. The traces of promiscuity belong the pre-Vedic stage, as the institution of marriage is well established by the time of the *Rg Veda*.

Marriage became an obligation to women, possibly as a reaction against Buddhism and Jainism. Dirghatamas ruled that women should not remain unmarried in future. Manu argued that woman should have all the sacraments, but without the Vedic formulas. The only Vedic sacrament for them is marriage. The smrtis condemn prolonged celibacy, and exalt the householder's status. A wifeless man is not eligible for sacrificial rites. It is in *Manu* and the *Dharmasastras* that the doctrine of the perpetual dependence of women on men is enunciated. For them woman is a fragile plant, to be cared for and nourished by man. The later commentators revel in increasing the restrictions on women. We, however, get exalted ideas of womanhood even in *Manu,* not to speak of poets like Kalidasa, Bana and Bhavabhuti. Though there are certain passages which declare that the woman has not equal rights with man for Vedic duties, the main view is that she is entitled to perform them, either as wife along with the husband, or as maiden independently. When later her position deteriorated, the bhakti religion arose, satisfying all the religious needs of women.

In spite of heavy disabilities from which they suffered, women enjoyed certain advantages. They are not to be killed, whatever be their crimes; they are not to be abandoned, even when guilty of adultery. Gautama prescribes that a wife guilty of adultery should undergo a penance, and be kept under guard. Vasistha says that "the wives of Brahmins, Kshatriyas and Vaisyas, who commit adultery with a Sudra, may be purified by a penance if no child is born, but not otherwise."

Love in Human Life

The great achievements of the world have for their inspiration a woman's love. Geniuses like Kalidasa, conquerors like Napoleon, scientists like Michael Faraday, and many other world-makers and world-forsakers, bear witness to the important part played by love in their lives. What stirs lyrical poets to their finest flights is the delight of the senses, the fruitful contentment as well as the fatal passion of love. A woman was the centre of the conflict between Rama and Ravana in the *Ramayana,* and the Trojan war was fought for the possession of a woman. The impulse of love is the fire at the heart of life itself; it is the voice of all creativeness. Many have missed achieving their life's work, worthy of their talents, for lack of a beloved presence by their side. The *Divina Commedia* was inspired by the love that Dante treasured for Beatrice, even when she had become the wife of another. The immortal poems of Candidas were inspired by his love for a young peasant girl; and a queen was the inspiration of Vidyapati's songs. Beethoven poured out his rhapsodies to the "immortal beloved."

In discussing the relations of men and women, Hindu legislators avoid the extremes of prudery and prurience. That famous student of sex, love and marriage, Havelock Ellis, writes that in India "sexual life has been sanctified and divinised to a great extent than in any other part of the world. It seems never to have entered into the heads of the Hindu legislators that anything natural could be offensively obscene, and singularity which pervades all their writings, but is no proof of the depravity of their morals. Love in India, both as regards theory and practice, possesses an importance which it is impossible for us even to conceive."

While nature provides the raw material, the human mind works on it. Without this our sex life would be as uninteresting as that of apes and dogs. When the natural instinct of sex is guided by brain and heart, by intelligence and imagination, we have love. Love is neither mystic adoration nor animal indulgence. It is the attraction of one human being to another, under the guidance of the highest sentiments. Marriage, as an institution, is a device for the expression and development of love. Marriage is not a mere convention, but an implicit condition of human society. Though its ideals have changed, it seems to be a permanent form of human association. It is an adjustment between the biological purposes of nature and the sociological purposes of man. Whether it is successful or not depends on the way it is worked. It can lead us to an earthly paradise, or in certain conditions it may turn out to be an organised hell.

The present tendency is towards greater individual freedom.

Restraints, physical and moral, are not popular. As our knowledge of the unconscious and of the nature of repression increases, conventional morality is becoming suspect. To the invitation to contribute to *The Book of Marriage,* edited by Count Hermann Keyserling, Bernard Shaw replied: "No man dare write the truth about marriage while his wife lives. Unless, that is, he hates her like Strindberg: and I don't. I will read the volume with interest, knowing that it will consist chiefly of evasions." On the social side increasing industrialisation and the democratisation of culture are diminishing the significance of the family life. Women are becoming economically independent; social and political privileges are getting equalised, and attempts are being made to endow motherhood. All this is likely to introduce radical changes in the pattern of domestic life.

If we are to think usefully on an ancient institution like marriage, if we are to distinguish the essential from the accidental, we should analyse the several tendencies and motives that have led to the origin and growth of the institution. We will then discover that many of the things we value in marriage, and in sex relations generally, are impositions of law or custom framed by our intellect and imagination.

So far as the origin of the institution of marriage is concerned, neither romantic love nor animal lust is at its basis. There was no reason for primitive man to limit his freedom in the exercise of the sexual instinct. He did not place any value on the chastity of woman or the paternity of man. He knew neither sexual jealousy nor romantic love. Primitive marriage was based on the subjugation of woman, and its durability rested on economic necessity, not on evanescent passion. Anthropologists tell us that the primitive husband willingly lent his wife, in her capacity of sex mate, to any guest as the merest act of hospitality. But he was jealous of his ownership of her as a worker. With the development of a more settled life, and the accumulation of possessions, the desire to perpetuate ownership through legitimate heirs gave additional support to the institution of marriage. Soon, with the growth of civilisation, the recognition of the wife as a person, not merely as a slave labourer or propagating animal, arose with far-reaching effects on the institution of marriage.

Physical Basis

To look upon sex as something unclean or indecent is a sign of moral perversion. Freud's emphasis on the sex basis of human life, though exaggerated, is not incorrect. Sexual instincts are not inherently disgraceful. The Hindu view has no sympathy with the relentlessly severed attitude adopted by Christianity. Jesus did not marry; and the whole idea of immaculate conception indicates that there is something unclean about normal sex life. "Marriage peoples earth," said St. Jerome, "but virginity heaven." He writes: "There are virgins in the flesh who are not in the spirit, whose body remains untouched but whose soul is corrupt. Only a virginity which has never been soiled, by a desire either of flesh or of the spirit, is a worthy offering to Christ." If we are to be perfect, we must cut out sex life and the normal family affections. Our vision and hope are restricted to a relative perfection. In the imperfect condition of married life, we are to live perfectly.

On the other hand, the Hindu looks upon sex life as sacred. The *Ramayana* opens with a curse on the hunter who separated the two birds lost in the ecstasy of sex union. Sex is not a disease or a perversion, but a natural instinct. The Hindu view exalts the state of the householder. As all living beings depend on the support of the mother, so do all the stages of life depend on the support of the householder. "The house is not the home, it is made by the wife; a home without a wife is to me like a wilderness." Home is not what is made of wood and stone; but where a wife is, there is the home." The Hindu view does not suffer men and women to become saints, striving for a vacuous perfection. It does not make of sexual abstinence an absolute virtue. If we do violence to natural forces, they will sooner or later seek their revenge. The author of the *Kama Sutra* gives us an account of the different sides of sexual life and attraction, presents us with those stirrings of the human heart that make life so full and poignant. His whole account, with its ardent love of life and passionate spiritual serenity, has nothing in common with the abstinence solicited by the votaries of suffering. Spiritual freedom is to be secured, not by the arbitrary suppression of desires, but by their judicious organisation. To purge the spirit from the dross of the flesh is not to destroy the flesh. Celibacy is like the ascetic discipline of fasting, and other quietings of the body. It is dangerous, since it recalls the mind to the subject which it would like to avoid. It produces a negative sort of bondage. The highest ideal, even in sex matters, is that of non-attachment, to use the relations when valuable and forgo them without trouble.

In Hindu practice marriage is not only tolerated, but extolled. The ascetic tendency to impose dangerous restraints on life is denounced. God, who made us male and female, is not to be mocked. Austere ideals of sanctity, which require us to save our souls at the risk of destroying the species, are opposed to our natural instincts. Though the physical urge is not to be mistaken for anything deep or permanent, it is essential as the basis on which a durable and satisfying relation is built. If the physiological aspects are unsatisfactory, marriages turn out unsuccessful. But they are not enough. Kant's definition of marriage as "the tying together of two persons of different sex to a lifelong reciprocal procession of their sexual qualities" is defective. If it were true, marriage would be dissolved with the coming of sexual frigidity. Even as life is not physiology, love is not sex. Gratification of sex impulses is not like taking a cup of coffee. It is not a trivial, inconsequential event which leaves no memory behind it. It results in affection, friendship and love. The casualness of modern sex life is a sign of growing vulgarity.

In man sex has acquired certain peculiar qualities. Man has no periodicity. He eats without being hungry, drinks without being thirsty, and indulges in sex at all seasons. This privilege is shared by the large ape, the orthograde primate. Secondary sexaul characteristics acquire primacy over the central features. We fall in love with a face, or eyes, or brains. The impulse can turn back toward the same sex. Human beings are capable of protracted parental care. Few animals care for the young. The partnership between the dog and the bitch is of short duration. The crane and its female take interest in the young, and so their relationship is of longer duration. But as soon as the young grow up, the relationship of the parents to the young is forgotten. There are no such ties as those of brother and sister.

The basic urges of human nature must be fulfilled. For normal people an intimate relation with an individual of the other sex is a necessity. Biologically, the failure to satisfy the sex instinct leads to nervous instability; psychologically it results in emptiness and misanthropy. Here and there, there may be individuals like John the Baptist, Jesus, St. Paul, or Samkara, who are able to divert the life-energy from its natural course, and use it for spiritual achievement; but for the vast majority of men and women, and for the race as a whole, the sex relation is one of the most urgent and important.

Racial Factor

What Fabre calls the "universal instinct of maternity" is the most marvellous side of even animal life, where we find love and sacrifice and protection of the weak. Even the ferocious tiger becomes a tender mother. The Hindu scriptures speak of the three debts we have to pay: to the risis by Vedic study, to the gods by sacrifices, and to ancestors by offspring. "Gifts that were made by a childless woman robbed the receiver of his life powers." "As long as man is not united to a wife, he is only half a man; the home that is not surrounded with children is like a graveyard." The feeling for the continuity of the family is one of the strongest of social forces. The family is a cell in the social body, and if the cell loses the desire to reproduce itself the race dies. France fell, said Petain, because France had too few babies. A declining birth-rate is a symptom of that indifference to the future which we find in the final phase of a dying civilisation. "Do not cut off the thread of offspring" is the advice of the Upanisad, and it must be followed if the race is to survive. Without children, the sex union, however, beautiful and sacred, will remain incomplete. Sterility is one of the grounds on which marriage with another woman is sought to be justified.

Marriage is more a social charter of the establishment of a legitimate family that a licence for sexual intercourse. The mutual attachment between husband and wife becomes stronger when a child is born. They may hurt and hate each other; but something stronger than their whims, something more enduring than their quarrels and hatred, has grown up between them. The parental instinct for the welfare of the child is common to both parents. This unity of interest is not artificial. It is the expression of a basic truth in human nature, nay, all nature, which has planted in the mother heart and enduring affection and readiness for self-sacrifice. Parenthood helps to build lifelong emotional bounds and complex cultural ties on biological foundations Social relationships of mutual obligation and service are established by its means. By the time the biological needs get weakened, affection for the children grows up; and through the exercise of parental affection we acquire a knowledge of the world and inward experience. Children are a source of spiritual sustenance to the parents.

The birth of a son was sought with eagerness and that of a daughter was looked upon with disfavour, possibly because, in the struggle for existence against physical forces, men were more useful than women. In patriarchal societies, and in primitive conditions, a son is economically more valuable than a daughter. This does not mean that parents loved their daughters less. Cultured people even then adopted a more healthy view. An educated daughter is the pride of the family. As interest in ancestor worship increased, sons alone were regarded as eligible for offering oblations to the *manes*. There is also the difficulty of procuring suitable husbands, and even after marriage there is a large element of chance in regard to the future. This difficulty of securing happiness for girls is the cause of preference for boys, and not any unfairness to the female sex.

Not all women have the maternal instinct. Some are better wives than mothers. The two are quite distinct. There are women who want sexual life without motherhood, and women with little or no sexual desire who want motherhood. The two tendencies attempt to be reconciled in the institution of marriage.

Friendship

Men and women are not superior animals, nor is the aim of marriage mere stock-breeding. Love is not a narcotic where the two are lost in each other and the biological level; nor are human beings mere instruments of race-preservation. Apart from the biological side, there is the need for comradeship which marriage supplies. There is the desire for awareness, for communication, for the sharing of intellectual pleasures, for tenderness, in short, for completeness of experience. We cannot live entirely to ourselves. We do want friends; but friendship is of spurious value if we cannot communicate and exchange our deepest ideas. If we succeed in getting friends in whom we have absolute confidence, with whom we can share our innermost thoughts and feelings, we deepen our individuality. If, on the other hand, we enter into relations with others, just to escape from the bonds of our individuality, it is a form of self-indulgence, a mere relief from boredom. We relinquish our life at the centre for a doubtful one at the periphery. Love, according to Rainer Maria Rilke, "consists in this, that two solitudes protect and touch and greet each other." When Omar cries:

Here with a Loaf of Bread beneath the Bough,
A Flask of Wine, a Book of Verse — and Thou

Beside me singing in the Wilderness — he means that he cannot live or enjoy life unless she is 'beside' him. It is good companionship. The song on the lips expresses staunchness, truth, loyalty and loving care, things that we strive after and seldom reach. Friendship is different from sexual attraction. Society of intelligent and sympathetic women for men, and of men for women, cannot be forbidden. As it cannot be had purely at the Platonic level, wives are expected to be friends also. It is said that "the wife should be of one mind with the husband, like a shadow, should be his companion in all good works, and should always remain cheerful and be mindful of household duties." The married woman of the *Rg Veda* is the comrade (sakhi) of the husband and has similar interests. What is called psychological complementation, or temperamental affinity, enables community of thought and feeling to arise and grow. Intellectual and aesthetic fellow-feeling, similarity of value scales, provide a promising starting-ground for a truly successful marriage. More even than community of ideas and aspirations, the sharing of sorrow serves as the foundation of human sympathy. Marriage does not aim, however, at producing identical individuals. Differences must be there, even as the difference of sex is there to start with. Only they must not be too great. If one is anaemic and the other fiery, if one is unimaginative and the other adventurous, the marriage will not be a success. The two should supplement each other, so that each is assisted to discover the self and grow into a genuine individual, and the two together achieve a harmony. The marriage relation is intended to contribute to both life and mind. While woman is entangled more in the activities which life has assigned to her, man is engaged more in the creations of mind. It is vital national service, to work hard, to serve and rear a family. If woman is engaged in activities which prejudice the work of preservation, she comes into conflict with her own inner nature. She is the giver of joy and the inspirer of activity, and she cannot do her part successfully if she imitates man. The modern woman is discontented with her role of child-bearing and home-making, and wishes to devote herself to some other 'higher' activity. While we should extend to women opportunities for education and employment, her main business will still be mother hood and the making of home.

If the institution of marriage does not provide for this essential relation of friendship, escapes are devised. In the great days of Athens, Pericles had for his concubine an accomplished Milesian woman, Aspasia. Demosthenes said in open court that "every man requires besides his wife at least two mistresses."

Love

The biological, the racial and the human elements are the foundations on which we attempt to build the beautiful temple of the creative life of the spirit. Love is more than sexual ease, propagation of the species or comradeship. It is a personal matter, in which intimate ties which are more valuable than the satisfaction of an animal need, or the founding of a family or selfish happiness, are found. Through love we create a spiritual reality, and develop our destiny as persons, through the pleasures of the flesh, the happiness of the mind and the joy of spirit. The tempests of the heart are taken over into the calm of the soul. Love is not merely flame meeting flame, but spirit calling to spirit.

In the concrete field of human life, equality is invaluable. The laws about marriage must be equal, no doubt; but at some point or other we have not only to acquiesce but delight in inequality. In true love there is that absolute surrender which alone can make it a success. Pure love asks for nothing in exchange. It throws itself out without restriction or reservation. It makes light that otherwise is heavy. It carries a burden without feeling its weight. It is never weary, considers nothing impossible, and is ready to suffer all things. Such love is eternal. We have it in the depths of our soul, a sacred inviolable flame, which we can carry to the end or our lives. Such love has nothing in common with human desire, low, brutal, selfish, violent or petty, or feelings brittle, superficial, exacting. It is the force sent down to earth that the earth might get back to heaven. Such a communion of mind and spirit, as well as of body, is immortal. It is the purest relation which makes us inwardly complete and contented. Love is all that one can call one's own. It is the one treasure of life, for everything else in life has been communised. It is life's supreme blessing, however, bitter its afflictions may be, however, lamentable its defects.

For most of us marriage is only a pairing, a resolve to tolerate each other for breeding purposes, a determination to live together on the principle of give and take. But once in a way a man and a woman meet whose lives are in complete accord; and such people live together for ever. True love is a union of soul and body, so close and so firmly established, that one feels that it will last as long as life lasts. It is a relationship so deep and binding, so gripping the heart by its tenderness, so transforming the life by the intensity of its fevour, that the thought of a second relationship of the same kind is a sacrilege. Savitri was asked by her father to choose another husband, as the one chosen by her was fated to die early; she answered: "Be he long-lived or short-lived, endowed with good qualities or utterly lacking in them, once my husband has been chosen by me, I will not choose another." Hanuman, who met Sita, who is said to be really devamaya born to bring about the defeat of raksasa maya, tells Rama that she is pining away in Lanka, and when he met her she was resolved on death. And yet Rama, after the victory over Ravana, looks at Sita filled with you and love as well as a sense of shame, and tells her that it was not his love for her that made him engage in war and win victory, but the desire to protect the good name of himself and his house. " I do not wish to take you back, you may go wherever you please, to Laksmana, Bharata, Sugriva, or Vivhisana." There are some who say that these shocking verses were a later interpolation. They indicate that the best of us are blundering amateurs in love and suffering, while women are supreme artists. When Sita is discarded by her husband, she says, according to Kalidasa, that "I shall, after the birth of the child, so try to practise asceticism with my eyes fixed on the Sun, that in the next life I may have you for my husband without separation." Those women are the greatest lovers who grow beyond the need of any love in return, who can say to the man who deserts them: "my love no longer depends on the way you treat me." Has not Spinoza taught us that to love God without expecting any return is the highest and purest love? For normal human beings, however, love requires to be shared.

Love is not something we command. The relationship between the two persons is exclusive and no other person can enter. Infidelity destroys the nature of a person, for it attempts to undo what has been the fulfilment of one's personality. This view of marriage is a matter of culture. For there are tribes where it is a mark of hospitality to offer one's wife to a stranger, and where it is legitimate for the wife to add to the family income. But there is a general reluctance on the part of most husbands to share their wives with others: and developed cultures foster the monogamic ideal.

Marriage is the easy, but not the only, way by which we can merge our natural instinct with the spirit to form a higher union. It has for its aim human fulfilment, the development of personality through love, which is an enduring bond. We undertake married life not for the sake of natural passion,, but for the sake of the spirit, atmanastu kamaya, for increasing the wealth of spirit, the richness of satisfaction. Under the spirit of love, our eager minds absorb impressions with new zest, all the senses thrill with keener joy, as if an unseen spirit had renewed all the colours of the earth, and inspired each living thing with a new vitality. It is possible to have love disengaged from the senses, not too much enslaved by the body, where the spirit dominates the roving animal in us. We love not the woman or the man, but the person behind ; not the position, fortune or employment, not the beauty, grace or charm, but the person. Marriage is the union of two independent and equal persons, striving through mutual relationship to attain a self-development which neither could achieve in isolation. Dissimilarity is there, and we must penetrate as deeply as possible into it. "The more we understand individual things the more we understand God," says Spinoza. No man can love God perfectly if he has not loved well a creature of God in this world. There is no source of happiness so sure and true as the love of one human being for another. Through in we become wiser than we know, better than we feel, nobler than we are. The heart in its hunger and helplessness feels that it must love at any cost, if only to know that it does not exist for nothing. The way to heaven is through earthly love full of woes and watered with tears.

The great God is said to have divided himself into the twofold aspect of husband and wife. Man is not a complete being without his woman. Husband and wife from one whole. The wife is ardhangi, half-self; Mahadev and Parvati are represented in one body in many places in India. Love requires a blending of two essentially different, solitary individuals through physical understanding, intellectual kinship and spiritual comprehension. Man and woman are not only one flesh but one spirit; not that they are identical in tastes and outlook, but harmonious. As the spiritual end receives empirical content, marriage is said to be sacramental. We aim at the union of two persons who love each other. They are of fulfilled desire (aptakama), and so of no desire (akama). This deep and tender communion is the best protection against any lapse. When we are with one whom we !ove deeply we are satisfied, and do not ask shy we live or why we were born. We know that it is for love and friendship that we are born.

Marriage and Love

There are marriages which remain at the biological level. They are cases not of love, but of sexuality or animal desire, cold and calculating. Sorrow at the death of a partner means more "regret for a lost habit than a lost person." If marriage is regarded only as a duty and convenience, it becomes a utilitarian institution of limited purpose. It imposes on natural man a restraint which is felt as such, because love is not there. Even marriages which are formed by the desire for riches and position may soon develop into something richer and deeper. The pleasures of affectionate union may grow up. To be one's wife is an accident; to be in love is the reality.

There is a view which holds that there is something fatal to marriage in the very nature of the institution. We seem to hanker after unhappiness. Teh forbidden fascinates us. Unorthodox love accounts for a good deal of human unhappiness—renunciation, compromise, separation, remorse and rebellion. Novels and pictures exaggerate the erotic aspects of life, which are regarded as a relief from mechanical boredom; illicit sex relationships seem to be the chief occupation of civilised peoples.

Deep love is sometimes confused with explosive passion. We think that we live more fully and intensely when we have a passionate experience, a giddiness, a cloud without discernment, without choice. It is looked upon as a transfiguring force, something beyond pleasure and pain, an ardent, fever, a frenzied living, which cuts across conventions and breaks all laws in the name of something elemental and sublime. There is something tragic about such relations, which are more exhausting than helpful. When we are under the power of passion, we are not ourselves. Passion is the enemy in our own hearts that we have to contend with. It is a morbid excess, a force of nature that seizes lovers and generally ends by destroying them. Love is no paroxysm. It is inward and deep surrender and identification with the beloved. We must not equate the sublime with the trivial; the hectics of passionate love are not to be confused with deep affection.

In his *Phaedrus* and *The Symposium,* plato speaks of a frenzy that, spreading from the body, infects the spirit with malignant humours. This sort of love he does not commend; but there is another kind of frenzy or delirium, which is neither conceived nor born in a man's soul except by the inspiration of heaven. It is alien to us, its spell is wrought from without, it is a transport, an infinite rapture away from reason and natural sense. It is called enthusiasm, which actually means "possessed by God," for the frenzy is not only of heavenly origin, but culminates at its highest in a new attainment of the divine. It is both madness and supreme sanity.

The ideal woman is the symbol of love drawing us away to the highest. We should not look upon woman as a mere means to pleasure. She is, it is true, a female; she is also a helpmate; but she is first and foremost a human being. With a sanctity and mystery about her, she is not to be treated as a mere chattel, or maidservant or housekeeper. She has a soul, and is for man generally the bridge to reality. If we make her a mere house-wife or a mother, and debase her to the service of common things, the best in her does not find expression. Every woman must have the chance, like every man, to develop the fire of passion, the transports of the heart and the flame of spirit. Tagore's Chitra exclaims: "I am Chitra. No goddess to be worshipped, nor yet the object of common pity to be brushed aside like a moth with indifference. If you deign to keep me by your side in the path of danger and daring, if you allow me to share the great duties of your life, then you will know my true self." The institution of marriage must recognise this. Happy love has no history, and we talk about it only when it is unfortunate and doomed by life itself.

There is an unformulated assumption that love and marriage are incompatible. It is sometimes asked: "What does a married man know of love?" "They could not have been married, for they are so interested in each other." Marriage is not the grave of love, but only a savage love or sensuality, as Croce says. The two go together when the aim is fulfilled; but the path is long and difficult. Love is not the starting-point of marriage relationship, but an achievement to be won by effort and endurance. Failures in married life are more common among those who start with a false ideal, determined by the excitement of early love and rapturous happiness. When the novelty of marriage wears off, the excitement of fresh experiences and romantic dreams is followed by the dullness and routine of life; the romantic lover is lost in the habitual husband, and the wild exuberance settles down to domestic contentment. Marriage is not an everlasting round of roses and dreams; it is a preparation for a quiet happiness. Pleasure is of the moment, and the accidents of time and peace affect it. The decay which awaits all mortal things has the power to destroy beauty of body and the fire of passion, but not the imperishable element of the happiness which is the reward of austerity. What we desire is not the body, which is an illusory and fleeting aspect of the actual complete life. The fidelity of the married couple is the acceptance of one's fellow-creature, a willingness to take the other in all particularity. After a few years the early rapture and wild excitement are replaced by trusting companionship, shared work and interests, tolerance and understanding. Happiness in marriage requires a generous self-abandonment, endless tolerance and gentleness, politeness of the heart.

The idea that marriage gives a proprietary right to each other is inimical to the development of true love. The very sense of security diminishes the passion. Habit deadens the perception, kills the emotions, and blinds the soul alike to satiety and to loss.

A faithfull monogamous marriage is the ideal to be aimed at, though its realisation is difficult. The great romances of the world are those of faithful love. It is fidelity through suffering and pain that has moved and won the homage of the world. One of the greatest minds of the world said that "the course of true love never did run smooth," though we may settle down to it by a happy accident, if we are lucky. Marriage is an art which involves both pain and joy. The difficulties of life do not not end, but begin, with marriage. It takes two to make marriage a success, but one can make it a failure. It is a partnership in which patience is called for; not an experiment, but a profound experience which, though tender and fragile at first, grows through pain and strain. Draupadi tells Satyabhama that "happiness is not derived from happiness, but a good woman experiences happiness through suffering". A woman unscarred by trouble is incomplete, for she lacks the consecration of suffering. Uma won Siva not through her personal beauty, but through austerity and suffering. Women have a genius for suffering, and if they are not true to it, they lose their great gift of cherishing life. Kalidasa in his *Sakuntala* shows how two loving souls are worked through suffering into shape, and moulded into fitness for each other. The gods are strange. They bring us to trouble through what in us is good, gentle, humane and loving. They send us sorrow to fit us for larger things. Centuries of tradition have made the Indian woman the most unselfish, the most self-denying, the most patient and the most dutiful woman in the world, whose pride is suffering.

Marriage is not an end in itself. It is the normal means of gaining self-fulfilment. Human relations are the most personal part of our lives, in which we can be ourselves completely. In our public life only parts of our being operate. Our personal life, which is love and fellowship, has no purpose beyond itself. It is natural for human beings to share their experience, to understand one another, to find joy and satisfaction in mutual confidence. Such relationships do not serve partial or limited ends and do not exist for society, but society and its laws exist for them. There are groupings of people, which are not personal, where the place of the individual is determined by his function in the group, by the particular service which he renders to the welfare of the whole. When we associate with others to achieve some common ends which we all share, we have functional groups and social co-operation. To avoid clashes and achieve common ends, we have to submit to rules and regulations enforced by law or maintained by custom. Since the individual is a member of society, the latter has the right to impose restrictions on the freedom of individuals. In a well-ordered society, these restrictions will not be felt as checks on individual liberty. Since marriage has consequences for society, social codes are formulated in regard to the contracting of marriages. Social laws by themselves do not constitute a universal panacea for social wrongs and evils. Man-made laws can never adjust themselves to all the caprice of the human heart. But if these are hard and inelastic, they may destroy us as individuals, and force us into mutilated and meaningless ways of living.

The Hindu Ceremony

The Hindu ideal of marriage is essentially a fellowship between a man and a woman who seek to live creatively in a partnership for the pursuit of the four great objects of life: dharma, artha, kama, and mokṣa. Its purpose includes the generation of children, their care and nurture, and co-operation in a better social order; but its main aim is the enrichment of the personality of husband and wife, through the fulfilment of their needs for a permanent comradeship, in which each may supplement the life of the other and both may achieve completeness. The married couple as persons are a mutual creation. The ideal has come down from Vedic times, and is preserved in the elaborate marriage ritual which is in force even today. The marriage ceremony marks the beginning of the great opportunity for the development of an emotional maturity, in which the sense of justice, of understanding, of consideration of, and forbearance for, others are born. It can be simplified, since the essential rites by which the ideals are impressed on the couple are only few.

The first stage is the *panigrahana,* where the bridegroom holds the bride by the hand and leads her thrice round the fire, reciting the appropriate verses. Oblations are offered to Pusan, Bhaga and Aryaman, who are the presiding deities over prosperity, good luck and conjugal fidelity, respectively. The parties touch each other's heart, and pray that they may be one in heart and mind, though two in bodies. "May you never admit sorrow in your heart; may your prosper in your husband's house, blest with his life and cheerful children". They ascend a stone and offer a prayer that their mutual love be as firm and steadfast as the stone they tread on. At night the polar star and Arundhati are shown. The bridegroom is enjoined to be as steady as the polar star, and the bride as faithful as Arundhati. In the *saptapadi* ceremony, the bride and the bridegroom take seven steps together, and pray that their married life may be full of love, brilliance, opportunities, prosperity, bliss, progeny and holiness. The husband addresses the wife thus: "Having completed seven steps, be my companion. May I become your associate. May none interrupt my association with you. May such as are disposed to promote our happiness confirm your association with me". The husband and the wife take vows that they will further each other's hopes and desires in the spheres of religion, love and worldly prosperity. The ceremony concludes with a prayer that the noble union be indissoluble. "May the universal gods join our hearts; may the waters join our hearts. May Matarisvan, Dhatar and Dvestri together blind us close." The woman is blessed to be a good wife with her husband alive. At the end of the *saptapadi* ceremony, the bride passes into the family of the husband. Marriage may be regarded as complete with it. Others argue that consummation is necessary. For three days after the marriage, the two are to sleep in different beds, but in the same room, and practise strict celibacy. This is to indicate that self-control is essential in married life. The bride and the bridegroom approach their marriage with lives that are chaste. They guard their chastity, and offer it as a tribute to the mate at the time of the marriage. No other gift can quite compensate for the loss of this.

The position of the wife is an exalted one. She is to be the head of the household, bearing full sway over the father-in-law and the mother-in-law, over her husband's sisters and others. She is the effective partner in life. She should not be discarded in religious duties, business matters and the emotional life. All religious acts should be performed together.

During the period of the banishment of Sita, Rama performed his rites with the golden image of Sita by his side. Kulluka, commenting on *Manu*, quotes a passage of the *Vajasaneyi Brahmana* which reads: "A man is only half his self. Till he takes a wife, he is incomplete and so not fully born. Only when he takes a wife is he fully born, and becomes complete." So Brahmins versed in the Vedas declare: "Verily he who is known as the husband is also the wife". The image of ardhanarisvara is India's recognition of the mutual relationship of man and woman, the idea of the co-operative, interdependent, separately incomplete but mutually complete masculine and feminine functions. "The husband and the wife are to each other the best of friends, the essence of all relationship, the fulfilment of all desires, the very life itself. So is the husband to the wife and the wife to the husband". Sita went into exile to share her husband's sorrows. Gandhari refused to use her eyes lest she should enjoy a pleasure denied to her husband. The ideal wife is a source of endless gratification to the husband, with her shy tenderness, winning smile and good companionship. Again, the wife who is devoted to the happiness and welfare of the husband, whose conduct is pure, who is self-controlled, attains fame here and incomparable bliss hereafter. Kalidasa makes out that husband and wife are as constantly united as are words and their meanings. Sita tells Anasuya that her husband loved her as a father and mother would. This is the vision and the ideal toward which both men and women strive.

The household is an essential element in the social structure. Through it the householder is enabled to attain liberation. Vasistha says that the life of the householder is a life of service and austerity, and is specially distinguished among the asramas. It is not the mere presence of wife and children that make a home into a home. It is the performance of social duties. "The householder who is intent on God shall seek true knowledge and consecrate to God whatever work he does."

Forms of Marriage

The Epics, the Smrtis and the Dharma Sastras mention eight forms of marriage, which include relics of earlier stages that have survived into the later. Many of these can be traced to the period of the *Rg Veda.* Hinduism has the tendency to preserve old beliefs and customs, without deleting them when they are outworn. Four forms are approved, while the other four are disapproved.

The Paisaca form of marriage, in which the bride is overpowered by the husband, is of a very low type. The bride is deceived, or loses control over herself by taking drugs or drink, and in such a frame of mind yields to the husband. Baudhayana says: "When one marries a girl while she is asleep or unconscious or mad, it is the Paisaca marriage". This form is discouraged and held as low, but because certain tribes resorted to it, it was regarded as legal. Besides, in society where virginity is regarded as sacred, any woman who loses it has no chance of respectable marriage. So the jurists required the culprit to marry the woman he wronged.

The Raksasa form of marriage refers to a period when women were regarded as prizes of war. The victor carries away the bride and marries her. In many cases collusion of the women occurs. Rukmini, Subhadra and Vasavadatta aided their husbands, Krsna, Arjuna and Udayana. In the *Rg Veda* the Aryan masters took slave girls, but these connections were also legalised.

In the Asura form of marriage the husband buys the bride for a price. It is marriage by purchase. It assumes that the woman has a value, and cannot be got for nothing. This form was in practice, but was not approved. A son-in-law who buys the bride for a price is called a vijanata. These three forms of marriage are entirely disapproved.

The Gandharva form of marriage is generally approved, as it is based on mutual consent. The lover chooses the beloved. *Kama Sutra* regards this type of marriage as ideal. No rites or ceremonies solemnise the marriage of free love. Marriages with midnight elopements, outraged parents, and other incidents of romance are brought under this class. The most interesting case of this type of marriage is that of Dusyanta and Sakuntala, which is the theme of Kalidasa's great drama *Abhijnana Sakuntala*. The poet suggests that this type of marriage, contracted under stress of passion, is not likely to be stable. As the secret union based on love at first sight is not enough, a curse falls on the bride, and exacts its penalty. In the King's court she is insulted and rejected. When she is purified by discipline, and the bondage of desire yields to the detachment of duty, Sakuntala is accepted as wife and mother. Through the rigour of renunciation, the passion of desire has to be transmuted into the austerity of devotion. As Gandharva unions were brought about without the recitation of mantras, to give them respectability it was laid down that ceremonies should be performed after the union, at any rate for the three upper classes. The formal celebration is an indication of social approval. When child marriages became popular there was no scope for mutual love.

In the Arsa marriage, the father of the bride is permitted to accept a cow and a bull from the son-in-law. This is a modified form of Asura marriage, and is held low among the approved forms of marriages.

In the Daiva form the sacrificer offers his daughter in marriage to the officiating priest. It is called daiva, because the marriage is settled during the course of the performance of a sacrifice to the gods. It is not held in high regard, since matrimonial alliances should not be mixed up with religious affairs. With the disappearance of Vedic Sacrifices, this types of marriage also has disappeared.

In the Prajapatya marriage the bride is offered to the bridegroom with due rites, and the couple are enjoined to be inseparable companions in the discharge of their religious duties. The father gives away the daughter with the injunction: "Fulfil ye the law conjointly". It does not seem to be different from the Brahma type, where the bride, properly decorated, is offered to the bridegroom, who is specially invited for the purpose. The husband takes the vow that he will always be closely associated with the wife in all spheres of activity.

Many marriages are like those of Urvasi and Pururava, merely contractual, where the woman yields her body but not her soul. This is abuse of sex relationship. The physical union is the outward sign of an inward spiritual grace. For spiritually evolved persons, the communion of bodies is the outward expression of the communion of souls. We must realise that sex union is the great sacrament of life. There are cases of spiritual chastity, though a woman might lose physical purity through force, or yield her body when it has ceased to have any spiritual existence for her.

The Brahma form of marriages is the one approved and popular among all classes, and in it the couple pray that their friendship and love shall be lasting and genuine. The other types of marriages which legalise even abduction (Asura), rape (Raksasa) and seduction (Gandharva) are distorted forms of civilisation, and deprive a woman of equality by reducing her to a sexual unit, and emptying her of personality. If the codes disapprove of these, it is because they desire that marriages should not be left completely to individual choice. They were recognised in the interests of women. The Vedic seers teach that great tolerance is necessary in matters of sex, since people are endlessly different. Morality has less to do with legal ceremony, and more with mutual relations. The current forms aim at the Brahma ideal, though here and there Gandharva and Asura forms are to be met with.

Early Marriages

The custom of child marriage was unknown in the Vedic and Epic periods. Susruta tells us that a man reaches the full development of his physical powers at twenty-five and a woman at sixteen, though signs of her maturity may appear at twelve. If marriages take place at any earlier age the effects will be injurious. "When a man, before he has reached the age of twenty-five, impregnates a girl less than sixteen years old, the embryo dies while in the womb. Or if a child is born at all it will not live long; and if it lives it will be weak. Therefore one should not impregnate an undeveloped girl". Ancient practice was in conformity with this medical advice. The Vedic rituals assume that the bride is a grown-up woman, mature in body and mind, ready to love the married life. The word udvaha conveys the meaning that the girl is in a position to live as wife. The marriage hymn assumes that the girl is blooming with youth and yearning for a husband. She is called a kanya, who chooses a husband for herself. Sita, Kunti and Draupadi were fully grown-up at the time of their marriages, which were consummated immediately. The *Grhya Sutras* lay down that the consummation of the marriage should take place on the fourth day after the marriage ceremony. The word nagnika means that she is a virgin, not a tender child who has not developed a sense of modesty and bashfulness. The bride and the bridegroom have to guard their chastity, and approach each other with the treasure of celibacy. Insistence on absolute chastity was responsible for prepuberty marriages in the first centuries after Christ. The analogy of upanayana for boys was applied to marriages for girls. The joint family system encouraged non-earning members of the family also to marry. Some smrtis argued that even if good bridegrooms were not available, girls must be given in marriage to men of inferior quality. Marriage was obligatory for girls, though not for men. The practice, however, was originally limited to the Brahmin class. The writers of the *Dharma sastras,* who flourished two or three centuries before the Christian era, advise that marriages of girls should not be delayed long after puberty. They allow that girls may be kept unmarried for a period of three years, if suitable husbands cannot be found, and Manu agrees with them. If, three years after attaining puberty, the guardians do not find a suitable mate for a girl, she can choose one for herself. Savitri remained unmarried long after puberty, and was granted permission to select for herself. She selected Satyavan, a very desirable young man in every sense, except that his horoscope indicated his death at the end of the year. Her father advised her against marriage with him; but she was firm, as she had given herself in mind to him. The marriage took place and the forecast proved incorrect. Even those who advocate early marriages (like Manu) permit girls to remain unmarried, if suitable husbands cannot be had. She can live till her death at her father's home, rather than be given in marriage to an unworthy man. Early and late marriages are both contemplated by the *Kama Sutra.* Even when the girls have the right to choose their husbands, they generally consult their parents and obtain their consent. Even when brides and bridegrooms are grown-up, the usual practice is for the parents to arrange the marriages, of course in consultation with their sons and daughters. In the *Atharva Veda* we read that parents entertain suitors in their homes, and the daughters choose their husbands from them. The Jataka stories give us many examples of consultations by parents with their sons and daughters in regard to marriages. The practice of *svayamvara* (self-choice of the husband by the bride) became popular in the Epic period. Personal inclination and parental advice combine to secure for the girls worthy husbands. It is very rarely that impatient young bridegrooms are flung upon shrinking and innocent brides. After all, in a matter where psychology, race, family traditions and education are involved, the decision cannot be left to individual caprice. Early marriages, as distinguished from child marriages, arranged by parents, in consultation with their sons and daughters, have been the norm in India. A good deal can be said in their favour. Love is predominantly a subjective experience, of which the essential components are imagination and desire. The lover is drawn irresistibly not by the real person, but by an illusory figure in his own mind. Every man bears in his heart the image of one woman, though not this or that woman. So too has woman an inborn image of man. In an early marriage, at a time when minds are receptive and malleable, the young man projects on the personality of his woman a force of attraction which has its being within himself. Even the most intelligent of us remain in ignorance of the real nature of the woman who has attracted us. Much of the cause of love is in the lover, and the object is only an accident. Whatever be the object, an almost identical passion would have been felt for it. The very intensity of passion blinds us to all objective vision, and causes us to conceal the features with a veil we cannot penetrate. Any woman, no matter how commonplace and devoid of intelligence or beauty she may be, has the power to subjugate us completely, when once we have permitted ourselves to project on her all those desires and dreams which we believe can be satisfied by union with another soul. So also girls project their dreams on the husband, who is more a principle than a person. The husband or the wife is our creation; we consecrate ourselves to the service of an ideal. With acquaintance, the quality of love becomes adapted to the person loved. The instinctive desire slowly matures and adapts itself to the other person. Compatibility is a process, not an accident. There is a natural tendency for a boy and a girl who are brought together to grow on each other, and achieve a harmony. A popular verse says that kings, women and creepers twine themselves round those near them. Women adjust themselves everywhere. They take root wherever placed.

The objection to parental leadership in marriages is due to its abuse, especially in a system which encourages early marriages for women, and remarriages for widowers. Some parents, who were eager for both making money and observing the orthodox conventions, have brought about marriages between young girls in the first bloom of their beauty and wealthy old men. All this is becoming impossible with the raising of the marriage age. The disintegration of the joint family system, the progress of women's education, the economic struggle, have brought about a gradual raising of the marriage age of boys and girls. The Sarda Act, which prescribes the minimum age for girls and boys at 14 and 18 respectively, is already the rule. For both men and women, marriageable age may be the same as the legal age for majority. In adopting post-puberty marriages. Hindus society is reverting to Vedic practice.

Choice of Partners

We have seen already that marriage is intended to be an adjustment of psychological, racial and human factors. But these are all external data which are very important, and on their basis we are called upon to develop responsible and mature love, which is the destiny of the individual and the true aim of marriage. We do not marry the woman we love, but love the woman we marry. Marriage is not a matter of nice calculation. We cannot foresee how the bride and the bridegroom will each develop and also both together. Society can lay down general rules regarding the choice of partners. "The bride yearns for beauty, her mother for wealth, her father for learning, her relations for family honour, and the rest for a feast". As marriage is the instrument for the perpetuation of the species, we must take into account eugenic considerations also. Since one who plants trees considers the soil and the climate, and does not permit himself to be led by caprice, marriages should become means for progressive life. We must not only perpetuate the species, but exalt it. Generally marriages should take place between members of families who belong to the same social and cultural level. Excessive inbreeding is wrong, but the present laws regulating Hindu marriages are hard. They insist that marriages should be within one's own caste (endogamy), outside the direct paternal line (gotra exogamy), and also outside certain specified degrees of blood relationship (sapinda exogamy), paternal as well as maternal. Membership of the same gotra does not mean consanguinity. Such a tie may have existed at the beginning, but it has no force when we are cut off from the original founder by a number of generations. There seems to be no valid reason for the taboo on marriages between sagotras, and it may be allowed to disappear by permissive legislation to the effect that a marriage between Hindus shall not be invalid only because the parties are descended from the same gotra, notwithstanding any text of Hindu law, or custom or usage, to the contrary. The prohibition regarding the interdiction of marriages between persons by reason of sapinda relationship within certain degrees need not be taken up now. Marriages among cousins are not to be regarded as irreligious or un-Hindu. Arjuna married Subhadra, the daughter of his maternal uncle. Krsna married Mitravinda and Bhadra, the two daughters of his father's sisters. Prince Siddhartha (Gautama the Buddha) married Gopa (Yasodhara), the daughter of maternal uncle. *Samskara Kaustubha* says that the great Manu, Parasara, Angiras and Yama permit marriages among descendants of the third degree on both the mother's side and the father's side. There have been violations from early times of the rules of sapinda relationship. Vaidyanatha in his *Smrtimuktaphala* says: "among the Andhras good people, deeply versed in the Vedas, follow the practice of matulasutaparinaya, and among the Dravidas respectable people allow marriage of a person with a girl who is fourth in descent from a common ancestor."

It is obvious that since the end of marriage is the enhancement of personality, though the development of mutual relationship based on sex attraction and affection for children, the qualities necessary for making it a success can be judged better by those who are detached, and whose emotions are not already engaged. We must be careful to marry not one who has just a pair of fine eyes and a pretty body to play with, but one who is worth while and has an attractive mind.

Anuloma marriages, where men of higher castes marry women of lower, were permitted; and the children born of such marriages were placed in an intermediate caste. Rules governing the shares of inheritance of sons born of wives of different castes are mentioned in the *Dharma sastras*. Hindu history records a large number of cases of anuloma marriages, though they were discouraged after the tenth century A.D. Pratiloma marriages, where women of higher classes marry men of the lower, were prohibited; and the children born of such marriages were not included in the four castes, but became candalas or nisadas. As certain castes are traced to these prohibited marriages, it is clear that they were not uncommon. In the *Rg Veda,* however, we have many instances of intermarriages. Cultural differences among castes are gradually diminishing; intercaste marriages will again be on the increase, and cannot be said to violate the spirit of Hindu dharma. Canakya says that the bride can be chosen from any caste or community, even if it is low. Several inscriptions state that Hindu princes married foreign princesses. Manu allows a man to marry a girl, from even inferior and bad families, if the girl is a jewel among women. *Mahanirvana Tantra* mentions the Saiva form of marriage, and lays down only two conditions: that the woman is not within the prohibited degree of marriage, and that she has no husband. Questions of age and caste need not be looked into. Such a rule justifies intercaste and widow marriages. Under present conditions, the Civil Marriage Act may be extended to cover marriages between two persons of different faiths, without demanding their formal renunciation of religion as at present.

Polyandry and Polygamy

The wife is called patni on account of equality of rights with the husband. Dampati means that the husband and the wife are the two joint owners of the household. It follows that there can be no third. Monogamy is the ideal, and there is no double standard of morality. The examples of Siva and Parvati, Rama and Sita, Nala and Damayanti, Satyavan and Savitri were impressed on the minds of the Indian people.

Polyandry and polygamy are forbidden, and yet there are occasions when both are permitted. Polyandry prevailed in certain communities. The famous instance is that of Draupadi's marriage with five brothers. Her father was aghast at the proposal, and said it was opposed to the codes (lokadharma viruddham); but Yudhisthira argues that family traditions justify it, and it is difficult to know what is right in all cases. Fantastic reasons are given to justify it; and the *Tantravarttika* goes to the extent of denying it, asking us to take it only figuratively as five persons marrying one rajyalaksmi or royal glory. The custom prevailed among the Ksatriya tribes. Tantrika writers, among others, protested against it. Even in Malabar communities, where it has survived, it is passing out of fashion.

As in other early societies, polygamy was the privilege of princes and noblemen. Common people were ordinarily monogamous. But the *sastras* allow a husband to contract a second marriage with the consent of his wife. It is justified, also, where the first wife is found to be imbecile or suffering from an incurable disease, or barren or adulterous. Though polygamy is becoming rarer, it is still practised. Legal recognition of polygamy has resulted in great unhappiness.

The unfairness to women in *Manu* comes out when he requires a good wife to adore a bad husband. This is a sort of slavery to the husband. By such exaggerated teaching he attempts to extol the duty of devotion to the husband. Of course, husbands who are unfaithful to their wives come in for severe censure. Apastamba requires them to wear donkeys' skin and beg for food. the practice has, however, been unkind to women. There is also a difference in the treatment of widowers and widows. Men obtain permission to marry, after the wife dies, by the device that they cannot discharge their religious duties except by marrying a second time, though the presence of the wife is not indispensable for the performance of religious duties. The *Aitareya Brahmana* states that a widower can continue his Vedic sacrifices, even if he has no wife. Sraddha or devotion will function as his wife. *Visnu* holds that the images of the dead wife can be used. In *Ramayana* it is said that Rama performed his sacrifices with an image of his wife by his side. Later on, Manu and others require widowers to marry again.

The Status of Widows

The position of widows has changed considerably from the time of the *Rg Veda*, in which we have references to the remarriage of widows. It is undesirable for a woman to have two husbands at the same time. A sentiment of reluctance to marry a woman who was taken by another is at the root of the advice given by Yajnavalkya to marry a woman "that has yet belonged to no man". But the Epic mentions several instances where this sentiment did not operate. Hayadratha wanted to make Draupadi his wife. Trisanku married the wife of a prince whom he killed, and had by her a son. King Rtuparna was eager to marry Damayanti at her second svayamvara, knowing her to be the wife of Nala. Satyavati was sought in marriage by King Ugrayudha shortly after the death of her husband. Arjuna accepted as wife the widowed daughter of Airavata, the Naga king, and had by her a son. The *Jataka* also contain references to this custom. A king of Kosala killed the king of Benares and made the widowed queen, who was already a mother, his wife. In the *Ucchanga Jataka* a woman prays for the release of her brother, who along with her husband and son has been sentenced to death, saying that of these three she can get a new husband, and a new son, but not a new brother whatever she may do. Kautilya in his *Arthasastra* writes: "On the death of her husband a woman wishing to lead a virtuous life shall at once receive not only her endowment, money and jewellery, but alo the balance of the dowry due to her. If she is desirous of a second marriage, she shall be given, on the occasion of her marriage, whatever her father-in-law or her husband or both had given her. If a widow marries any man other than the person selected by her father-in-law, she shall forfeit whatever had been given to her by her father-in-law and her husband."

In the smrti books we find growing opposition to the remarriage of widows. Apastamba decrees that "if a man lives with a woman who has once been married before, or belongs to a different caste, they both commit sin". Aparently both intercaste and widow marriages were to be met with. Manu knows of such marriages, since he mentions that a son born of a remarried widow (paunarbhava) by a Brahmin father does not cease to be a Brahmin, though he is to be regarded of the same rank as a Brahmin who lives by trade. *Gautama* admits the existence of widow marriages; for the concedes the right of the son of a widow, by her second husband, to inherit one-fourth of his father's property, in the absence of legitimate heirs. For *Vasistha* and *Visnu* the son of a married widow, by her second husband, is fourth in order of preference in the matter of inheritance among the twelve kinds of sons, and is regarded as better than an adopted son. A rigid life is prescribed for widows for a short period. "The widow of a deceased person shall sleep on the ground during six months, practising religious vows...then her father shall appoint her to raise issue to her deceased husband." Regarding the remarriage of women, *Vasistha* lays down very liberal rules. "If a damsel has been abducted by force, and not wedded with sacred texts, she may be lawfully given to another man; she is even like a maiden. If a damsel at the death of her husband has been merely wedded by the recitation of sacred texts, and the marriage has not been consummated, she may be married again". Amitagati in his *Dharma-pariksa* (A.D. 1014) refers to widow marriages. "Even if a woman is married once, when through ill luck the husband dies, it is fit that she should go through the ceremony (of marriage) again, provided there has been no sex union. When the husband has gone away from home, a good wife should wait for eight years, if she has already borne a child, and for four if she has not. If, on five such occasions, husbands are taken when there is justification, the women do not incur sin. This is what Vyasa and others says." While remarriage of widows is permitted, Manu and others hold that a life of asceticism is the ideal for them. Even Parasara, who holds that remarriage of widows is legal, contends that "the woman who, when the husband is dead, observes the vow of chastity, goes to heaven after death like a Brahmacarin." Later commentators like Hemadri, Raghunandana and Kamalakara forbid widow remarriages. In earlier times, the practice of remarriage of widows prevailed. Chandragupta II murdered his elder brother Ramagupta and married his widow Dhruvadevi, and his son by that marriage, Kumaragupta I, succeeded him on the throne. There are other instances of this kind, which did not outrage the orthodoxy of the time. Voluntary consecration to an ideal is different from its compulsory imposition. The chastity of women is praised as the highest virtue, and widows might refuse to remarry on account of their deep love for their dead husbands.

Widow remarriages became unpopular in the period between 300 B.C. and A.D. 200. Even then child widows were permitted to remarry. Alberuni records that remarriage of widows was prohibited by custom, and this prohibition became extended to child widows also.

The difficulties of widows were to a certain extent relieved by the practice of niyoga, which was fairly common till 300 B.C. The custom of the remarriage of a widow with the brother of the deceased husband, devara (dvitiyo varah), prevailed. When the husband's dead body is about to be burnt, the dead man's brother seizes the hand of the widow with the following words: "Arise, woman thou art lying by one whose life is gone; come to the world of the living away from thy husband, and become the wife of him who grasps thy hand and woos thee as a lover". A reference to this practice is found in the *Mahabharata*: "As a woman married her brother-in-law after the death of her husband, so, the Brahmin having failed to protect her, the earth made the Ksatriya her husband." The son raised for the deceased husband by intercourse with the brother, or near kinsman, is called ksetraja. The production of offspring was the main purpose, and the sanction terminated as soon as a son was born. When the widow has a son she gets a share of the family property. In the *Mahabharata* Pandu and Dhrtarastra and the five Pandavas were born of niyoga.

As the practice was inconsistent with the ideals of purity and constancy in sex relations, Apastamba and Baudhayana opposed it. Manu condemned the practice as animal. It is one of the practices condemned in our age. The practice of niyoga gradually fell out of use. Though Dayanand Sarasvati, the founder of the Arya Samaj, sanctioned it, his followers adopted the straight course of widow remarriage.

Regarding the practice of Sati, or self-immolation, there is no direct reference to it in Vedic literature. *Grhya Sutras,* which describe in great detail important ceremonies of domestic life, including the cremation ceremony, are silent about it. Later commentators and lawgivers quote a verse of the *Rg Veda,* in support of the rite of sati. It reads: "Let these women who are not widowed, who have good husbands, applying collyrium to their eyes, enter; without tears, without disease, and full of ornaments, let these first enter the house." The verse cannot be addressed to the widow, but to the assembled women; and by substituting agneh (of fire) for agre (first), its meaning becomes distorted. Possibly this custom prevailed among several branches of the Indo-Germanic race, and so among some Indo-Aryans; but it is clear that the *Rg Veda* viewed it with disapproval. There is Greek evidence for its prevalence in India, and *Visnusmrti* commends it. The practice prevailed among the members of the princely class. The *Mahabharata* mentions two instances of sati. Madri immolated herself on the funeral pyre of her husband Pandu. The wives of Vasudeva burnt themselves with the body of their lord. Even among the princes, however, it was not the usual practice. The widows of the Kuru family duly performed the sraddha ceremonies, after the cremation of the dead bodies of their husbands. During the early centuries of the Christian era, when the sakas and the Hunas invaded the country and created havoc, the princely families resorted to this practice to save the honour of their women. Hindu codes of conduct include practices of different ethnic groups, and their modes of living, who all aspire to adopt the Brahminical code. In the matter of vegetarian food, and the non-marriage of widows, even the lowest classes imitate the highest. With the increase of confusion, instance of sati also increased; but all through protests were uttered. Bana in his *Kadambari* declares that "this is a path followed by the illiterate, is a manifestation of infatuation, a course of ignorance, an act of foolhardiness and shortsightedness, a stumbling through stupidity, that life is put an end to, when a parent, brother, friend or husband is dead....If it be properly considered, this suicide has a selfish object, because it is intended to obviate the unendurable sorrow of bereavement". Madhatithi, commentator on Manu, condemns sati as an act of suicide, not of dharma. The *Adigranth* of the Sikhs says: "They are not satis who perish in the flames, O Nanak: satis are those who live on with a broken heart". Deep love may be shaken to its depths when the lover is removed, and death may be resorted to in such cases. This is not peculiar to any race or country. Thanks to the awakening of the social conscience, brought about by the spread of Western ideas, Isvara Candra Vidyasagar and Rammohan Roy got the necessary legislation, in 1856, permitting widow marriages under certain conditions; it is in accordance with the spirit of Vedic tradition and practice.

Divorce

We have referred already to the provision for the remarriage of men, even when their wives are alive. The *Yajur Veda* says that one man can have many wives, but one woman cannot have many husbands. In other words, a man can have more than one wife at the same time, but a woman cannot have more than one husband at the same time, though she can have more than one husband at different times. Remarriage of women is also permitted under certain conditions. "The wife of an emigrant shall wait for five years. After five years have passed she may go to seek a husband." *Narada Smrti* says: "When the husband is lost or dead, or turned a recluse, or impotent, or fallen from caste, in these five kinds of distress, a woman can take a second husband. The Brahmin shall wait for eight years for her husband who is gone abroad; if she has no issue she shall wait for four years; after which period she may marry another. The Ksatriya woman, having issue, shall wait for six years, and without issue for three years. The Vaisya woman who has issue, four years, and without issue two years. The Sudra woman has no rule for waiting. If it be heard that the husband is alive, the waiting period shall be twice as long. Such is the order of Prajapati." If the woman is unwilling to go to her husband, when he returns after five years, she is permitted to marry a near relative. While the *Dharma Sutras* require a Brahmin woman to wait for her husband for five years, Kautilya reduces it for ten months. Katyayana follows Vasistha and Narada and holds that "if the bridegroom be of a different caste, an outcaste, impotent, of vicious occupation, of the same gotra, a slave, constant invalid, the bride, even if married, should be given in marriage to another." The well-known verse,

> naste mrte pravrajite klibe ca patite patau
> pancasvapatsu narinam patir anyo vidhiyate

allows remarriage in certain circumstances. Kautilya writes: "If a husband is of band character, or is long gone abroad, or is guilty of high treason, or is dangerous to his wife, or has become an outcast, or has lost virility, he may be abandoned by his wife." He gives detailed instructions for the separation of couples who find it impossible to live with each other, though he limits the privilege only to those married according to the Asura, Gandharva, Rakasasa and Paisaca forms. The permission for separation and divorce was superseded by the doctrine of the indissolubility of the marriage bohnd, due perhaps to the fear of the fascination of the monastic life exalted by Buddhism. Even when divorces were denied to the upper classes others were allowed the privilege. In the pre-Christian era, divorces and remarriages took place in all sections of society. Vatsayana admits the remarriage of women, when he states that "union with a woman of lower caste, and a twice married woman, in neither desirable nor forbidden." In other words, while marriage is sacred as a human institution, circumstances may arise in which dissolution is the only way of saving the couple from perpetual misery. For two people to remain together in unhappiness, because they have entered into a bond which only death can break, is a sin against the best in us. It sometimes blasts the soul. It is better for the children that unhappy parents should not live together. Our laws make havoc of our domestic intimacies, in defference to dogmas we no longer respect. To allow divorces freely would be to damage social stability. It is a question whether increased divorce facilities in the West have added appreciably to the sum of human happiness, or at any rate diminished human unhappiness. On the sanctity of marriage depend the practice of the domestic virtues, the integrity of the family, and the rearing of children. If marriage is a sacrament, not a contract, it is not to be lightly entered upon. If we approach it in a sacramental spirit, there is a better chance of making it a success. The prevailing sentiment for centuries in Hindu society has been opposed to the remarriage of woman.

In some Hindu castes divorce and remarriage are permitted. The grounds for divorce among these are ill-treatment, continual quarrel, impotence of the husband, or any irregularities in the first marriage itself. In permitting the remarriage of widows, and the remarriage of women after divorce, we are acting in the spirit of our ancient legislators. J.D. Mayne writes: "The prohibition against second marriages of women, either after divorce or upon widowhood, has no foundation either in early Hindu law or custom. The second marriage of women who have left their husbands for justifiable cause, or who have been deserted by them, or whose husbands are dead, is expressedly sanctioned by the early writers."

As things are at the present day, the husband has the freedom to marry again and again, while the wife is denied the liberty to marry again, even when she is forsaken by the husband. The marriage bond cannot be regarded as indissoluble, when the husband can marry again when the wife dies, and sometimes even when she is alive. Loveless marriages and empty parodies of matrimony, which are tolerated by convention, hurt sincere spirits. There are many deserted wives who have no relief. Some of them are obliged to change their religion in order to contract a new marriage. They must be allowed to remarry, if they so wish. Liberal divorce laws are not sufficient by themselves. A few unhappy situations, stinging words, resentful brooding on real or imaginary wrongs, incompatibility of temper, may all lead to separation. They may also be overcome by a little sacrifice and adjustment, which easy divorce laws do not encourage. In the early days of the Bolshevist revolution, maarriage ceased to be the binding thing it was once. A simple declaration of intention to separate was all that was necessary for divorce. It was, however, open for husband and wife to stick to each other in the hope of making something out of it. A couple could be married and divorced on the same day at the same Registry office. "But the statistics of short-time marriages became so alarming that recently a new regulation was put into effect stipulating that a divorce can be granted only a certain length of time after marriage—some weeks I believe. The charges for registration and divorce are nominal only about five dollars."

The marriage relation should be regarded normally as permanent. Divorce should be resorted to only in extreme cases of hardship, where married life is absolutely impossible. It is a drastic remedy which uproots one's whole life, involves other lives as well. We expose children to a divided life and loyalty. In the interest of the children, the marriage tie must be regarded as permanent. Conscientious parents will put up with a good deal of suffering rather than expose their children to emotional strain and nervous damage. Even when a marriage is childless, divorce is not to be freely granted. Marriage is not a mere contract; it is a part of the life of the soul. Risk and hardship are part of human life, and we must be prepared to face both. We must meet as human beings and companions full of faults, weakness and desires common to bothy; and adjustment is a long process. In the Catholic Church, the parties contracting marriage receive the Cross and the Sword on their heads bent towards each other, the one as the symbol of their tragic courageous trust in a higher order than the human, the other as the symbol of the unfailing wrath for every infraction of the law of the Cross. In the faith that love is the sign and pledge of the loveableness of the ultimate ground from which all things arise, the sacramental view requires us to face risks, and not to admit defeat in the great enterprise. We enter into the marriage relationship for the development of individual integrity, for that adaptation to reality, without which there is no happiness for individual or society. This traditional view has still a strong hold on Indians, among whom stable marriages are more numerous, and family affections much stronger, than perhaps in any other country. This is due largely to the character of Indian women, who are miracles of dignity, graciousness and peace. For many of them the object of life is to endure life. Faith in the Supreme has endowed the hearts of men and women with hope that endurance will have its reward, and suffering meekly borne will melt the stoniest heart. Divorces are much easier for men to bear than for women; for a man can throw himself into his work, and forget to a certain extent the disruption of his domestic life. For a woman it is loneliness. By casting off the chains we do not acquire wings.

The dogma of indissolubility of marriage is not final; yet it is the ideal. Deviations from it should occur only in very exceptional circumstances. Many laws and customs which were once significant and necessary have lost their meaning, and are merely empty husks. Some of them, which stifle the spirit, will have to be given up. A law establishing monogamy among Hindus is long overdue. Such a statute can be equitable only if permissive legislation for obtaining dissolution of marriage under certain conditions is adopted. Dessertion, habitual cruelty, adultery, insanity and incurable disease should be the only grounds for the dissolution of marriage, at the option of either party. Such a law will help to establish, so far as law can do, a clean, healthy and happy life; and it will not be inconsistent with the general spirit of Hindu tradition.

Social Reform

There are anomalies in our social legislation. A Hindu with more than one wife can retain them even when he adopts Christianity, if the wives do not object, though it is a crime for the Christian to have more than one wife at a time. A Hindu, when he is converted to Islam, is governed by Muslim Law in matters of succession, unless he establishes the prevalence of a custom showing that the Muhammadan law of succession has been varied. If a Muhammadan husband gives up his faith, his marriage is dissolved. A Hindu convert to Christinity retains his wife. A Christian embracing Islam can marry another woman during the lifetime of his first wife while as a Christian he would be guilty of bigamy. A Hindu cannot divorce his wife, but can do so if he becomes a Muslim. Again, anuloma marriages were treated as legal and valid in 46 Bombay, 871 and 55 Bombay I. This view is rejected by A.I.R. 1941 Madras 513. Again, Section 2 of the Widow Remarriage Act (Act XV of 1856) prescribes forfeiture of the interest of the widow in her first husband's property after her remarriage. When the question was raised whether this section applies to those widows who are permitted by the custom of their caste to remarry, the Allahabad High Court held that it does not, while others contend that it does. There are difficulties, too, with regard to the Hindu women's Right to Property Act. What is needed is a codified general system of laws which is in accordance with the modern spirit of freedom and equality and applicable to the whole society. The Hindu Law Committee is attempting the codification of the laws of Inheritance and Marriages.

The woman is called abala, the weak. In a civilisation where physical superiority was the determining factor, she, the weak child-bearer, had to be protected from the violence of strong men.

Until recently it was admitted that women were weaker and more delicate, and so required protection; nor was it necessary for her to earn her livelihood, as the value of the work which she rendered at home was quite as important as any other type of work. So long as the home is the centre of human life, woman will continue to be the most important member of family life. But home is gradually being displaced by an hotel, a peasant cottage by a suite of rooms. We are leading a vagrant life; but the Hindu ideal is that the family should be perpetuated. Man is rooted in his soil. The Indian woman is the mother. That is the vocation for which she has yearned from childhood. There is a good deal of emphasis laid in recent times on economic independence for women. We must admit that marriage and a sheltered home are the aims of most women the world over, even today. If women become wage-earners, nothing great is likely to be gained. The tasks at home are sufficiently heavy, so that women cannot undertake other occupations without detriment to the work at home. Economic independence must be found for women within the home. Attempts should be made to give them the same rights as men have in regard to property, owning, inheritance, and disposing of property, real as well as personal. Legislation with regard to the property rights of women is urgent. The care of the destitute and the dependent, especially children, old men and women, has been the special concern of Hindu dharma. The dependent woman was a charge first on the family, and then on the clan (kula). Kautilya recommends workhouses for women, and makes male relations repsonsible for their maintenance. The rights of a wife in the husband's property, movable and immovable, must be liberally admitted. The scriptures proclaim that the wife is half the husband's person, and his partner in the pursuit of the ends of life. She has a right to the dead husband's estate as long as she lives. Childless widows, according to Brhaspati, have a right to inherit the husband's property in preference to agnates. The inheritance of the maternal grand-father's property, when he has no son, by the son of the daughter and not by her daughter, will have to be modified. That the grand son will perform oblations, which the daughter cannot, is no serious obstacle. Daughters' rights to inheritance along with the sons will have to be admitted.

Maternity must be protected, whatever be the conditions regarding marriage. It is not right to penalise children for the faults of their parents. All children are legal, and equal in the eyes of the law.

In the old days, the smritikaras and their commentators, by a judicious process of selection and interpretation of ancient texts, moulded the law to suit the needs of changing times. Their place is now taken by the Courts of Law and legislative bodies. The former have not the same freedom of interpretation as ancient commentators had. So, if the growth of law is not to be arrested, legislatures have to intervene.

Whatever be the origin of devadasis, or temple girls, the system of prostitution, to which it has given rise, is vicious and requires to be put down. It has been opposed by all champions of social purity, and has already been suppressed by law in Madras presidency. In the ancient civilisations of Egypt, Greece and Rome, the practice of consecrating virgins in honour of the gods prevailed. The girls lead a loose life; and it is an institution which has grown up, not merely as an accident, but as an integral part of our social codes and marriage laws. Every temple in India has, in addition to the central holy of holies (garbhagrha), a natyamandir, a dance-hall. *Siva purana* lays down in connection with the building of a temple dedicated to Siva, that it should be provided with thousands of excellent girls skilled in the arts of song and dance, and numerous male musicians skilled in palying stringed instruments.

There are some who argue that, in many cases, even marriage is a form of prostitution: a more fashionable form, perhaps, of disposing of a sexual commodity for monetary considerations, a form sanctified by law, custom and religion. Only the prostitute is a blackleg, who is accepting less than the market rate of wages—that is, marriage—for the service she renders. For the sake of the advantage of economic dependence, a woman gives up her work, and her person which she enjoyed, as an unmarried person. Having sold their bodies and their accomplishements for the best price they would fetch, they stick to their bargains without complaint, whatever their secret repining may be. The education which many people give to their daughters is to enable them to interest some male while her youth is still there, and to use her resources to make herself a valued member of a family. To trap a man into a contract to support her is the aim of marriage.

This is taking an unfair view of marriage; for the possibility of developing fidelity and family life are ingrained in that institution.

To argue that the system of prostitution protects decent women, safeguards public health and prevents scandals, is to put a cloak on iniquity. To degrade women to satisfy men's depravity is wrong. When women are thus misused there is hardly a spark of soul left in them. Individual failings are one thing; official recognition of brutality another. Women are not to be treated as commodities. If we look upon women as persons, then prostitution is a crime against their personality.

Birth Control

Malthus wrrote an *Essay on Population,* in which he urged that disaster would rapidly overtake the human race unless something were done to check the natural capacity of man to increase geometrically, while the produce of the soil on which he lived could at best increase arithmetically, and could do even that only for a limited time. He advised the means by which this calamity could be averted: late marriage (with absolute continence prior to marriage), followed by copulation only at such times as it was desired to have a child. Many of the assumptions made by Malthus, however, are incorrect. It is not established that over-population is the cause of poverty. It is untrue, also, that the resources of nature are unequal to the rapid increase of population.

Mahatma Gandhi, though he is anxious to give relief to women from excessive child-bearing, feels that the use of contraceptives is dangerous to the nervous and moral health of the community. He does not wish us to adopt the old wasteful method of child-bearing, when we produce twelve of whom only half a dozen survive. For him, the means for checking too frequent births is sexual abstinence. To use contraceptives is to regard sex as an end in itself, and evade the responsibilities associated with it. We cannot regard indulgence as an end in itself. By the use of contraceptives we pervert the sex act. The end of the perpetuation of the race is frustrated, and pleasure becomes an end in itself. Clement of Alexandria says: "To have intercourse except for procreation is to do injury to Nature."

Here, as in other cases, what is ideal is different from what has to be permitted. The indissolutbility of marriage is the ideal;

but, in certain circumstances, divorces have to be permitted. So also control of births by abstinence is the ideal, and yet the use of contraceptives cannot be altogether forbidden. It is not right to think that a man and a woman should not take physical delight in each other for its own sake, and should do so only for the sake of children. It is wrong to think that sexual desire in itself is evil, and that virtue consists in dominating and supressing it on principle. Marriage is not only for physical reproduction, but also for spiritual development. Men and women want each other as much as they want children. To remove from the lives a masses of men and women their one pleasure would be to produce an enormous amount of physical, mental and moral suffering. Lord Dawson writes: "To limit the size of a family to, say, four children would be to impose on a married couple an amount of abstention which for long periods would almost be equivalent to celibacy; and when one remembers that, owing to economic reasons, the abstention would have to be more strict during the early years of married life, when desires are strongest, I maintain that a demand is being made which, for the mass of people, it is impossible to meet; that the endeavours to meet it would impose a strain hostile to health and happiness, and carry with them grave dangers to morals. The thing is preposterus. You might as well put water by the side of a man suffering from thirst, and tell him not to drink it. No; birth control by abstention is either ineffective or, if effective, pernicious."

It is sometimes argued that birth control is an unnatural interference with the process of Nature. But we have interfered with the process of Nature by inventions and discoveries. Our habits are different from savage practices; and this is due to our interference with Nature. If we argue that ancient things are more natural than modern, then polygamy and promiscuity should be regarded as more natural. Birth control is fast becoming, in some countries, as natural as wearing clothes, on account of the present social climate with its economic insecurity, and the desire of parents to give their children a good start in life.

The objections to the practice of birth control are due to its abuse. Women who wish to avoid the trouble of pregnancy, birth and rearing, and men who wish to escape the responsibilities for their acts, resort to it. The abuse of a thing does not affect its proper use. If the methods of birth control are adopted by those who cannot afford to have children, we cannot condemn them. The poorer classes do not mind having children, but they do not wish to bring them up in conditions of pain and poverty. The proper remedy is that they should be provided with the means of nourishing children in a proper environment. We must improve the circumstances, not assume them to be permanent. We are not animals. The use of sex should be governed by the mutual consent of the parties, as responsible beings. If the needs of the children require self-control, it is to be employed. If parents feel that to safeguard their mutual happiness they may risk the future, they need not be prevented from taking the risk. We do not deny that sex control is better than birth control; but men are not all saints, though they may aspire to become saints. In the present conditions, in the interests of social economy, facilities for birth control must be available, especially to the poorer classes.

Attitude to Failures

The test of a civilisation is its attitude towards the inconsistencies and foibles of human beings. Whatever rules we may adopt in regard to marriage, extramarital relations will also occur. As a rule, the Hindu sages had an immeasurable tolerance for human weakness and vulnerability. Ofteh what is called crime is not the manifestation of a debased and brutal mind, but the expression of a sensitive and affectionate nature. Disregard of the law is not real wickedness. A good deal of current morality is unsound and conventional. Our codes have stagnated into mechanical habits by reason of flagging vitality. Convention is the general taste of the community. The morality of law or duty is not the highest type, though it is essential for soical order and decency. Its inhibitions are intended to stimulate moral insight, not to break one's spirit. But life is not a mechanical observance of moral precepts. When a man and a woman are brought together in a deep unity of soul and mind, whenever he or she, looking deeply into the eyes of the other, sees mirrored there the one person before whom he or she is utterly lost in speechless adoration, wonder and love, whenever they come together in spirit before they come together in body, them everything they can do one with the other is holy. Anyone who utters a word against the sanctity of such love has not a right mind. The dictum of Augustine: 'Love God, and do what you like,' indicates that in the true life of love there is something above rules and conventions. If traditional taboos and institutionalised attitudes sometimes thwart a life of love and happiness, they may be violated. The marriage laws are intended to discipline one's nature, and bring about a harmony of physiological, racial, social human and spiritual elements. This involves restraint and discipline. Failures may arise at any level; the physiological, the human or the spiritual. We assume that monogamy is natural. It is not quite so simple. We have passions. Fidelity, though essential, is not easy. There are some who look upon it as an absurd and cruel prejudice, the consequence of an inability to live to the full, a spiritless liking for the conventional, a contemptible timidity and lack of imagination. We sometimes think that a woman has everything she wants if she has a husband and children. She may fear to be undeceived, to be relieved of the delusion. Honourable feeling, domestic affection and a stern sense of duty that social life depends on the observance of conventions, however faulty they may be, may keep her straight; and yet there may be no full flowering of her whole nature. Her desire may be awakened, but not stilled. This tension leads to the 'problem' of marriage. The tribulations of love are admitted to be beautiful, but not moral. Unless we have tolerance for breakdowns we are not sufficiently human. Socrates was more significant than Miletus, who was only a moral person. Jesus had greater goodness than the Pharisee, who was only conventionally correct. If love without marriage is illegal, marriage without love is immoral. Many aspirations are crushed and many lives destroyed on account of rigid and imperfect social rules. We attach more importance to the absolute fidelity of the body than to the unswerving loyalty of spirit. Once upon a time a young man sat by the wayside, and said to a guilty woman: "Neither do I condemn thee. Go, and sin no more." By trying to play the Puritan we often act in inhuman ways. There are two kinds of morality, the absolute one of right and the relative one of social convention, which each society construes in its own way. Through the observance of moral rules we must approximate to the ideal, which is the holy more than the moral, the beautiful more than the correct, the perfect more than the adequate, love more than law.

Even the *Ramayana* sometimes sets a wrong ideal. Rama refuses to take Sita back after the fall of Ravana, because she had stayed so long in his house. Sita protests that in captivity she was no longer the master of her person. Her mind was under her control, and that was always faithful to him. This harsh code was not adopted by the Smrti writers. In *Yajur Veda* a woman is asked at a certain step in a sacrifice: Who is thy lover? (kas te jarah?), and when she names her lover, that is, admits her misconduct, she is absolved from sin. Manu, while enumerating different kinds of sons, mentions one born of a lover (jara). If women are made prisoners or molested criminally, they should be treated with sympathy and accepted after certain purificatory rites. Vasistha holds that if a woman is taken captive by an enemy, or spirited away by robbers, or ravished against her will, she ought not to be abandoned. Atri expresses the same view. Even cases of criminal assault followed by conception are taken into account, and the woman, according to Atri and Devala, is taken back into the family after childbirth, though the child is to be given up, which is unfair. After the thirteenth century practice became more rigorous, and violated women were not readmitted. Hindu society has suffered as the result of this great wrong, and paid heavily for it.

In Vedic times women who had gone astray were permitted to take part in religious service, if they confessed their error. Vasistha was willing to readmit women who had committed adultery, provided they repented and performed a penance. Parasara holds that adulterous women should be abandoned only if they are confirmed sinners. Even for adultery the man is more responsbile than the woman.

Past ages were filled by actual human beings, not abstractions, persons with passions in their hearts, sensitive and tender, who pass through dawning love, blind passion, ardent tenderness, doubt, apprehension, defiance, sorrow, despair, beings who abandon themselves to passion, and do not scruple to violate moral rules. Even in the *Rg Veda* we find references to women going astray, faithless wives, elopements, lawless unions. Our Epics are full of stories like that of Visvamitra and Menaka, where even great heroes falter and stumble in the narrow path of conventional duty. Men much better than many of us, who have done things which we never dream of doing, are also the victims of our common frailty. Vyasa was born of an unmarried non-Brahmin girl, whose beauty was too much for the ascetic Parasara. Bhisma was the son of an unmarried woman. Puru was the youngest son of Sarmistha, who was a princess in attendance on the Queen, and therefore not exactly the wife of King Yayati, and yet sage Kanva, according to Kalidasa, when sending Sakuntala to her husband's place, asks her to behave as Sarmistha did for Yayati. We have the case of Madhavi, who was the daughter of Yayati. She was under the guardianship of an ascetic, Galava, who placed her under four kings in succession, on condition that each must give her up after having one son. Thus she became the mother of four sons. When she was restored to her parents, and Galava forced on her marriage and arranged a svayamvara, she placed the garland on a tree, indicating that she had resolved to lead the life of an ascetic in the forests. Arjuna was sought by a widowed woman Ulupi, and had Iravan by her. The Epic *Mahabharata* is distinctly in favour of women. Sexual wrongdoing becomes a crime or a sin by its circumstances and, after all, the sins of the flesh are not greater than those of the spirit. We must approach things human in a spirit of piety. Sexual life on its positive side is a very personal matter, guided by taste and temperament, and affair of desire and artistry. Personal conduct must be released from all taboos and restrictions, except those imposed in the interests of society, especially the weak and the young. The *Mahabharata* had a definite social attitude towards what may be called non-marital or experimental relations between men and women. The chief objections to such relations are that they tend to promote a habit of sexual irresponsibility, or a cynical promiscuity. But we are not dealing with the promiscuous type, which cannot be changed into something different by any means. Promiscuity is a disease which has to be treated. There is no danger of sensitive men and women degenerating into promiscuous perons.

Non-marital relationships are, in very exceptional cases, perhaps the only way for some to make their sex life satisfying, precious, and even permanent. The time when men and woman can be kept faithful by making it difficult for them to be unfaithful is long past. The greatest gift in our possession is our true self. Without this integrity the individual is worth nothing to anyone, not even to himself.

Adultery on the part of the husband is generally regarded as more venial than on the part of the wife. This is because men have had the run all these centuries. They cheat their wives by saying that their lapse is of no importance, it does not álter the fundamental relations, it is passing affairs, an act without a sequel. If the wife is bitter and complaining, the husband adopts the high and mighty attitude that it is vital for him, that his happiness is more important than all our petty morals. This double standard is due partly to a sense of ownership. Woman is property. Adultery is an offence against property. It is an illegitimate appropriation of the exclusive rights which the husband had acquired over the wife. Galsworthy has written wonderfully of the Forsyte conception of woman as property. In the name of marriage we acquire vested rights in the wife's person. The woman also feels the right of property in her man. If a man commits marital infidelity he does not introduce any new blood into the family, as women's infidelity does, so the latter is regarded as more sinful. We cannot say, however, that ideas or property are at the root of all sex restrictions. Sex jealousy implies more than an infringement of one's personal property. It is a feeling of grief. There is also the idea that chastity and holiness go together.

Discipline, or the imposition of limits an our natural tendencies, is essential for human dignity. Plate in the *Philebus* says: "The goddess of the limit, my dear Philebus, seeing insolence and all manner of wickedness breaking loose from all limit in point of gratification and gluttony and greed, established a law or order of limited being; and you say this restraint was the death of pleasure; I say it was the saving of it." If we aspire to life, true, good and beautiful, we must lead disciplined lives. The oveflowing violence of passion demands it. Otherwise we will justify, in the name of love, whatever is nasty, gloomy and shameful. Dirt cannot purify us. It is clear that, for normal human beings, compliance with conventional rules is the easiest way to gain the end. Only those who are well disciplined, and have developed the delicacy of apprehension which is conspicuous in the saints, have the right to go beyond the rules.

There is a notion that free love, in the wrong sense, is advocated in Russia. To give is the lie direct, it will be enough to quote what Lenin wrote to Clara Zetkin as early as 1920. "The changed attitude of youth people to the problems of sex is naturally is `question of principle' and depends on a theory. Some talk of their attitude being `revolutionary' and `communist.' They sincerely believe this to be the case. But this does not impress me at all. Although I am by no means an austere ascetic, this so-called `new sexual life' of young people, and sometimes of older people also, seems to me often enough to be a merely *bourgeois* business, an extension of the bourgeois brothel. It has nothing whatever to do with freedom of love as we communists understand it. You know, of course, the notorious theory that in communist society the gratification of sexual passion is. . . as simple and commonplace an act as drinking as glass of water. This `glass of water' theory has made our young people totally and utterly crazy. It has been the doom of many a young lad and lass. Those who support it say they are Marxist. Thank you! But Marxism it is not. Things are not quite so simple as that. It is not merely something natural to us that is fulfilled in the sexual life, but also something which we have acquired through culture, however lofty or low that may be. Thirst must, of course, be satisfied. But is there a normal man in normal circumstances who would lie down in the mud and drink from a puddle? Or say, from a tumbler the rim of which many lips have made greasy? And the fact which is of greatest importance is the social aspect of the problem. The drinking of water is an individual act. In love, on the other hand, two beings are involved. And a third, a new life, many appear. It is just here, in this fact, that the interests of society are involved. There is the duty to the community. The revolution requires concentration, an increase of strength, both from the masses and from individuals. It cannot tolerate such orgies as are normal to the heroes and heroines of d'Annunzio. Sexual licentiousness belongs to the bourgeois world. It is an evidence of decay. But the proletariat is a rising class. It has no need of intoxicants as narcotics or as stimulants. Self-control, self-discipline, is not slavery. No, even in love it is not that." We must free ourselves from the illusion that primitive lusts are a novel form of advanced thought. Civilisation of man's gradual mastery over savage nature. A nation in which chastity and self-control in sexual matters are widely observed will be a strong and creative nation.

There are only two ways of life: the easy and broad way of self-indulgence; the difficult and narrow way of self-restraint. The latter calls for risk, heroism, desertion and misunderstanding; but it alone is worthy of the spirit of man. Life is not meant to be easy. Its aim is not excitement or fun, but liberation of the spirit. Marriage is a means to this. India is every generation has produced millions of women who have never found fame, but whose daily existence has helped to civilise the race, and whose warmth of heart, self-sacrificing zeal, unassuming loyalty and strength in suffering, when subjected to trials of extreme severity, are among the glories of this ancient race. Women as mothers are more directly sensible of the iniquity and injustice of the present order, and can bring about a deep and far-reaching change of spirit, and work it into the new style of life. Then will the New Man be born.

A stage will arise when even home ties are snapped for the pursuit of spiritual freedom. We transcend even social bonds by accepting them. Married life is not essential to salvation. In the moral growth of the human being, a stage arises when we overcome sex desire, develop chastity of mind and body, and identify ourselves with the well-being of the whole universe.